To Be Near the Fire

# To Be Near the Fire

Demonic Possession, Risk Analysis, and Jesus' War on Satan

ROGER S. BUSSE

Foreword by
STEPHEN J. PATTERSON

RESOURCE *Publications* · Eugene, Oregon

TO BE NEAR THE FIRE
Demonic Possession, Risk Analysis, and Jesus' War on Satan

Copyright © 2014 Roger S. Busse. All rights reserved. Except for brief quotations in critical publications or reviews, no part of this book may be reproduced in any manner without prior written permission from the publisher. Write: Permissions. Wipf and Stock Publishers, 199 W. 8th Ave., Suite 3, Eugene, OR 97401.

Resource Publications
An Imprint of Wipf and Stock Publishers
199 W. 8th Ave., Suite 3
Eugene, OR 97401

www.wipfandstock.com

ISBN 13: 978-1-62564-811-2

Manufactured in the U.S.A. 07/02/2014

With love for my family and children, and to my mother and father, this book is dedicated to my wife Tami Busse, whose love, encouragement, rigorous discussion, and unfailing support made this project possible.

# Contents

*Foreword by Stephen J. Patterson* | ix

1 Introduction:
Demonic Possession, Risk Analysis, and Jesus' War on Satan | 1

2 Roman Imperialism, Occupied Palestine, and Perilous Risk:
Qualitative Risk Analysis and Contemporary Sources | 8

3 Palestinian Judaism and Ecstatic Activity:
Demonic Activity and Possession | 31

4 The Beelzebul Controversy: Countermeasures to Perilous Risk | 54

5 Reconstructing the Conflict of Perilous Risks | 60

6 Disarming the Strong Man:
Jesus' Attack on Satan and Demonic Imperialism | 70

7 The Risk Context of the Controversy Dialogues:
The Collision of Countermeasures to Perilous Risk | 89

8 Jesus' Exorcisms and the Risk Context of His Mashal | 131

9 Confirming Findings: Perilous Risk, Jesus to Paul | 166

10 Qualitative Risk Analysis and Faith | 171

11 Summary | 175

*Bibliography* | 179

# Foreword

IN THE 1990S, ROGER Busse was a rising star in the world of big-time banking. His was a real-life bootstraps-to-boardroom success story. He had a young family to support. His life was full and the future looked promising. Imagine, then, the surprise at US Bank when he strode into the office of the Chief Credit Officer and said he wanted to take a leave of absence. Since college, his dream had been to do graduate work in Religious Studies. Now he wanted to take some time off from banking to go to Harvard Divinity School to study Christian origins. Was he unable to see the risks in such a move? Hardly. Busse was a specialist in risk management. He just believed that following his dream would be worth the risk.

I came to know Roger Busse only many years later, now back in banking as president of one of our local Pacific Northwest banks. He went to Harvard, studied with the same scholars I had studied with there, earned a degree, and then went on with his life—a life in banking. But each night he would return to his studies, puzzling out questions that his Harvard education had led him to ponder. A few years ago, he came to me with a manuscript of several hundred pages, the result of years of study that had brought together his twin passions: Biblical Studies and risk management. I was skeptical. But as I read, I began to see that Busse had something valuable. He could see that whatever Jesus was, historically speaking, he was taking big risks with his life. He was saying and doing very risky things. Why?

In the final product, Busse finally settled on one extremely risky thing that Jesus did. He exorcised demons. In recent years, more and more scholars have come to the realization that Jesus probably did cast out what he believed were demons. They also understand that exorcism was, by and large, an illicit activity in the Roman world. So why would Jesus risk official condemnation, arrest, and even death for the sake of the demon-possessed? A typical answer might be that he was compassionate. Busse, however, has

*Foreword*

another answer, and it comes from the world in which he lives: risk management. People engage in risky activities only when not doing so would pose even greater risks. What was the greater risk for Jesus? He believed that his land—his home, then under foreign occupation—was filled with demons. He believed that if he did not drive them off, all might be lost and the forces of darkness might win after all. That, by the way, is pretty much how an ancient peasant who believed in demons might actually think.

I am still not sure why Roger Busse thought it was worth the risk to jeopardize a promising career in high finance for a few years spent learning the arcane ropes of real Biblical scholarship. But it turns out that he was right. You can be both a banker and a scholar. What I have learned is that banker-scholars sometimes say the oddest things. And sometimes they're right.

Stephen J. Patterson<br>
George H. Atkinson Professor of Religious and Ethical Studies<br>
Willamette University

# 1

# Introduction
## Demonic Possession, Risk Analysis, and Jesus' War on Satan

"To be near Jesus is dangerous. It offers no prospect of earthly happiness, but involves the fire of tribulation and the test of suffering. But, it must indeed be born in upon every one who, yielding to fear, turns away from the call of Jesus, that he excludes himself from the Kingdom of God."

—Joachim Jeremias[1]

Is this correct? Was it dangerous to be near Jesus, and if so, why? Did the young Jewish Galilean peasant and exorcist, Yeshua ben Yosef, embrace the "fire of tribulation," reject earthy happiness, and demand the same of those who, having witnessed his expulsion of demons, chose to respond to his proclamation? What perilous risks did he perceive that would have led him to demand such a radical response? Can these risks be recovered from their historical context, and if so, how? What were the perilous risks of his generation, and how did he confront them, even at risk to his own

---

1. Jeremias, *Parables of Jesus*, 196. See Jeremias' discussion of the saying, "He is who near me is near the fire, and he who is far from me is far from the kingdom" (*Gos. Thom.* 82).

life? What do they tell us about his undisputed confrontation with demonic possession and the religious elite, as well as his death?

These are questions that have plagued me for over thirty years, because risk is something I deal with every day. Now I manage a $1.5 billion community bank, but ten years ago I worked at the highest levels of risk evaluation and analysis in a multibillion-dollar organization, analyzing all types of perilous risks, quantitative and qualitative.[2] During those years, I developed and employed proven methodologies for evaluating and mitigating risks, presenting countless seminars to all levels of risk managers and leaders. This included working with nonprofit and religious organizations, as well as speaking on the subject at Harvard Divinity School. Analyzing risk and evaluating historical countermeasures to peril have permeated my thinking.

Many years ago, I thought I had risked everything. I left my career so that I could attend Harvard Divinity School in search of a deeper understanding of risk and historical resistance to evil, even at one's own peril. It was there that I read about Jesus of Nazareth and Paul of Tarsus—people who risked everything. Only then did I begin to understand the human drive to neutralize risk, and that certain analytical methods were useful in uncovering consistent patterns of risk response, regardless of culture or time. I eventually finished my studies at Harvard, and thanks to the support of my advisor, Helmut Koester, I was armed with a new understanding of how to apply my skills to New Testament studies.

As a result, risk analysis of the New Testament has become my lifelong passion. I have applied various risk methodologies to interpreting the New Testament, leading me to believe that a specific application of risk analysis uncovers a fascinating, detectable pattern of conflict between Jesus and his opponents, particularly in his confrontations with them over demonic possession, pollution of the land, and imperialism. These findings suggest that there is a core tradition surrounding Jesus' activity that is reliable and recoverable through risk analysis.

Let me describe a framework for researching the New Testament from a risk analysis perspective. First, I take the Gospels, particularly the Gospel of Mark, holistically. I do so because there are several indisputable historical facts that virtually all scholars accept. They provide a "wisp of history"[3]

---

2. See Busse, *Essentials of Commercial Lending*.

3. Stephen J. Patterson (Willamette University George H. Atkinson Professor of Religious and Ethical Studies) in discussion with the author, February 2013.

*Introduction*

that even the most ardent critics embrace, and it is important to note that subsequent practices of the community in which the memory of Jesus is preserved confirm aspects of his risk actions, including the practice of exorcising demonic possession. As Helmut Koester states,

> Historians are therefore treading on very thin ice if they try to recover the historical person of Jesus through a critical analysis of the sayings tradition. A person of past history can only be understood if the extant sources reveal the traditions to which such a person belongs as well as the subsequent structures, practices, and institutions of a community in which the memory of this person is preserved.[4]

Second, Jesus' risk practices can be correlated using our methodology. In fact, there is a direct connection between practice and ritual instituted by Jesus himself—which, as we shall see, should include his own ritual practice related to exorcisms, particularly among the exorcists he trained, who later made up the first post-Easter community.

When aggregated, these historical facts provide a general historical context that confirms that there was a significant risk conflict between Jesus and his opponents. In my experience, the presence of risk conflict between competing or embattled parties universally points to historical conflict that a rigorous analysis of context can successfully unravel, even in documents that layer and obscure the original conflict. This is particularly true when the conflict includes historical elements that are internally awkward for one of the parties, and would be omitted if possible. If we take such a core set of facts, introduce a proven risk methodology, and then use it as a basis on which to reevaluate these traditions as they are reflected in the Gospel of Mark, what new findings might be suggested? Furthermore, what are the implications as to their meaning? I will use these facts as a common ground to begin the risk analysis and then let findings fall where they may. So what are these facts?

The historical facts accepted by virtually all scholars can be divided into context and conflict. With regard to context, there is no disputing that first-century Palestine was occupied by brutal and corrupt Roman rulers. The Jewish aristocracy and religious elite of Jerusalem were Roman collaborators. They participated in this brutality and accepted Roman rule as the will of God. Resistance to this rule was tantamount to blasphemy,

---

4. Koester, *Jesus to the Gospels*, 231. A risk context enriches our understanding of the practice of exorcism and its meaning in the activity of Jesus. See ibid., 222–23.

a rejection of the order divinely set forth. Unlike the wealthy aristocracy, Jesus was a poor, reclusive, and dispossessed Galilean peasant, Jewish ecstatic, and exorcist. For Jesus, his exorcisms evidenced that the land was possessed by demons and spirits introduced by Satan, whose activity and power had been augmented by the invasion of pagan, foreign imperialists and their supporters. Jesus left Galilee to become a disciple of John the Baptist. John rejected the Jerusalem elite, calling them "vipers" (Matt 3:7), that is, those possessed by Satan. At baptism, Jesus had an ecstatic experience and was possessed by the Spirit given by God. Jesus was then able to command demons and angels at will, for which he was feared. The Jerusalem elite murdered John, leading Jesus to flee to the Galilee. Jesus then began an assault on Satan, exorcising demons and spirits by his Spirit, which he called the "finger of God" (Luke 11:20). He recruited and trained other men to be exorcists. For Jesus and others who witnessed them (in experiential encounters), these exorcisms had meaning. Jesus announced that God was coming as king (or was already becoming present), and that he would claim his people, his children, in the powerful and transformative intervention of the kingdom, leading to the general resurrection and judgment of the apostate. The rule of Satan was ending.

The context of conflict then becomes clearer based on other undisputed contextual facts. Exorcists were well-known, but Romans considered them to be charlatans. Indeed, exorcism was considered to be demonic dark magic, was illegal under Roman law, and was punishable by death as a capital crime. Jesus was therefore an outlaw under Roman law, not just an annoyance. Worse, to associate demons with Rome and the elite amounted to sedition. Thus, the Jerusalem elite accused Jesus of being a seditious magician, possessed by Beelzebul. His family also rejected him and publicly accused him of being mad—that is, possessed. So it was that Jesus and the Jerusalem elite, together with their supporters, were in perilous conflict.

With this context established, we can assess risk responses to crises that are expressed in Jesus' conflict with his opponents, which included Satan.[5] The response to dire conflict in the perception of dangerous risks is historically consistent. Indeed, the human response to risk has not changed in millennia, only the source of those risks and the types of countermeasures we employ to cancel them out.[6] In the world of first-century

---

5. For analysis of the human response in recent studies, see Paul Slovic, et al., "Risk as Analysis."

6. Risk analysis—and the human responses to perilous risks that have influenced

*Introduction*

Palestine—a world widely believed to be filled with onerous spirits, demons, and unmitigated evil that caused pain, sickness, and death—the ultimate countermeasure was exorcism, or expulsion of those forces. Those who could control or command the spirits were revered by the afflicted as more powerful than evil, or alternately, were feared, hated, and often killed by those who were threatened by powers they considered subversive. We may arrogantly believe that we are different from our ancient ancestors, but we are anything but different when it comes to our fear and the response countermeasures we take to annihilate perilous risks that we perceive as real and present. We want fearful risks ended and will use whatever means necessary. In short, our response is to react with effective countermeasures. So, when perilous risks arise, human responses can be evaluated objectively and historically. To explain this, let me set the stage by providing the basic tenets of risk analysis so that we may apply them to this context.

Effective risk analysis, when applied to uncovering perilous risks and conflict, is generally framed in two methodological categories. The first is quantitative risk analysis, based on numbers, ratios, trends, and statistics. This method, which is associated with traditional mathematical due diligence, is obviously not fruitfully applied to the New Testament except in terms of word counts to help determine authorship. The second methodology is qualitative risk analysis. I believe this method has real value in analyzing the New Testament context outlined above and for evaluating the implications of this historical conflict.

Qualitative risk analysis generally follows a standard evaluative pattern that is iterative. To begin with, there is a perception of what those in the industry call "perilous risk," or danger of imminent, serious material harm, which is thought to be a real threat to the stability or survival of an entity under analysis. This threat is usually an assault on the entity's religious, social, economic, or political environment(s). Qualitative risk analysis assesses both the scope of those threats and the entity's vulnerability, then evaluates the effectiveness of potential measures employed to cancel them out. If they are successful, these countermeasures are usually patterned, replicated, or embellished by the entity, thereby attracting other

---

the application of qualitative and quantitative risk analysis—has been the topic of both classic and contemporary research. See Kahneman, Slovic, and Tversky, *Judgment under Uncertainty*; Drabek, *Human Systems and Response to Disaster*; Fischoff et al., *Acceptable Risk*; Bernstein, *Against the Gods*; Slovic, *Perception of Risk*; Pidgeon et al., "Social Amplification of Risk"; and Sunstein, "Laws of Fear."

adherents and standard practices. However, when countermeasures fail, devastation, catastrophe, or even physical harm or death can ensue.

Where there are two conflicting entities, additional criteria come into play that are particularly applicable to studies of the New Testament. When two entities in a common historical context perceive one another as a perilous risk, the countermeasures each employs to cancel the other out almost always isolates a verifiable historical conflict.[7] In almost every case, the core risk issues are uncovered, and often they provide a basis for assessment of the factual nature of the escalating conflict and the countermeasures employed (e.g., actions, sayings, or events). Many times, obscure, distracting, or irrelevant issues (such as later embellishment and exaggeration of the original conflict) can be identified and set aside. The goal of each of these two conflicting entities is victory, rarely a negotiated settlement (which usually occurs only when perilous risk assures mutual annihilation). Even if a negotiated settlement is reached, it is usually temporary, since each opponent urgently seeks and ultimately employs any advantage to eliminate or neutralize their opponent. In case of failure, the entity or its followers may shift to a different strategy, usually more clandestine, in order to survive.

Most interestingly, when this method is applied, the results can provide unqualified conclusions about the materiality and likelihood that events will or have occurred in highly specific ways. The qualitative method is applicable to any historical conflicts of crisis and peril, even those set in a different cultural context, as long as that risk context can be adequately recovered.[8] This has important implications for the application of qualitative risk analysis to the New Testament, for I believe the core context is available. Qualitative risk analysis suggests conclusions as to the activities of Jesus and his contemporaries in countering perilous risk, all in a new context of historical risk and human conflict over combating competing perils. It can also provide clarity to the original conflict between Jesus and his opponents, as well as to the nature and intent of his activity, including the sayings that defined that activity and resulted in his capture and execution. The pattern and methods of his activity are also made available by such means.

Our analysis, then, will seek to apply qualitative risk assessment to the Jesus tradition surrounding demonic possession and exorcism, with

---

7. Paul Slovic (Professor of Psychology, University of Oregon, and founding president of Decision Research, http://www.decisionresearch.org) in discussion with the author, November 2013.

8. See Slovic et al., "Risk as Analysis," 313–17.

particular reliance on the most original form of the traditions and practices of Jesus that can be recovered. We must first establish the reference point of perilous risk and conflict using those elements accepted by scholars noted above. We will primarily rely on Mark, Q,[9] multiple attestation, and other critical methods, as well as non-biblical sources and sociological studies when appropriate. This will ensure that we start with elements accepted by virtually all scholars as we identify conflict and countermeasures that are undisputedly historical, and thus, identify events and sayings that are characteristic of Jesus' activity within a risk context. In this way, we can consider how this perspective better informs our understanding. We may discover that in the context of first-century Palestine, even Jesus' most dramatic actions, including his public exorcisms, would not necessarily engender perilous risk and deadly response from opponents. Like virtually all countermeasures to peril in dangerous conflicts, it was what he said those actions *meant* that defined the measure of threat to his opponents. This is where qualitative risk analysis can be most revealing. To arrive at this level of understanding, we must supplement the New Testament with independent historical sources—Jewish, Roman, and pagan—as well as current research on exorcism, magic, and ecstatic religion within various cultures.

Our first step is to establish the historical context of Roman-occupied Palestine in which Jesus operated and acted, identifying the core conflict and perilous risks perceived by his various opponents which ultimately led to his execution on a Roman cross. I recognize that this analysis calls for consideration of several controversial findings. But the hope is that such consideration may open new insights based on risk analysis, many of which I am sure will be challenged. Frankly, the results unintentionally fall squarely between the liberal and conservative interpretive camps. I trust that this analysis of risk in the New Testament, its trajectories, history, and sources offers a bridge for discussion, not a rejection out of hand. Finally, the evidence of core risk and tension is undeniable in the New Testament, but the perilous risks embraced by Jesus, including the possibility of his capture and execution, must bring clarity to the conflict between Jesus and his opponents.

---

9. Since the publication of John S. Kloppenborg's, *The Formation of Q*, critical scholarship has generally acknowledged that any study of the Jesus tradition must include analysis of Q materials because the content of this lost gospel, which traces its formation through various redactions, includes early forms of Jesus' sayings that are contemporary with and yet independent of Mark. For further discussion on the importance of studying Q, see Koester, *Ancient Christian Gospels*, 128–35; and Borg, *Lost Gospel of Q*, 9–12.

# 2

# Roman Imperialism, Occupied Palestine, and Perilous Risk

## Qualitative Risk Analysis and Contemporary Sources

WE BEGIN BY EMPLOYING the tenets of qualitative risk analysis. Our first task is to analyze the historical context within which perilous risks arise, leading to the adoption of countermeasures to mitigate and cancel out those risks. Proper analysis must bring to bear all appropriate contextual sources, but especially sources that are independent from the conflicts that ultimately arise from the perspective of those entities employing countermeasures. Fortunately, there are several historical sources written independently of the New Testament, including pagan, Roman, and Jewish texts. By applying qualitative risk analysis, new insights into the countermeasures to context are made possible.

The first setting to analyze is the Roman-occupied Palestine of the first half of the first century, as best as it can be recovered. These independent sources discuss the Jerusalem Jewish aristocracy (including the high priestly families, the scribes, and the Herodians), which ruled over the second Temple period in Palestine prior to the Jewish war and destruction of Jerusalem by the Romans in 70 CE, both in relation to the scope of the Roman occupation as well as their collusion with Roman imperialism. We will use these sources to build a view of the Roman-occupied Palestine contemporaneous with Jesus' activity, and then move to evaluate the risks that led to conflict between Jesus and this religious and secular aristocracy, which we will call the "elite."

## HISTORICAL SOURCES

The first-century Jewish historian, Flavius Josephus (37–100 CE), was roughly contemporary with the first generation Christians, and clearly knew of John the Baptist, Jesus, Herod Antipas, Pontius Pilate and other Roman procurators, Jesus' brother James, the various Jewish religious sects, the priestly elite and aristocracy of Jerusalem, and other historical figures from the New Testament period in first-century Palestine. Consequently, we must recognize the importance of Josephus while still exercising caution regarding his own biases, since he was a Roman sympathizer (although not sympathetic to the Jerusalem elite)[1] at the time of his books' composition.[2] Josephus' two literary Jewish histories were *The Jewish War* (ca. 75 CE), his seven-volume treatise on the history of the rebellion and war with Rome, and *Antiquities of the Jews* (ca. 94 CE), an apology on behalf of the Jews recounting their glorious history in twenty-one volumes. Since Josephus claims to have been a member of the first-century Jerusalem priestly aristocracy,[3] his is an invaluable eyewitness account of the life, practices, and events of the first century, including the disastrous destruction of the temple and slaughter of the inhabitants of Jerusalem by Titus in 70 CE.

We are also indebted to Josephus for the unparalleled insight he provides into imperially-controlled Palestine. Josephus documents the cruelty and deceit of the Roman procurators, including Pontius Pilate. He describes how Pilate detested the Jews, but was complicit with the Jewish aristocracy

---

1. Wasserstein, *Flavius Josephus*. See also Horsley and Silberman, *Message and the Kingdom*, 28–29, 42.

2. Josephus himself fought in the war against Rome, taking command of a Jewish army in Galilee. When Vespasian arrived with his legions, Josephus' crude defense and conscripted army was crushed at Jopata (where forty thousand Jews are said to have died). By 69 CE, Josephus was back in Jerusalem working for the Romans as a negotiator, pleading for the surrender of the city, which of course failed. By 71 CE, Josephus was brought back to Rome by Titus and was adopted into the ruling Flavian family. After being made a Roman citizen, he was given a pension and a home in Judea. He then compiled his apology for the Jews, as well as his histories.

3. Josephus describes himself as such and even calls himself a priest of the Jerusalem temple (Josephus, *J.W.* 1:13).

in order to procure access to their informants. This allowed him to keep the peace and so fulfill his primary role: collecting Roman taxes.[4] Moreover, Josephus details the sway that John the Baptist[5] held over the lower classes, which led to Herod's fear of rebellion, John's arrest and murder (a different casting of events than that provided by the gospels), and the resulting hatred of Herod Antipas, who was considered a corrupt Roman minion. Josephus also describes the attempted murder of Jesus' brother James, a man who was clearly respected by the people for his piety but who became a target of the aristocracy and high priest during the interim appointment of Roman procurators. These Roman procurators were free to murder those who publicly rejected their authority (or were related to a man who had, namely Jesus).[6]

Furthermore, Josephus provides his own version of the class divisiveness and hatred of the Jerusalem elite, particularly during the Jewish war. Examples are numerous. The office of high priesthood itself was obtained by bribing the Romans. Even the high priest's vestments were kept in storage controlled by the Romans. Josephus describes how the collusion between the temple aristocracy and the Romans led to violence in the later years, due to the bitterness (to say the least) over the austere wealth and power they had obtained through corruption and support of the Roman hegemony.[7] This sentiment is most aptly portrayed in the deposition of Ananus (a.k.a., Annas or Ananius) in 36 CE.[8] The lower classes considered the hated aristocracy to be traitors to the nation, as exemplified by their attempt to persuade the peaceful surrender of Jerusalem to the Romans during the rebellion. This hatred is also underscored by the burning of the

---

4. Josephus, *Ant.* 18:3.2. See also Evans, "Jesus' Action in the Temple."

5. He writes, "Herod, who feared the great influence John had over the people might put it into his power and inclination to raise a rebellion, for they seemed ready to do any thing he should advise, thought it best, by putting him to death" (Josephus, *Ant.* 18:5.2).

6. As Josephus writes, "Festus was now dead, and Albinus was but upon the road; so he assembled the Sanhedrin of judges, and brought before them the brother of Jesus, who was called Christ, whose name was James, and some others; and when he had formed an accusation against them as breakers of the law, he delivered them to be stoned: but as for those who seemed the most equitable of the citizens, and such as were the most uneasy at the breach of the laws, they disliked what was done; they also sent to the king, desiring him to send to Ananus that he should act so no more, for that what he had already done was not to be justified" (ibid., 20:9).

7. Ibid., 18:1.1.

8. Ibid., *J.W.* 4:3.

temple records by rebels in order to obliterate any documentation of debt owed to the elite.⁹

Because Josephus composed his books after the Jewish war, and because he expresses his personal devastation at the loss of Jerusalem due to the treachery of the Jewish aristocracy and high priestly families, he speaks freely on political issues and openly criticizes the corruption of the elite (although not the priesthood in general).[10] Indeed, Josephus apparently considered himself the victim of bribes that had been accepted by the high priest Ananus—so much so that he remained bitter three decades later.[11] Thus Josephus, however biased in his view of Jewish history as a result of his adoption and Roman citizenship, provides a window into first-century Palestinian Judaism that opens our study of historical context to support an application of qualitative risk analysis.

Consequently, as the following excerpts will demonstrate, Josephus provides compelling evidence for the period's political volatility—characterized as it was by popular hatred for Rome and hope for redemption, as well as by the Jewish religious sects' shifting alliances with the elite as they competed for control of the temple, power, wealth, and Jerusalem itself. It is no wonder that any man who came to Jerusalem and publicly charged the elite with hypocrisy and blasphemy, particularly a charismatic Galilean peasant, would be in extreme danger as a target for a quick, violent death. This also begs the question of why he would take such a risk.

We begin with Josephus' passage on John the Baptist.[12] It is important to evaluate several important insights he provides regarding John's activity, particularly since this is the only independent discussion of John outside of the New Testament gospels. Such an evaluation will afford us deeper insights into the potential risks John posed to the elite of first-century Palestine. While Josephus' account dates from the first century, it unfortunately does not come from an eyewitness. Nonetheless, John was important enough, and indeed popular enough in the 90s CE (some sixty years after his murder), to still be remembered and revered by the scattered Palestinian Jews of the Diaspora and included in Josephus' *Antiquities*.

---

9. Ibid., 2:17.6. See also Horsley, "High Priests."

10. Josephus, *J.W.* 4:3.3–6 are good examples, revealing Josephus' emotion at the unfolding events.

11. Ibid., *Life*, 38–39.

12. Ibid., *Ant.* 18:5.2.

## JOHN THE BAPTIST

> Now some of the Jews thought that the destruction of Herod's army came from God, and was a very just punishment for what he did against John called the Baptist. For Herod had him killed, although he was a good man and had urged the Jews to exert themselves to virtue, both as to justice toward one another and reverence towards God, and having done so, join together in washing. For immersion in water, it was clear to him, could not be used for the forgiveness of sins, but as a sanctification of the body, and only if the soul was already thoroughly purified by right actions. And when others massed about him, for they were very greatly moved by his words, Herod, who feared that such strong influence over the people might carry to a revolt—for they seemed ready to do any thing he should advise—believed it much better to move now than later have him raise a rebellion and engage him in actions he would regret.
>
> And so John, out of Herod's suspiciousness, was sent in chains to Machaerus, the fort previously mentioned, and there put to death; but it was the opinion of the Jews that out of retribution for John, God willed the destruction of the army so as to afflict Herod.[13]

Josephus describes John as a "good man" who "commanded" his fellow Jews of all social standing to practice righteousness towards one another and piety towards God. According to Josephus, it seems John's almost prophetic standing with God was confirmed by the divine destruction of Herod's army; that is, by God's divine punishment for his murder of John.[14] Josephus' implication is clear—Herod was not considered pious, but an apostate, and the destruction of his army was seen as a direct result of murdering God's prophet. John's murder was also motivated by a potential loss of control, implying that Herod, who was appointed by Rome, feared loss of his standing if he did not act on behalf of his patron and silence John.

According to Josephus, John's baptism was not for "remission of sins" as it is in the gospel tradition (Mark 1:4),[15] but instead was the outcome of responding to his "command" to come to Aenon (Bethabara) in piety

---

13. Ibid.

14. This is clearly the implication of Josephus' introduction to the story of Saint John the Baptist (ibid.).

15. This is in conflict with the synoptic tradition established by Mark 1:4, in which Mark states that John's baptism was for the forgiveness of sins.

## Roman Imperialism, Occupied Palestine, and Perilous Risk

and righteousness, traveling perhaps as far as forty-nine Roman miles away from Jerusalem. Coming to the Jordan meant accepting the demand to practice "piety," or love toward one another, and to recommit to God (as king) in special baptismal rites, as a protection from apostasy in preparation for the coming final judgment of God.[16] It is interesting to note that when Jesus challenges the scribes and Herodians about why they went such a distance to see John, he charges that they did so to determine whether he was "mad," that is, possessed by demons—a charge that Jesus later dismisses while confronting the scribes and high priest in the Temple (Luke 7:25). For the crowds that made the journey, John was held to be a Spirit-empowered (i.e., Spirit-possessed) messenger of God in the prophetic tradition. This implies that John was considered a charismatic, although not an exorcist. Consequently, it is clear that John's authority was considered to be independent from that of the temple elite and that he rejected Jerusalem's authority altogether, implying corruption and apostasy had overtaken Jerusalem and the temple. John refused to set foot in the city. It was doomed.

We must be cautious with Josephus, for we cannot diminish John's baptism as simply a washing "sanctification" of the body. Indeed, John's baptism "where there was much water" (John 3:23) was intended to fully immerse the Jew, and must have included special words or rites now lost. Clearly, Josephus diminishes these rites by claiming the washing was for the body only, since contemporary uses of water immersion were considered a sacred rite of purification and unification with the Spirit and law—a mystical and spiritual reuniting with God that would purify and protect from evil.[17] In fact, "sanctification" can also imply the exorcising of evil spirits as well as ritual impurity. If so, John's baptism could have been an intentional charismatic act to drive out deception and apostasy arising from the pollution of the temple. This would not have been dissimilar to others' rejection of the high priests of Jerusalem.[18]

Supplementing Josephus with segments of gospel tradition provides some important risk insights. Here we also must be cautious, since John was seen through the eyes of the later, post-Easter community as the precursor of Jesus, the prophetic fulfillment as the one to "prepare the way"

---

16. Koester, *Jesus to the Gospels*, 237.

17. Another example is found in 1 Cor 10:2 with Paul's description of baptism as uniting with the Spirit of Christ.

18. See 1QpHab 12:3–5, 8–9; 1:13; 8:8–12; 9:9. See also Ehrman, *New Testament*, 239–40; Vermès, *Dead Sea Scrolls in English*, 30–33, 47; and Eisenman, *Dead Sea Scrolls*, 130, 168–169, 180–185, 249.

for the Christ (Mark 1:3). There are, however, elements within the tradition that seem to correspond with Josephus' account. For example, John intentionally took his followers (perhaps a new community) a safe distance from Jerusalem to a location on the River Jordan—away from Herod's soldiers, to be sure. However, this action was also a public rejection of the authority of Jerusalem, specifically the high priest and temple elite and the general evil he perceived to be present there. The gospels rightly define this rejection. John characterizes the Jerusalem elite not just as liars and hypocrites, but also as a "brood of vipers" (Matt 3:7; Luke 3:7). John publicly asserts that they were possessed and evil, deceivers who were complicit in accepting the rule of foreigners and their foreign gods.[19] The Essenes at Qumran (40 km south of Jerusalem) also rejected the high priest and temple elite as apostates (led by the "wicked priest"), and moved their community to the shores of the Dead Sea. And like John, they refused to set foot in the city (until called upon to defeat evil in a holy war as the "sons of light").[20]

Contextual analysis of the sources available therefore suggests that John saw the Jerusalem elite as the progenitors of a crisis: the perilous risk of apostasy that had defiled the temple.[21] Apostasy demanded a radical countermeasure to the perilous risks present in Jerusalem, namely, John's urgent call to all pious Jews to make a pilgrimage to the location chosen by God's appointed prophet (far from corrupted, possessed Jerusalem). He was enabled by the Spirit of God to cleanse apostasy by immersion in water, thereby allowing the repentant to enter into God's favor. Needless to say, this activity implies that John was calling God's people to publicly submit to God as their forgiving king, thereby democratizing access to God apart from the temple and high priesthood. This made John dangerous. As such, John was considered a radical, and the collision with elite, whose countermeasure was his arrest and execution, confirms that he was considered a perilous risk.

It is no wonder why John drew radical disciples and charismatics, and why these disciples immediately gravitated to others—particularly exorcists like Jesus, who also supported baptism on the Jordan—when John was imprisoned and then killed by Herod Antipas. According to the gospels, John considered Herod a foreign blasphemer and adulterer, the epitome of

---

19. This is as recorded in the gospel tradition, but is certainly implied by Josephus by means of his call for popular religious uprising.

20. See 1QpHab 12:3–5, 8–9; 1:13; 8:8–12; 9:9.

21. See Ehrman, *New Testament*, 255. See also, Crossan, *Historical Jesus*, 313–20.

pagan apostasy, and the very symbol of imperialistic corruption as an elite Jewish ruler and Roman puppet (John 4:1).[22] To be clear, John's baptism was an act of public repudiation of Herod and imperialism, and as such was a call to purification, implying that baptism was an individual's public rejection of sin and apostasy.[23] In essence, John's proclamation was the dramatic countermeasure to the pollution brought to Judaism by the religious elite, who had embraced Rome and a pagan king.

Herod's fear of John was well-founded. While his call was an internal Jewish religious matter, it nonetheless posed the risk of Roman intervention since John's proclamation inferred displacement of the elitist patrons of Rome by the rule of God. Public gatherings and mass baptism away from Jerusalem were forbidden as tantamount to rebellious activity. John was explicit as to the meaning of baptism. It was a commitment to walk in rightness with God through piety, which John defines as a loving relationship with others, including the disenfranchised, the fringe of society, and those rejected by the ruling classes. John not only democratized access to God (regardless of social status, position, or wealth), he also assured that judgment was coming against those who had created injustice. Imperialism's inequities, and therefore its oppression, were apostasy. The rule of the elite was soon to be replaced by God's rule and judgment of the oppressors. Consequently, as Josephus observes, John's activity constituted a perilous risk to the elite, particularly given the rising support he was receiving.

Would John become political and raise a rebellion? Or even if he were silenced, might another revive his spirit? Ultimately, John's criticism of Herod and the elite *was* silenced—he was swatted like a fly. These passages and our analysis confirm a contextual view of the elite's corruption and apostasy that aligns with John's own criticisms: that Jerusalem was occupied by evil demonic and pagan forces, and that the Jerusalem's priestly rulers and aristocracy were deceived and possessed by Satan. Countering this view was the elite's accusation that John was "mad," or possessed by

22. Ehrman, *New Testament*, 255.

23. Josephus, *Ant.* 18.5.2. While Josephus does not directly make this connection here, it will be come evident later in his writings when he links the corruption of Pilate with Ananus, both of whom were deposed. See ibid., 18.3.1–2, 4.1–3. John had abandoned Jerusalem, and with it, the temple. His call to the people to join him at Aenon, rather than in Jerusalem, and practice "justice toward one another and reverence towards God and having done so join together in washing," verifies that righteousness could no longer be found in Jerusalem. Consequently, Jerusalem was under control of religious leaders who were apostates, implying that the temple also had been corrupted. Of course, Jesus agreed with John and ultimately attempted to retake the temple (Matt 21:12).

demons. Both accusations reflect the classic conflict between countermeasures to perilous risk.

## HEROD ANTIPAS

Josephus reports that Herod Antipas "feared John," primarily because he believed John's followers would do as he "commanded,"[24] which may have reflected Herod's fear of open rebellion, but much more likely, was a fear of devastating political sabotage directed at Herod himself. From a risk perspective, we must not always assume fear of an overt uprising (i.e., that John's followers would simply become a violent mob), which the Romans would have certainly crushed without hesitation. Herod, too, had supporters: the "Herodians" who, aside from those who publicly supported his rule and the aristocracy, included sympathizers who were infiltrators, informants, and spies who trailed through all social and religious strata.[25] Paranoia was rampant in the camp of Herod and the Herodians. Consequently, for Herod to "fear John" because his followers would do "as he commanded" undoubtedly meant that Herod's informers found growing and widespread support for John's criticisms and that this support was not just from the rabble; it included higher social strata, even among the ruling elite, the Sanhedrin.[26] Only this degree of political intrigue could have displaced Herod and turned his Roman patrons against him. Indeed, Josephus is very clear in all his writings that John had nothing to do with armed political resistance or violence—his motives were prophetic and religious reformation in opposition to apostasy, which clearly included the corrupted Jerusalem elite and Herod.[27] Nonetheless, John's call for piety and righteousness was fraught

---

24. Josephus, *Ant.* 18.5.2.

25. Horsley and Hanson, *Bandits, Prophets, and Messiahs*, 30–33. This may have included brutal men like Judas the Sicarii, perhaps an infiltrating paid informant and assassin of the elite, a man who convinced Jesus of Nazareth to admit him into his inner circle. It is clear that Jerusalem was filled with political turmoil and intrigue for much of its Roman historical period, all of which was fostered by fearful concern over maintaining political control and power, as exemplified by Herod the Great slaughtering members of his own family. For more information, see our forthcoming discussion of Judas under the heading, "The Origin of the Assassin in Jesus' Band."

26. This is evident by the gospel tradition that at least two of the Sanhedrin were "secret" disciples of Jesus.

27. For a comprehensive study of evidence of corruption in the first-century temple and among the elite, including the high priests, priestly families, and the aristocracy, see Evans, "Jesus' Action in the Temple." Evans use of contemporary evidence and resources

with risk. Consequently, Herod's murder of John was based solely on political expediency. Beheading was considered a merciful death, but it did nothing to aid Herod's reputation as a bloodthirsty autocrat and murderer.

It is apparent that Herod presumed that murdering John would end the spiritual leader's social influence. This presumption was based on historical experience. Other religious and messianic movements had disbanded once their leader was either captured or killed by the Herodians or Romans. The list of these messianic pretenders crushed by Rome in Palestine is impressive.[28] Yet John's popularity endured in equal measure to the reverence Jews held for him in life, as demonstrated by the writings of Flavius Josephus sixty years after his death. Herod's chilling indifference to John's murder not only demonstrated his detached elitism (i.e., that he was out of touch with the anti-elitist sentiments entrenched in Palestine), but also surprisingly showed no concern that his brutal act would itself trigger armed rebellion. This indifference is somewhat remarkable, and suggests that the assassination took place early in John's career, before he gained widespread support.

Unlike other religious factions, John's disciples did not disband. Some became activists who even more radically rejected apostasy and demonic possession by turning to the exorcist, Jesus of Nazareth—and many took to carrying weapons. Also, it is interesting that Herod did not pursue any of John's close followers, just as after Jesus' murder there was no sweeping search for Jesus' disciples by the Romans, Caiaphas (with Ananus, former high priest and father-in-law to Caiaphas), Jonathan ben Ananus, or the religious elite (John 18:13). This means that both John and Jesus' brutal deaths had been expected to disband their followers and end their movements, thus neutralizing the risks they presented, just as it had done for Athronges, Judas, Theudas, and other messianic pretenders. Herod, as an elitist and Roman-Hellenist, was interested in John's prophetic message only to the extent it was an annoyance that would present a political risk if allowed to continue growing in popularity.

---

is overwhelming: "Taken together, the above evidence clearly demonstrates that various groups, such as some tannaitic and early amoraic rabbis, members of the zealot coalition, Qumran sectarians and Josephus viewed various priests, high priests, or priestly families as wealthy, corrupt, often greedy, and sometimes violent" (ibid., 342).

28. These include Athronges in 4 BCE (Josephus, *Ant.* 17); Judas the Galilean in 6 BCE, whose rebellion against new taxation brought about the death of thousands of Jews by the Romans (ibid., 20:5.2); the grandsons of Judas; and Theudas from 40 to 46 CE; to name the most well-known movement leaders. John the Baptist and Jesus of Nazareth should be added to the list of those radicals crushed by the elite—specifically, by Herod and Pontius Pilate, respectively.

## JESUS OF NAZARETH

What about Jesus of Nazareth? Josephus included a short paragraph on Jesus:

> Now there was about this time Jesus, a wise man, if it be lawful to call him a man; for he was a doer of wonderful works, a teacher of such men as receive the truth with pleasure. He drew over to him both many of the Jews and many of the Gentiles. He is the Messiah. And when Pilate, at the suggestion of the principal men amongst us, had condemned him to crucifixion, those that loved him at the first did not forsake him; for he appeared to them alive again the third day; as the divine prophets had foretold these and ten thousand other wonderful things concerning him. And the tribe of Christians, so named from him, is not extinct at this day.[29]

One would expect Josephus' report to mirror his passage on John, and it does to a point. Jesus was a good man; he was wise and taught the truth; he had a following and, due to concern about his control over a growing rabble that might follow his instructions, he was captured by the elite and murdered by the Romans. Importantly, Josephus notes that Jesus was a charismatic, a "doer of marvelous deeds."[30] This report is also different: Josephus explains that Jesus' death came at the suggestion of the local elite, and that he was the "Messiah." It is quite clear that the report as it stands today is completely corrupted by later Christian emendation (though no extant manuscript indicates this). Josephus, a Pharisaic Jew, would never have described Jesus, a crucified Roman criminal, as the Messiah.[31] Consequently, Josephus' original report is lost to us, but a remnant can be recreated using risk analysis.

There are elements of an original core tradition. Just as Herod's army was punished for John's murder, it seems plausible that the conspiracy of the "leading men among us" to hand Jesus over to the Romans led to the deposition of Pilate and Caiaphas in 36 CE, as Josephus later reports. While various recreations of the *Testimonium Flavianum* have been offered, none

---

29. Ibid., 18:63–64.

30. This is the same designation for charismatics and exorcists was given for Hanina ben Dosa: "When Hanina ben Dosa died the men of deeds ceased" (*m. Soṭa*, 9:15).

31. In his passage on John, Josephus is interested only in how John's death at the hands of Herod was unjust and, consequently, how many Jews believed Herod's loss in battle was divine punishment. John was an anecdote, nothing more. The passage on Jesus should reflect the same emphasis, language, style, and format as the report on John.

is particularly satisfactory. What is certain, however, is that Josephus did include a description of Jesus in *Antiquities*, that he mentioned his death under orders of Pontius Pilate, and that he acknowledged that Jewish leaders were responsible for capturing and turning Jesus over to the Romans to be killed. Josephus would only include these elements in his passage if, indeed, (1) he wished to explain why Pilate and Caiaphas were deposed, similar to the punishment the people ascribed to the defeat of Herod's army for killing John; (2) Josephus was writing an apology for the Jews at height of Roman Emperor Domitian's presumed Christian persecution (81–96 CE) because Josephus wanted to identify the origin of the seditious Christian movement as distinct from Judaism, explaining that both the Jewish leaders and Romans had cooperated in attempting to crush it while Pilate (however vile) was procurator; or (3) prior to Domitian's persecution, Josephus provided his report as an apology for Jesus the Jew, whom Josephus claims was never a danger to Rome, but was handed over by the same leaders who were ultimately crushed by Rome during the Jewish war, which in turn led to Jesus' followers' stalwart love of for him and precipitated the still-extant "tribe of Christians."

It is my opinion that the first and third explanations above reflect the original emphasis and context of Josephus' passage based on qualitative risk analysis. These explanations fit the life situation of the original passage, the risk context of other reports in *Antiquities* such as that of John the Baptist, and would be the only valid explanation as to why Josephus includes a report of a crucified Jewish criminal in his Jewish history. The perilous risk Josephus himself faced was the growing disdain for the Jews as a race. His urgent defense was an attempt to explain how and who corrupted Judaism, which included the Jerusalem elite and several corrupt Roman authorities who were complicit in actions that ultimately fomented the rebellion between 68 and 70 CE. This would mean that Josephus' report was likely issued before the persecution under Domitian. As an apologist for Judaism, Josephus wrote his report in its original form as a countermeasure—an apology for the Jews and for Jesus of Nazareth, and for how he was silenced under the corrupt Jewish leadership and brutal rule of the banished Pontius Pilate (who may have been known to have committed suicide in Gaul). The extent of Josephus' negative reports on Pilate can now be explored.

## ROMAN PROCURATORS AND PONTIUS PILATUS: BRUTALITY AND CORRUPTION[32]

What gives this assessment additional credence is the support we find by placing the passage in its original context. The section preceding the *Testimonium Flavianum* is focused on Pontius Pilate, the Roman procurator of Judea (26–36 CE) under Tiberius.[33] This passage underscores the hatred the common Jew had for Pilate's Roman imperialism, which was based on his brutal disdain for them as shown by arrogant acts intended to belittle and insult them. Based on Josephus' passages, Pilate considered the Jews, particularly the Jerusalem aristocracy, to be corrupt and inferior. Pilate's primary role was to collect taxes and impose Roman justice on those who failed to pay, but also to subdue the Jews so that they feared Rome. The Roman procurator appointed the high priest, held the vestments in the fortress of Antonia adjacent to the temple (releasing them only for festivals), and was authorized to dispatch unlimited force against any act of sedition. Pilate also controlled the temple treasury. The Jerusalem elite owed their wealth, position, status, and religious authority to Pilate, which included the membership of the Sanhedrin, the ruling council of seventy.[34]

Immediately upon his arrival in Palestine in 26 CE, Pilate placed Roman standards in Jerusalem[35] to honor Caesar, and did so secretly, overnight. In the account by Josephus, it seems these standards included not just the *Aquila*,[36] or eagle standards, but also either images or actual busts[37] of Tiberius Caesar that were imprinted, stamped, or carved on these gilded plates. Philo states that there were no images: "They bore no figure and nothing else that was forbidden, but only the briefest possible inscription, which stated two things—the name of the dedicator and that of the person in whose honor the dedication was made."[38] Images or dedications

---

32. See Horsley and Hanson, *Bandits, Prophets and Messiahs*, 29–32, 41–42.

33. Josephus, *Ant.* 18.3.3.

34. Evans, "Jesus' Action in the Temple," 320–41.

35. Josephus recounts this in *J.W.* 2:169–179 (70 CE) and in *Ant.* 18:55–59 (94 CE). Philo writes of this event in 44 CE, the *Embassy to Caligula*.

36. The *Aquila* was the symbol of power that appeared in images and sometimes slogans, which Pilate knew were forbidden in Jerusalem and were offensive to the Jews.

37. This is how it is described in Josephus, *Ant.* 18.55–59. Here the images are described as busts of Caesar as opposed to the more vague reference in ibid., *J.W.*, 2.175–203.

38. Philo, *Embassy*, 299–305.

to Caesar were strictly forbidden to be placed anywhere within the walls of Jerusalem in accordance with Torah restrictions on graven images, an observance that had been honored by previous Roman procurators, including Pilate's predecessor, Gratus. The standards were discovered the next morning. Josephus reports that hundreds of Jews went to Caesarea,[39] demanding that Pilate remove them. Noticeably, there is no mention of the Jerusalem priestly elite or aristocracy at these protests. Expecting such a reaction, Pilate had set a trap and was prepared to kill all of those who refused to yield. When his soldiers rushed in and surrounded the Jews, the Jews fell to the ground in unison and laid bare their necks, prepared to die. Astonished, Pilate ordered the standards removed. The scandal of such a public slaughter would have been too much for Pilate to bear if reported to Rome. Clearly, Pilate was hoping to incite a riot so that he could violently crush an incipient rebellion, thereby elevating his position with Caesar. His intent was also political, that is, he wanted to identify those who resisted and quickly kill them, using a riot as a pretext to do so.

Even a cursory review of these events, employing qualitative risk analysis, confirms that the dramatic collision of the perilous risk created by Pilate (along with the Jewish mob's traveling to Caesarea and their nonviolent, high-risk countermeasure of bearing their necks) suggests a reliable tradition of historical conflict. We must recall that Josephus, an adopted Roman and imperial sympathizer, is here criticizing a Roman procurator openly and vociferously. Pilate was thus being shown as a cruel and barbaric Roman ruler in contrast to the peaceful Jews. As noted, the passage that follows this report centers on Jesus of Nazareth. This can only mean that Josephus did wish to cast Pilate as complicit with the Jewish elite in another barbaric act of cruelty: killing a "good man" who was not only peaceful, but a healer and a charismatic worker of wonderful deeds, whose followers still persisted as a peaceful tribe at the time of Josephus' writing. As we shall see, Josephus avoids using terms like "exorcism" or "magic," instead employing "wonderful deeds" to elicit sympathy for Jesus. In essence, Josephus was writing an apology for Jesus of Nazareth, a fellow Jew and Galilean of good standing and character, and for those who followed this "good man." Josephus would never have gone further than this characterization.

---

39. Caesarea was the principal Roman city on the Mediterranean coast where Pilate was headquartered and garrisoned as procurator.

A second passage[40] relates Pilate's unilateral seizure of temple funds. According to Josephus, Pilate confiscated some of the Jewish treasury to build a water aqueduct into the city of Jerusalem, although this may have been a ruse, since the aqueduct is unknown. This resulted in a public protest of some significance. Josephus records that Pilate's soldiers infiltrated the crowd in disguise and waited for a signal from him to strike, mercilessly slashing the unarmed Jews with swords, all under an accusation of sedition. This accusation allowed Pilate and his forces to respond violently and at will. As in our previous example, informants must have warned Pilate of the protest in advance, including when and where it was to occur, since it is clear that he had time to prepare and place his undercover men in the crowd. It is difficult to imagine Roman soldiers being able to infiltrate a Jewish crowd even in disguise, particularly if that crowd included Zealots and other Roman antagonists—those who would be able to identify the hated enemy! Consequently, it is certain that the Herodians and temple police were involved and that the informants could only have been Jews sympathetic to imperialism. Pilate would have warned the Jerusalem elite, particularly the high priest, Sadducees, and aristocracy about the attack,[41] and based on Josephus' account, they were absent from the demonstration.

Once the crowd of protesters formed, Pilate gave the signal. Without hesitation, his men killed dozens of the defenseless protesters, slaughtering countless innocent bystanders in the process. As Josephus notes: "There were a great number of them slain by this means and others ran away wounded; and thus an end was put to this sedition."[42] It is important to stress that Josephus only records those events that build contextual momentum towards a pre-revolutionary Palestine—that is, events that contributed to the revolt against Rome. Thus, Josephus' account of the obscure attack is not just to show that Pilate had a sadistically brutal nature, but that Pilate typified the corrupt and brutal regime that precipitated other significant events that led to rebellion in occupied Palestine, thereby explaining *why* imperialism was hated in Palestine. For Pilate to openly and freely crush opponents at will, and do so with the help of Jewish sympathizers from the

---

40. Josephus, *Ant.*, 8.60–62.

41. Recall that the high priest was appointed by the Roman procurator, and the vestments of the high priest were kept by the procurator in the fortress of Antonia adjacent to the temple, except on certain festival days. This demonstrated Roman imperial control over the elite, the temple, and Judaism.

42. Josephus, *Ant.* 18.62.

elite class, helps later explain the devastating events leading to the destruction of the temple.

Thus it is documented that the elite would inform against and hand over fellow Jews, whether a whole mob or an individual, under the mantle of "sedition." Whenever they concluded there was a perilous risk or threat to the control Roman of authority, they did what was necessary to protect their imperial patron. This leads to an important observation, namely, that the Romans, certainly Pontius Pilate, held the Jewish aristocracy and priestly elite responsible for any impending public actions that could be perceived as seditious. Moreover, if they did not inform the Romans of risk, the elite would be considered culpable, and their authority, wealth, position, and even the leadership of the high priest and the Sanhedrin would be at risk. Thus, the well-known statement of the high priest, Caiaphas, is not only contextually coherent with the facts portrayed by Josephus, but is also shown to be historically reliable: "Then one of them, named Caiaphas, who was high priest that year, spoke up, 'You know nothing at all! You do not realize that it is better for you that one man die for the people than that the whole nation perish'" (John 11:49–50). Evidence is overwhelming that in Josephus' view, Pilate represented an imperialistic oppression even worse than that of his predecessor Valerius Gratus (15–26 CE), a man who changed the high priest six times until he finally installed Joseph Caiaphas. This confirms that Caiaphas was by far the most conciliatory of his predecessors to Roman imperialistic rule.

Independent sources confirm that Pilate was a cruel and harsh Roman procurator, known to be vilely corrupt and intolerant of any act that might be reported as seditious. Philo writes: "in respect of his corruption, and his acts of insolence, and his unlawful seizures, and his habit of insulting people, and his cruelty, and his continual murders of people untried and innocent, and his never ending, and gratuitous, and most grievous inhumanity."[43] Under threat of marginalization and loss of status and wealth, he expected the Jewish elite to help inform and crush resistance, and he relished every opportunity to do so. He took pleasure in humiliating the very Jewish elite he installed in powerful positions by holding them responsible for *any* insurrection—he ridiculed them. Recall that Josephus was in fact writing to Romans as an apologist for the Jews. For him to be comfortable portraying a Roman procurator so negatively would indicate that Pilate had long held a negative reputation among the Roman elite and that his banishment

---

43. Philo, *Embassy*, 302.

was widely accepted to be based on cruelty and corruption. Indeed, Philo (20–50 CE) heard of Pilate's character in Alexandria, Egypt, where he wrote *The Embassy* (ca. 40 CE) within the four years following Pilate's deposition. Thus, it is difficult to deny that his reputation was known far and wide as a violent and brutal imperial ruler, and that he detested the Jews, Samaritans, and the Jewish elite.

Are there implications from these findings that shed light on Jesus' arrest and execution? As noted, a reconstruction of what was originally in the *Testimonium Flavianum* makes it undeniable that Jesus was both condemned and killed under the personal authority of Pilate by the charge of sedition. Applying our findings regarding Pilate's brutal and vile character to the events related to Jesus' death, it is now clear that he used Jesus' crucifixion as an opportunity to taunt and insult the high priest and temple elite. This is why he placed the accusations plaque on the cross in not one, but three languages (Aramaic, Greek, and Latin) that read, "This is the king of the Jews."[44] Normally, such an accusation would be in Latin, the official and legal language of the Romans, or perhaps in Hebrew in Palestine, although most Jews were illiterate and so such signs would have been directed at the scholars and educated aristocracy. The *titulus*, or inscription, was customarily written on a gypsum plate or board and placed by the head or near the foot of the cross to identify the capital accusation. It was a warning to others of what would happen if they committed a similar crime. The number of letters that would have been required to write Pilate's accusation would have made this *titulus* unusually large, and the reason is clear—to ridicule the Jews and the elite. For Pilate, the Galilean they turned over to him was the perfect foil to crucify as the king of the Jews. Given what we now know, who can doubt the authenticity of Pilate having ordered a centurion to create this *titulus*? It is contextually coherent with his other insulting acts, for he treated the elite as pathetic pawns. The high priest demanded he take the plaque down immediately, or change the wording. The chief priests are said to have protested to Pilate, "Do not write 'The King of the Jews,' but that this man claimed to be king of the Jews. Pilate answered, 'What I have written, I have written'" (John 19:21–23). Ironically, it was Pilate who first publicly named Jesus a "king" and then publicly crucified him as a "king," *not because he was a messianic pretender* but because Jesus could be used to make a bloodthirsty, horrific insult as the crucified "king of the Jews."

---

44. Found in both the synoptic (Matt 27:37; Mark 15:26) and Johannine traditions (John 19:19).

*Roman Imperialism, Occupied Palestine, and Perilous Risk*

Given that Pilate's actions corroborate our qualitative risk analysis' findings regarding the corruption and control of the elite by Roman imperialism, as well as the vile nature of imperialistic rule (particularly under Pilate), are there other elements of the gospel tradition related to Pilate that are contextually coherent? For example, is it possible that Pilate sought to release Jesus, as reported in John 19:12? Yes, it is absolutely possible, particularly given the risk context and the opportunity Jesus' arrest provided to him. For the Jewish elite to turn Jesus over and accuse him of sedition on the eve of the Passover, when thousands of pilgrims were in Jerusalem,[45] would have been a welcome opportunity to Pilate, but a risky one—his penchant, which the elite understood and Josephus validates, was to use an individual or event as an pretext to draw out opponents to Rome, then slaughter those who showed up in support. This arrangement was expected of the elite.

How would Pilate have countered the risks associated with Jesus' arrest to his advantage? As was his practice, he would have employed Jesus as bait in an attempt to draw out his supporters at a public event—why not set a ruse to offer to release Jesus, and lay in wait to attack his supporters? Pilate would have publicly offered to release Jesus, planted men in the crowd to call for crucifixion, and hoped that Jesus' supporters would cry out for him in protest so that they could be identified and slaughtered. This plan failed. He had Jesus scourged and brutalized, then presented. Pilate offered to release a Roman murderer, Barabbas or Jesus. Pilate's infiltrators in the crowd cried out to release the murderer, hoping to draw out Jesus' supporters (and for that matter, Barabbas' supporters as well). Presumably without success, Pilate simply proceeded by acceding to the high priest's request for Jesus' death. Coherent with his character, Pilate was sinister in his political savvy, using every step in his execution of Jesus as a means to get what he wanted: to satisfy his violent pattern of behavior and identify anti-imperialists. Ultimately, the execution of Jesus the Galilean did satisfy Pilate.

As a result, Pilate likely did seek to release Jesus, but only to identify enemies of Rome, and secondarily, to obtain a public endorsement from the Jewish elite that he must die. Pilate was then free to humiliate the elite with the *titulus* in front of thousands of pilgrims. We will never know if Barabbas was released (likely not—my guess is that he was one of the other men

---

45. This is why Pilate had come to Jerusalem from Caesarea. He garrisoned the fortress of Antonia to ensure peace during the volatile festival, while he stayed in the Palace of Herod on the western hill (located on the opposite side of the city from the fortress) within the area of other elite structures.

crucified with Jesus). Pilate's action to then crucify the "king of the Jews" was another ruse. Would others respond or rebel at the crucifixion site? It was within Pilate's savage nature to identify those who cried or scoffed at the cross when they read the *titulus*.

Despite Pilate's taking Jesus' arrest and crucifixion as an opportunity to taunt his political allies, the fact remains that Josephus confirms the "leaders among us," that is, the Jewish aristocrats and religious elite, did hand Jesus over to Pilate to be executed. This is not a condemnation of the Jews, but as we have seen from an application of qualitative risk analysis, was instead a critique of the corrupted elite, who were themselves complicit with corrupted local Roman rulers. Certainly, the elite acted for their own benefit to maintain their uncomfortable alliance with Rome and thereby retain power and control. According to Josephus,[46] about three years after Jesus' crucifixion, Pilate learned that a messianic pretender was leading Samaritans to the top of their holy mountain, Mount Gerizim. Pilate dispatched soldiers and brutally *attacked the crowd*, killing several and executing the leaders of the event. The viciousness of the attack led the Samaritan high council, their Sanhedrin, to appeal to Vitelleus, the Roman legate in Syria, Pilate's superior. Vitelleus dismissed Pilate and ordered him back to Rome in early 37 CE to appear before Caesar.

Since this betrayal of Jesus was retained in the oral tradition of the early church, it might be suggested that Jews in Palestine and the Diaspora were assisting later Roman authorities in the identification of Christians,[47] just as the "leaders among us" three generations before had handed Jesus over to Pontius Pilate. Perhaps, but there is a much more certain implication: Josephus wanted to emphasize that the Jerusalem elite handed Jesus over to the Romans. This was *not to their credit*, but to their dishonor. The name of Jesus' betrayer is never mentioned, but only that "leaders among us" turned him over to Pilate. The implication is that Judas was an informant to these leaders. As such, Judas would have been a detested figure in ancient Judaism, a murderer and assassin considered complicit with the corrupted

---

46. Josephus, *Ant.* 18.85–89.

47. Such as the Praetors of Phillipi (Acts 16:12–20). A saying of the risen Lord also addresses this issue: "When you are brought before synagogues, rulers and authorities, do not worry about how you will defend yourselves or what you will say, for the Holy Spirit will teach you at that time what you should say" (Luke 12:11). In Matt 10:8, they are brought before governors and kings, thereby demonstrating an expansion of the oral tradition when Matthew was compiled in order to better fit the current life situation of the community.

elite. Since the leaders certainly captured Jesus through the action of an informant, Judas Iscariot,[48] and he clearly knew the leaders (insofar as he was fully aware of exactly who to visit and was paid a spy or slave's wages), it was highly likely that he was a Roman secret agent, a *frumentarii*, or a Jewish informant working for the elite. In either case, it is certain that Judas was an infiltrator. Indeed, Judas' betrayal of Jesus presents a startling incongruity that is historically problematic and demands a legitimate evaluation in an attempt to solve an enigma.

## THE ORIGIN OF THE ASSASSIN IN JESUS' BAND

Given our contextual analysis, several contextual observations can be made concerning Judas Iscariot. First, Jesus' betrayal by Judas, one of his inner circle of twelve apostles,[49] is an undisputed historical fact. No one would have created such a troubling and problematic story if it were not true.[50] Contextual analysis has demonstrated that betrayal, intrigue, corruption, and bribery were common in Roman-controlled Palestine. Palestine was filled with spies and collaborators. Opponents were crushed without mercy with the help of these spies. Yet, if Judas were a Zealot (a Sicarii, or assassin), why would a violent Jewish nationalist bent on the destruction of Rome and the end of Roman occupation ever betray an opponent of Rome to the very people he hated for crucifixion? Furthermore, if Judas was a legitimate and publicly known member of Jesus' inner circle and fellow exorcist,[51] he had accepted the perilous risk of opposing Roman occupation

---

48. It is possible that "Iscariot" identified the Jewish village of Kerioth in Judea (there were two, and also possibly a region by this name), because the translation in Hebrew can be either "iS-Kryroth," or "a man of Kerioth," for his father Simon is identified in the same way (perhaps in John 6:71). If so, this would mean that Judas was the only apostle from Judea. He was an outsider to the Galileans and others who originally formed Jesus' inner circle.

49. See our discussion on the Twelve in the next chapter. These twelve apostles were charismatics and exorcists who appear to have employed Jesus' name and authority to expel demons. Jesus specifically chose others who were either known to be or would become exorcists (Mark 3:13–19; Matt 10:1–4). Luke drops the tradition that the Twelve were originally exorcists like Jesus.

50. This is, this is "negative historical" fact, i.e., so problematic that later Christian communities would not have invented or added this to the tradition, similar to Jesus' baptism by John.

51. There is evidence that Judas was an exorcist, like the other eleven apostles, at this calling. Certainly he became one immediately afterwards, and that was the purpose of his

and embraced the countermeasures of Jesus. By entering Jerusalem with Jesus, Judas publicly criticized the religious elite and aristocracy, placing his life in perilous risk.

Given these facts, it is clear that Judas was not a Zealot, nor could he have been a committed follower of Jesus while in Jerusalem. In the context of qualitative risk analysis, his behavior betrays two possible motivations. In either case, Judas no longer perceived perilous risk because he had come to a resolution of that risk through an acceptable countermeasure.

**Possibility 1:** Judas was disappointed that Jesus did not raise an army of resistance and decided to abandon him to the authorities as a traitor to the movement.

- Would even a disenchanted follower of Jesus have accepted payment for his betrayal, particularly given that he proclaimed the imminent arrival of the kingdom of God and justice against the apostate elite? Possibly, if the expectation of God's arrival was no longer thought to be a viable countermeasure to the risk faced. If this were Judas' motivation, then he would have believed Jesus' proclamation to be a lie. Out of fear for his life, he would have exchanged Jesus' for his own survival.
- Yet, what changed in Jerusalem that would have led Judas to such an action? There is no indication that Jesus' countermeasures to demonic domination and apostasy had suddenly failed, for his exorcisms as evidence of the inbreaking of the kingdom of God continued.
- Judas could have simply left the city, given the throng there for the Passover.

**Possibility 2:** Judas never feared death, even as a member of Jesus' band of exorcists. This can only mean that there was no need for a countermeasure to perilous risk. Therefore, Judas must have been a Roman sympathizer, an informant, perhaps a Herodian, who profited from turning troublemakers over to the elite. Jesus may not have been his first victim, meaning that Judas could feign magic or exorcism and infiltrated the work of other exorcists and charismatics, perhaps even John's movement. In this case, he waited until arrival in Jerusalem to collect his fee and so be free of the Galilean magician and blasphemer.

---

calling. See Mark 6:7, 3:13–19; Matt 10:1–4.

- Jesus admits that Judas was possessed (John 6:70), a fact later repeated by the other exorcists in Jesus' band (Luke 22:3). In terms of this language, Judas was therefore considered a Roman sympathizer, as he was possessed by a foreign demon.

- Moreover, Judas was able to make contact with the elite without fear. He was recognized and welcomed as an informant, meaning that Judas had previously informed for money. This confirms that Judas clearly had no perception of perilous risk in approaching the elite as a follower of Jesus.

- Judas took payment. The payment was equal to the price for freeing a slave (perhaps payment to secure his own freedom), but more likely would have been used to pay a creditor to avoid imprisonment, or simply to secure two-to-three months of funds on which to live. Judas was found dead, his money gone, having supposedly bought a field. Likely, the elite killed him in order to silence him and took the money back.

The second scenario fits the risk context. His motivation in acting as a Roman sympathizer was money. Judas did protest to Jesus for allowing expensive perfumed nard to be poured on his feet. Since Judas was responsible for the band's common donation "purse" and was later accused of keeping its contents, he likely pilfered from the money donated for each exorcism (John 12:1–8). Judas would have likely planned to sell the perfume to supplement his bounty on Jesus, being so near Jerusalem and his planned betrayal. There is clear evidence for this in the Gospel of John. The passage reads as follows:

> "But one of his disciples, Judas *Iscariot*, who was later to betray him protested saying, 'Why wasn't this perfume sold and the money given to the poor? It was worth a year's wages.' He did not say this because he cared about the poor but because he was a thief; as keeper of the moneybag he used to help himself to what was put into it." (John 12:4–6)

Consequently, the notion that Judas was an idealist who became disenchanted when Jesus did not proclaim himself the messiah, and then remarkably decided that Jesus' life was worth a spy's wages, is not supported either by the evidence or by an analysis employing qualitative risk. But Judas' pilfering of the common funds was an indication that he was a spy just waiting for his opportunity to betray Jesus.

Thus, Judas was not a Zealot, but an infiltrator, a "dagger man" in the sense of a paid assassin and informant. His betrayal was premeditated, which further evidences that he was a professional spy acting according to the common practice of killing his victim under cover of night. The cruel realities of first-century life in Palestine—a dangerous, intrigue-filled country occupied by Roman garrisons, spies, and aristocratic rulers that hated their fellow Jews—paint a sobering portrait of the grizzly world in which Jesus and John sought to spread their rejection of apostasy and imperialism and demand that people turn to God as king.

## SUMMARY

As a result of this contextual analysis, we are confronted with independent sources that provide a clear portrait of Palestine under Roman occupation. The Jerusalem aristocratic elite were tacitly Romans.[52] The corruption and brutality of the ruling class, as confederates of their Roman occupiers, is fully documented. Their drive to crush any opponent of Rome, which they asserted was implicitly established by God's will and power, was demonstrated by (1) the murder of John the Baptist, (2) the murder of Jesus of Nazareth, and (3) the placement of assassins and informants among the followers of possible opponents. Thus, Romans and the Jewish elite collaborated to prevent unrest or opposition, however insignificant, especially when it approached or entered Jerusalem. Jesus and John were victims of this historical context.

---

52. Other sources include *Tg. Isa.* 5:1–7, 28:1–13; *Apoc. Adam* 27:1–8, Habakkuk, and many others.

# 3

# Palestinian Judaism and Ecstatic Activity
## Demonic Activity and Possession

HAVING EVALUATED ROMAN IMPERIALISM and its brutality, we now continue our contextual risk analysis by turning to first-century Palestinian Judaism. As noted, the pre-Christian form of the *Testimonium Flavianum* recovered in the last chapter constitutes independent confirmation that Jesus was known as a "doer of wonderful deeds [*paradoxa*]," a characterization applied to other Jewish charismatics and exorcists as well.[1] Josephus is not alone in this characterization. In the writings of pagan and Jewish historians as well as in rabbinic literature, exorcism and charismatic acts were all activities ascribed to Jesus of Nazareth *and* his followers—including Paul, by his own admission (1 Thess 1:4–5). It is important to note that not all of these reports about Jesus were intended to be negative, but rather to explain why he was so controversial, both to his supporters and his opponents.[2] Consequently, since Jesus was universally acknowledged to be a charismatic, we will focus our attention on the activity of contemporary Jewish ecstatics, exorcists, *goetes*,[3] and *magoi*, or magicians.

---

1. Hanina ben Dosa; see *m. Soṭah* 9:15. See also Vermès, *Changing Faces of Jesus*, 169–74; ibid., *Jesus the Jew*, 53–82; Ehrman, *New Testament*, 262–63.

2. Jesus was a known exorcist and this was most certainly a central feature of his historical ministry (Koester, *History and Literature*, 78–79).

3. There is no convincing evidence that there were Jewish sorcerers, or *goetes*, in Palestine that apply to this study, although some may claim it. A thorough review of Daniel Ogden's recent *Magic, Witchcraft, and Ghosts* supports this conclusion. The closest we

With the affirmation of Josephus, we must question how easily this ascription is taken for granted as a common practice in Palestine. Was the world of demons, angels, magic, and possession the norm in Palestine, particularly among the Jews? Moreover, we must uncover whether the historical context of exorcism and demonic activity among Jesus of Nazareth's contemporaries defined the accepted countermeasures to the capricious world of evil powers and foreign gods that threatened the very lives of his fellow Jews. If so, was exorcism the equivalent of magical activity, and were both "normalized" in society or condemned? How did Jesus' actions relate to this world and those of his contemporaries? Were his practices distinct, or linked to eschatological expectations or claims? Finally, can contemporary examples help us confirm whether Jesus was taking inordinate risks in his aggressive assault on the demonic world and Satan? That is, what appears to be his deliberate itinerant mission to expel foreign gods and demons? Looking to these sources, we begin with Jewish and pagan contemporaries of Jesus.

## THE MILIEU OF JEWISH CHARISMATICS, MAGICIANS, AND EXORCISTS: 65 BCE TO 75 CE

To begin, demonic activity that caused maladies and insanity in first-century Palestinian Judaism was a feared and recognized reality that was evident everywhere.[4] It struck every social stratum and gender (especially women[5]), but was particularly prevalent among the lower castes, the poor, ill, and dispossessed—those assumed to be deserving of poverty and punishment for sin or some evil they had committed. Spells, magical potions, exorcisms, and the control of demons and angels ("angels" being a term often interchanged with "gods" and "demons" in pagan rites), including negotiation with them to leave a victim, were commonplace among pagan

---

come is Pibechis, an Egyptian sorcerer of the fourth century CE, whose exorcism spell includes numerous Jewish-Christian references and may date from much earlier. We do find a Jewish magician, or *magos*, named Bar-Jesus in Acts 13:6–12 while Paul and Barnabas are traveling through the city of Paphos in Cyprus. While some translations use the word "sorcerer," there is little doubt that the author's intent is that Elymas (from the Hebrew for a "divine counselor") is a magician.

4. See Smith, *Jesus the Magician*, 94–139; Lewis, *Ecstatic Religion*, 37–99; and Crossan, *Historical Jesus*, 303–53.

5. Typically the dispossessed and powerless, commonly women (Lewis, *Ecstatic Religion*, 32–33).

*goetes*, or sorcerers, as well as Jewish *magoi* and exorcists such as Jesus and other contemporary charismatics. Because possession and "infection" by evil spirits was an accepted reality, magicians, exorcists, and "sons of gods" (who possessed the spirit of a god or demon) commanded spirits by various means, sometimes by their own possession of a spirit superior to other demons, or by taking spirits into their soul and using them to overtake others.

One need only read The Acts of the Apostles to confirm from early Christian sources themselves that magicians and ecstatics were pervasively active in their attempts to control spirits and conjure them as they willed.[6] Jesus was always assumed to have a spirit, but a holy one, from the days of his itinerant activity as an exorcist (about 30 CE) to the compilation of the Gospel of John (96–110 CE).[7] A review of various Jewish sources, including an eyewitness account of an exorcism by Josephus, confirms that there were charismatic Jews, ecstatics, and magicians operating at the time of Jesus' itinerant ministry. We will first look at those sources with the best documentation, although as we will see, their records have been "cleaned up," as it were, to make them more acceptable to later generations and rabbinic sources that wished to use their sayings for instruction and paraenesis.

---

6. Act 13:6–17 details the blinding of Bar-Jesus, "son of the savior," a magician who was powerful and an advisor of a local Roman pro-counsel, Sergius Paulus. Paul is summoned, but Bar-Jesus forbids him to speak to the pro-counsel. Paul is possessed by the Holy Spirit, then silences and blinds Bar-Jesus. The point is clear: Paul's Holy Spirit is greater than that of Bar-Jesus. Paul practiced as an exorcist in Ephesus, and became so famous that other Jewish exorcists began using Jesus' name in their rites and practices. This confirmation that Jesus' name was powerful (as evidenced by calling on the spirit of Jesus to drive out demonic spirits) and was associated with exorcism among Jewish ecstatics should be quite revealing, particularly insofar as theirs was an attempt to conjure Jesus' authority. In Acts 19:13–16, the demon that the seven "sons" of Sceva (exorcists who served a supposed Jewish "high priest"—likely a stolen title since there is no record of him) attempt to cast out turns on them and possesses them, abusing them physically. Paul encounters the Spirit of Jesus, who forbids him to travel certain places and provides instructions during ecstatic encounters (Acts 16:7). In Acts 16:16–24, Paul and Barnabas encounter a *pythia*, a women who can read and speak with spirits to conjure future events and events of the past. She is owned and enslaved for money. For days, she follows Paul and Barnabas and publicly cries out that they represent the "most high God," a saying also found in magical papyri and stories of magicians who claim to represent or be empowered by the "highest god." Paul exorcises her spirit. She is thus rendered worthless to her owners, who have Paul and Barnabas—"these Jews," or Jewish exorcists—beaten.

7. See Smith, *Jesus the Magician*, 33–34, and our discussions to follow. Also see Sanders, *Historical Figure of Jesus*, 149–54.

## JEWISH CHARISMATICS

There were at least three renowned Jewish charismatics in Palestine who were fairly close contemporaries of Jesus (one even living in Galilee within a day's walk from Nazareth). Two had the "authority" to perform various cures and exorcisms, and the third was able to influence nature: namely Hanina ben Dosa (ca. 60–80 CE),[8] Eleazar the Exorcist (ca. 70 CE),[9] and Choni Ha-Me'aggel, or Choni "the Circle-Maker" (ca. 65 BCE).[10] The numerous events associated with just these charismatics, combined with Josephus' tacit acceptance of demonic activity based on his own encounter with Eleazar (while he was serving Vespasian and his son, Titus), are sufficient historical confirmation of the pervasive presence of demonic activity. Illness, insanity, evil influence, and death were all associated with spirits and demons. Ecstatic experience by holy men and exorcists included testing and even possession by demons who wanted to destroy them. Survival of such a confrontation (such as Satan's attempt to destroy Jesus in desert wilderness of Judea) meant the exorcist might obtain authority over demons, whereby defeated demons would serve the exorcist as slaves or the exorcist would use the spirits' fear of torment to negotiate with the demon to permanently vacate the victim. Others reported experiencing visions and hearing voices as spirits descended and possessed them, or wherein

---

8. Hanina, who was from Galilee and very poor, was roughly contemporary with Paul, having died after the destruction of the temple. Hanina was very popular among the people and was famous for miraculously healing the extremely ill sons of Johannan ben Zakkai (himself a famous wise man, or *Tannaim*, a sage of the first century) and Gamaliel II (the second critical leader of the Sanhedrin after the destruction of the temple in 70 CE) through prayer. Hanina knew that his prayer had been heard if his prayer flowed freely. The fever left Gamaliel's son immediately upon Hanina finishing his prayer, not unlike reports surrounding Jesus' healings, such as the tradition of the healing of the Centurion's son. Hanina is also associated with the nature miracle. That is, he asked God, "master of the universe," to cease the rain during his travels and produce rain upon reaching his destination and performed other wonders, such as burning vinegar in a lamp (*Pesaḥ.* 122b). Undoubtedly, Hanina was Onias in Jospehus, *Ant.* 14:22–24.

9. Josephus, *Ant.* 8:45–48. Here, Josephus describes the exact manner in which Eleazar performed his exorcisms and the effect on the individual.

10. In the case of Choni, God had not sent rain even into the winter. Choni drew a circle and stood in it, saying to God that he would not leave the circle until he made it rain. A light rain fell, and Choni complained that it was not satisfactory and refused to leave the circle. The rain then fell hard, and Choni complained that it was too much. Finally, normal rain fell. For his action, Choni was threatened with excommunication, but was saved because "Choni had a special relationship with God" (*m. Ta'an.* 3:8; Josephus, *Ant.* 14:2.121).

the spirit of that god or God was made available to act to control evil, such as Jesus' authority given by "the finger of God" after his baptism and the descent of the Spirit of God upon him (Luke 11:19–21). "Finger of God" was a term used by some ecstatics and magicians to identify possession of the power and spirit of a god, or God. However, as we shall see, Jesus' linkage of his charismatic authority as the "finger of God" with the arrival of God's eschatological kingdom (a kingdom that displaces satanic rule and, by implication, eradicates apostasy and imperialism) was completely unique in its contemporary setting.

"We have just seen that 'the finger of God' was a power in magic; that the kingdom of God should be identified with the accessibility of such power is noteworthy."[11] Clearly, the world of Jesus as portrayed in the gospels was also permeated with demons and possessions. Jesus is reported to have successfully exorcised all demons but one: curiously, the possession of Judas Iscariot. Satan possessed him, and Jesus knew it (John 6:7; Luke 22:3).[12]

There were multiple forms of demonic affliction—whether mental, physical, or spiritual—motivating every conceivable action from self-mutilation to living among the tombs. Demons entered one's heart to persuade one toward murder,[13] make one deaf and mute,[14] or terrorize their victim by inflicting physical abuse, pain, and debilitating mental anguish.[15] Many of these instances cannot be completely attributed to psychosomatic events. Illness was ascribed to evil possession, spells, sin, and punishment. Jesus' reported success in expelling demons of all manifestations was so widely known that it appears the gospel writers had begun to suppress and balance this activity, emphasizing his prophesy, didactic wisdom, and other charismatic aspects of his activity.[16] Many of Mark's exorcisms are muted or omitted by Luke and Matthew. His own followers, whom he empowered and trained to be exorcists by his authority, granting them the use of his

11. Smith, *Jesus the Magician*, 130.

12. See also John 13:27, for it is when Judas eats the bread (i.e., a substance that had become infested with evil) that Satan enters his heart.

13. As was the case with Judas (Luke 22:3).

14. A blind and mute man who was "possessed" and brought to Jesus (Matt 12:22).

15. The Gerasene demoniac "Legion" (Mark 5:1–20).

16. The suppression of the charismatic for the prophetic cannot obscure the core tradition that underscores Jesus' differences with the prophets. For a full discussion of this topic, see Smith, *Jesus the Magician*, 158–64. Clearly, Jesus did not understand his role as prophetic, but rather as something greater than that of a prophet: the charismatic son of God who not just announces, but also brings the kingdom of God into history.

name, often failed—but not so with Jesus. Indeed, his authority to expel demons and illness was as renowned as Hanina's is thought to have become. It was Hanina who forbade the "queen of the demons" (a demon equivalent to the feared Beelzebul, prince of demons), from passing through inhabited places after she threatened him. This underscores that Hanina's reputation likely needed refinement in rabbinic traditions, as there may have been a contemporary charge, much like those leveled at Jesus, of his being possessed.

Jesus' charismatic success over demons and spirits implied a direct and powerful relationship with God, which was variously depicted in the gospels through the angels, divine spirits, or the Spirit of God available to him at his call.[17] For Jesus, the event that established his authority over evil spirits and demons and gave him access to the authority of God was universally ascribed in all of the canonical gospels to an ecstatic experience at his baptism—a trance or spiritual ecstasy, actually a Shaman-like experience,[18] wherein he was possessed by the Holy Spirit in an event Jesus later shared with his fellow exorcists. They too reported an ecstatic experience in witnessing the transfiguration of Jesus and hearing of the voice of God.[19] When John finished his baptismal rites over Jesus (the actual words and actions of which are now lost), the Spirit of God appeared to him as a dove[20] and touched him, thereby giving him possession of the Spirit, as a voice proclaimed him as a beloved son of God. In Palestine's Judeo-pagan milieu, the resulting exorcisms were associated with such divine men, or "sons of god," and so the description found in Mark 5:7 of Jesus as "son of God," was tantamount to naming Jesus a god by pagan-influenced Jews, and of course, by the Gentiles he healed.[21] The ascription and identification of Jesus as a "son of a god" would be acceptable to them, and also fit the social setting of Jesus' activity as an accepted charismatic. Of course, this application of god-like status was blasphemous to the Jewish elite.[22] Ultimately, it was the

---

17. Some of these traits were also ascribed to other charismatics and so-called "divine men," such as Apollonius of Tyana.

18. Smith, *Jesus the Magician*, 77.

19. For example, Paul being caught up in the third heaven (2 Cor 12:2), a Shaman-like experience familiar to other cultures as well (Smith, *Jesus the Magician*, 97–98).

20. See Morton Smith's discussion of the appearance of birds in visions and the provision of power (ibid.).

21. Ibid., 100–101.

22. Recall that Jesus quickly ordered the possessed to be silent about this. He quiets the possessed Gerasene man and asks the name of his demon (Mark 5:7–8).

charge, "son of God," leveled against him before Pilate, which made him a criminal, an "evildoer" (Mark 14:61; Luke 22:70; Matt 26:63; John 18:30).[23] This is a technical term found in contemporary literature applied to magicians who were arrested for practicing exorcism or incantation and spells, which were offenses punishable by death under Roman law. The gospels also use other familiar spiritual images common to the first-century Palestine: either God's angels or the Spirit of God "descended on him" to possess Jesus and come under his command, or, as Jesus' opponents accused, his ability to control demons meant that Jesus was himself possessed by Beelzebul, prince of demons, or that he was a dark magician of Satan. Indeed, some scholars believe Jesus' detractors identified him as Beelzebul.[24] This was a charge commonly leveled against some of Jesus' contemporaries who were believed to be able to command spirits or compel demons to drive out other, weaker spirits. This accusation is still brought against shamans today (for example, among the *samans* of the Tungus reindeer herders of Siberia) who command spirits: namely, that evil spirits possess them.[25]

The conflict over the source of an exorcist's authority is well documented. Anthropological studies have detected an interesting pattern of response to maladies and illnesses within cultures that accept demon possession as the norm. For example, identical illnesses associated with possession in "superior" and "subordinate" classes of society are attributed to dramatically different sources.[26] For the "subordinate" class, such as the peasant class of Palestine, the source is considered to be malevolent spirits that attack capriciously, demonstrating their loathing for the gods, greater spirits, or, as in Judaism, God. Among Jesus' contemporaries, Beelzebul and Satan represented such malevolent spirits. The subordinate class will desperately seek out shamans for protection and help in questioning the spirits to divine the cause of their malady, then ask shamans for assistance in negotiating with the spirits or in driving them out via exorcism. For the "superior" classes, the cause of the same illnesses is considered to be due to the malice of subordinates who have mastered spirits by witchcraft, dark magic, or spells. Consequently, for the superior class, exorcists like Jesus

---

23. One of the accusations leveled against Jesus by the religious elite was that he claimed to be the Son of God. This accusation was certainly repeated before Pilate among the "many things" brought against him (Mark 15.3), and Pilate questioned whether he was an "evildoer" (Mark 5:13), a term associated with magicians and exorcists.

24. Smith, *Jesus the Magician*, 32.

25. Lewis, *Ecstatic Religion*, 33, 54–56.

26. See ibid., 120–21; and Crossan, *Historical Jesus*, 315–18.

were thought to be the cause of many maladies, since they controlled the evil spirits and might use them to deceive others and make money. Even today, shamans are often accused of being dark magicians who are themselves possessed by evil and may manipulate spirits in order to gain control over others and make a living off their magic. This is precisely what we witness in the Jerusalem elite's accusations against Jesus and their determination to eradicate him for fear of being attacked by the evil he might conjure—their primary concern being the rise of subordinate classes in response to his call for their rejection as "vipers."[27]

Just as Matthew and Luke redact or edit out some of the more controversial aspects of Jesus' charismatic activity found in Mark, miracle traditions about Hanina and Choni were significantly "softened" as sayings from both were accepted into rabbinic tradition. The final form of these traditions suggests that that each had an intimate relationship with God, not that they were possessed by spirits or commanded demons by the authority of God, which is otherwise evidenced in multiple contemporary examples of charismatics and exorcists. Instead, both were described as speaking with God informally. God himself *listened to them*—they were said to "have his ear."[28] They spoke to him as if in conversation, and also through special forms of prayer. The latter observation suggests ecstatic behavior stood behind these traditions as the norm. Both Jesus and contemporary exorcists practiced controlled prayer that may have been tantamount to a spiritual trance familiar to charismatics.[29] Spiritual trance is less palatable than speech or prayer. Interestingly, an intimacy with God is also ascribed to Jesus according to the gospels: "*Abba*, oh father, everything is possible to you" (Mark 14:36).[30] Here, Jesus' prayer may reflect a spiritual trance, as it is a request that acknowledges God as the active power via direct speech to God, which was witnessed by others in his band. Alternatively, in multiple

---

27. Lewis, *Ecstatic Religion*, 120–26. Jesus' accusations in Matt 23:3 reflect this conflict.

28. "Father, I thank you that you have heard me. I knew that you always hear me, but I said this for the benefit of the people standing here, that they may believe that you sent me" (John 11:41–44).

29. Vermès, *Jesus the Jew*, 74. Hanina prays with his head bowed between his knees and knows that when his prayer is "fluent," it has been heard. For a discussion of trance and possession, see Lewis, *Ecstatic Religion*, 31–51.

30. See also John 11:41–44, where Jesus statement acknowledges that he is in such a familiar relationship with God that his words are immediately heard and responded to by *Abba*.

examples, Jesus acts on his own volition because the Spirit of God has already possessed him (Mark 2:10–11). As the Son of God, given the "finger of God," Jesus is able to command that Spirit to overwhelm demons at will. Indeed, Jesus' address to God as *Abba* implies both respect and the familiarity that comes from his endowed charismatic authority. It is unlike any other of his contemporaries. While not uncommon in ancient Judaism,[31] here it is unique, for it is an affirmation of Jesus' ability to call upon this authority at will for exorcism.

Clearly then, Jewish exorcists and ecstatics such as Choni and Hanina were remembered in oral lore because of this power to command spirits and demons as shown through their memorable actions.[32] And while their ability to perform miracles is never portrayed in the rabbinic traditions as the result of magical spells, incantations, or formulaic actions that were intended to force out demons or merit God's response, these are the very traits attributed to other Jewish exorcists[33] such as Eleazar, who was active from approximately 60 to 90 CE. Eleazar used secret incantations that had been passed down from the "wise and blessed" King Solomon, who was thought to have been an exorcist *par excellence* by these charismatics and other contemporaries.[34] Josephus describes Eleazar's exorcisms as follows: Using special magical "rings" (which may have been inserted into the nostrils of the possessed victim), Eleazar would pull the demon out through the nostrils of the possessed.[35] He would then invoke the name of Solomon, followed by secret incantations to prevent the demon's reentry. Eleazar's

---

31. *Abba* did not mean "daddy," but rather "respected father," the address of an adult Jewish child for his parent or elder. This understanding differs from the claims of Joachim, *Abba*; and ibid., *Proclamation of Jesus*. See Barr, "Abba Isn't Daddy."

32. Described as "one of the men of deeds" (*m. Soṭah* 9:15), as Jesus was also called by Josephus, "the doer of wonderful deeds" (Josephus, *Ant.* 18:63–64).

33. Rabbi Johanan ben Zakkai, who lived about the time of Josephus, records the following: "Has an evil spirit never entered into you? Have you never seen a person in whom an evil spirit has entered? What should be done with the so affected? Take roots of herbs, burn them under him and surround him with water, whereupon the spirit will flee (Pesik., ed. Buber 40a)" (*Jewish Encyclopedia.com*, s.v. "Exorcism," updated August 1, 2002, http://www.jewishencyclopedia.com/articles/5942-exorcism).

34. This idea is fully developed in the *Testament of Solomon* (which possibly dates to the first century, but is only found among Christian writings). Solomon's wisdom derived from his ability to use special rings to perform magic, including the ability to control demons.

35. Josephus, *Ant.* 8:45–48. As noted earlier, Josephus describes the exact manner in which Eleazar performed his exorcisms and their effects on the individuals.

actions were not unique. Other Jewish exorcists like Eleazar also employed Solomon's incantations. Indeed, Jesus knew of them: "Someone [an exorcist] greater than Solomon is here" (Luke 11:31). Jesus is directly addressing Jews that expected him to practice exorcism like those who employed the ecstatic and secret incantations of Solomon. Indeed, he was likely called "Son of David," for this term was associated with exorcists and charismatic activity associated with Solomon at the time of Jesus' activity.[36] As we shall see, Jesus did occasionally use special methods in his exorcisms—whether words or the use of spittle for ointments—not unlike those contemporaries used to expel evil spirits that caused illness or blindness. It is no wonder that Jesus, like Hanina and Choni, was respected as well as feared.[37] To be near Jesus was to be "near the fire" (*Gos. Thom.* 82). There was danger: the conflict over the entry of the kingdom of God was present, and evil, and Satan would prevent it if possible.

## JESUS, EXORCISM, AND THE INBREAKING KINGDOM OF GOD (AND DISPLACEMENT OF THE ELITE)

Unlike his contemporaries, it is what Jesus said about his exorcisms that ultimately led to his arrest and execution. Helmut Koester states, "It is quite likely that the saying connected with the driving out of demons contains several genuine words of Jesus (Mark 3:23–25, 26, 27; especially Matthew 12:28; see also Luke 10:18)."[38] Indeed, the distinction between Jesus and other Jewish charismatics is that he claimed they signaled (if not activated), the beginning of a catastrophic eschatological event. Jesus very publicly and repeatedly, announced that every exorcism and healing were proof that the "kingdom of God" was inbreaking—a kingdom that by implication was displacing the present demonic "kingdom of Satan," namely, the pagan imperialism that occupied Palestine and was embraced by the Jerusalem elite. This claim, combined with such sayings as "the kingdom of God is in your midst" (Luke 17:21) or "is upon you is upon you" (Mark 1:15), was considered seditious.

---

36. Ahearne-Kroll, *Psalms of Lament*, 141. The naming of Jesus as "Son of David" during his ministry by witnesses to his exorcisms and healings is most certainly coherent with contemporary associations made with other charismatics.

37. When Jesus was being arrested, he identified himself to his captors, only to have them back away and fall over each other in fear (John 18:5).

38. Koester, *History and Literature*, 79.

Consequently, to associate the exorcism of demons and evil spirits with the ouster of Satan, and thus with the arrival of the kingdom of God, is to condemn the current kingdom and its rulers as demonic. Herein lies a direct conflict of perilous risk between Jesus and his opponents. Jesus did just this; he made and expounded on the current rule as a kind of "demonic imperialism" that was ending: "I see Satan fall like lightening" (Luke 10:8).[39] Jesus' exorcism in Mark 5:1–17, wherein he casts the demons of Legion into the herd of swine, is a reflection of the expulsion of demonic imperialism in its purest form. Jesus is able to free a possessed and abused man from torment as the "master of spirits."[40] He does so by negotiating with the demons of Legion—a name synonymous with imperialism—not only to leave, but also to be cast into a herd of pigs, the unclean food of pagans and gentiles,[41] which then race off a cliff to drown in the lake.[42] Whether this exorcism is historical or not, it confirms that Jesus' exorcisms were characterized as anti-imperialistic and that demonic possession was synonymous with imperial rule. Moreover, Jesus' association of Rome and the Jerusalem's elite with demonic possession could not have been more strongly tied together. The demons flee—exactly what Jesus claims is happening in his successful exorcisms of the forces opposing God. Thus, Jesus' countermeasure to apostasy, namely exorcism, was linked with the most powerful and anticipated eschatological countermeasure of all: the long-expected inbreaking of God into history, the judgment of the wicked, and the reward of the righteous. As John Crossan says, "There is therefore a 'symbiotic relationship' between 'possession and protest' from the weak to the strong and accused possession as control from the strong to the weak."[43]

For Jesus, the association of exorcisms with the presence of the kingdom of God was therefore unmistakable. The Spirit that possessed him, and that was available at his command, gave him the authority to exorcise demons and end demonic rule. Not only did Jesus demand the rejection of apostasy from those who witnessed or were participants in his exorcisms, he also demanded that they must also become a "child" of God and turn

---

39. See Crossan, *Historical Jesus*, 313 on the Book of Similitudes, or Parables of Enoch, in *1 En*. 37–71.
40. Lewis, *Ecstatic Religion*, 33 and 52.
41. Such as found in the ancient concept of "scapegoat."
42. Ibid., 33.
43. Crossan, *Historical Jesus*, 317.

away from the kingdom of Satan.[44] They must accept great risk and act with precipitous trust that what they witnessed was altering the current order in their favor. This demand on the new child was given in terms of specific and significant social actions, all of which were time-bound and measureable due to the urgency of the crisis situation:

- For the upper classes and wealthy: To renounce all titles or claims to social or religious standing, to repatriate stolen wealth, to give abundantly to the poor, to accept the disenfranchised and outcasts of society equally as fellow children by admitting them into the synagogue and to table fellowship (even, perhaps, without regard to gender[45]), and to reject the authority of Jerusalem elite's in religious matters pertaining to God and his judgment.

- For the poor and lower classes: To renounce maladies and demonic possession as God's rejection of them, to forgive the oppressor and surrender hatred to the coming judgment of God, to give to those in need as they are able (e.g., a drink of water, a morsel of food, a cloak), to pray for their enemies because they are controlled by Satan, and to love others as their neighbor, which included prohibition for seeking retribution on those who stole from them.

It is to these new children of God that Jesus directs sayings concerning joy and celebration, often making allusions to the celebration of the marriage feast and a release from fasting. These sayings are coherent with the proclamation of the impending kingdom (Matt 22:1–4), and are an outcome of his countermeasure to apostasy:

> "Can the wedding guests fast while the bridegroom is with them?" (Mark 2:19)

> "Congratulations to you poor, for yours is the kingdom of heaven!" (Q/Luke 6:20; *Gos. Thom.* 54)[46]

> "Go to your house, to your friends, and tell them what great things the Lord has done for you, and how he had mercy on you." (Mark 5:19)

---

44. For a full discussion of the term "kingdom of Satan," see ibid., 319–20.

45. The women who financially supported and travelled with Jesus as he went from village to village with his band of exorcists (e.g., Mary of Magdala and the wife of Zebedee) are abundantly well-documented.

46. See Stephen Patterson and Marvin Meyer's translation of the Gospel of Thomas in Miller, *Complete Gospels*, http://gnosis.org/naghamm/gosthom.html.

> "Again, the Kingdom of Heaven is like a treasure hidden in the field, which a man found, and hid. In his joy, he goes and sells all that he has, and buys that field." (Q/Matt 13:44)

> "The (Father's) kingdom is like a person who had a treasure hidden in his field but did not know it. And [when] he died he left it to his [son]. The son [did] not know about it either. He took over the field and sold it. The buyer went plowing, [discovered] the treasure, and began to lend money at interest to whomever he wished." (*Gos. Thom.* 107:1–3)

> "Most assuredly I tell you, there are some standing here who will in no way taste death until they see the Kingdom of God come with power." (Mark 9:1)

Jesus allowed his fellow exorcists and these children to address God in terms of having been adopted by him, something shocking and radical for those formerly considered untouchable, outcasts, sinners and possessed by Satan. Jesus demands that these people are under God's protection; he is their father, *Abba*, the loving one who preserves and provides for his children.[47] This was a charismatic association, an event that was part and parcel of the inbreaking kingdom and unlike the claims made by any of Jesus' contemporary exorcists or activists. For the Jerusalem elite, giving the outcasts and socially depraved such expectations engendered perilous risk. Such "children" came from the oppressed lower castes and the disenfranchised fringe of society made up of avowed enemies of the aristocracy. These were the poor, zealots, and disciples of the executed John the Baptist—those classified as outcasts, sinners, and the condemned under the law. Jesus was therefore dangerous, an outlaw exorcist, and an enemy of the aristocracy.

Thus, Jesus' rejected a claim to his own authority, but pointed to what his exorcisms indicated: the joy of the coming kingdom of God for those who embrace his demands. Justice and judgment were on the brink. As such, Jesus drove out demons to begin displacing the kingdom of Satan, end possession of the land brought about by pagan imperialism and foreign gods, and inaugurate the inbreaking of the kingdom of God—a kingdom occupied by the new children of the Father, *Abba*. Thus, Jesus' exorcisms were a countermeasure to demonic imperialism.[48] To more thoroughly explore this connection between exorcism and the rejection of Satan's kingdom, we turn to Luke 11:20.

---

47. See Rom 8:14–17 for the earliest rendering of this assertion.
48. Crossan, *Historical Jesus*, 313–32.

## JESUS, EXORCISM, AND THE KINGDOM OF GOD—LUKE 11:20

"But if I drive out demons by the finger of God, then the kingdom of God has come upon you."

—Luke 11:20

We begin our study of Luke 11:20 by analyzing its claim to authenticity. To do so, we will begin examining the evidence by first drawing on the analytical tools of critical scholarship.

New Testament scholar Norman Perrin was successful in isolating a group of Jesus' *logoi* (words or sayings) that are more than just a reflection of the faith and needs of the community. Applying specific literary criteria originally suggested by Rudolf Bultmann,[49] namely, the "criterion of dissimilarity,"[50] and a corollary criterion, the "criterion of coherence,"[51] Perrin was able to show that Luke 11:20 was dissimilar to both the early church and Palestinian Judaism, meaning that is was unique to Jesus.[52] In his analysis of "'I' Sayings,"[53] Bultmann concluded this saying contained the "full eschatological power [of Jesus' proclamation], which must have characterized the activity of Jesus,"[54] For both Bultmann and Perrin, the

---

49. Bultmann, *History of the Synoptic Tradition*, 205. As noted, Rudolf Bultmann has been considered the foremost (and most controversial) German liberal New Testament scholar of the twentieth century, at least until the emergence of German-born scholar Helmut Koester, one of the final doctoral students Bultmann produced. The "criterion of dissimilarity" and "criterion of coherence" are terms applied to Bultmann's suggestion by Perrin, *Rediscovering the Teachings*, 38–43.

50. A saying could not have any claim to be Jesus' own words—a claim to "authenticity," or *ipsissima vox*—if it were dissimilar from the sayings, beliefs, and context of first-century Palestinian Judaism and the early church.

51. As will be explained further, use of the criterion of coherence may bring other sayings to the level of Jesus' own words, provided that such sayings were coherent with those sayings found to be authentic under the criterion of dissimilarity and other "testing" tools.

52. Perrin, *Rediscovering the Teachings*, 63–68.

53. Bultmann, *History of the Synoptic Tradition*, 162–61.

54. Ibid., 162.

saying was also coherent with the Jesus proclamation of the eschatological event of the arrival of the kingdom of God, and therefore had "the highest degree of [claim to] authenticity."[55] Needless to say, the outcome renders fascinating insights into Jesus, his charismatic activity, and the content of his eschatological proclamation. Here too is clear evidence that Jesus' exorcisms and their linkage with the kingdom of God were both a factual and relevant part of his radical teaching—indisputably so.

Jesus states he can oust demonic forces.[56] He is possessed by the Spirit of God, able to employ the "finger of God" as a divine man or a Spirit possessed exorcist.[57] Exorcisms, or successful negotiation with and commanding of demons, confirmed the overthrow of Satan's kingdom. Jesus warns those present that the current order is ending. By implication, Jerusalem's elite and imperialism are doomed.

Jesus' teachings were therefore seditious in the eyes of the elite. As noted, his exorcisms, illegal under Roman law as magic (which his actions could be understood to reflect in their contemporary setting),[58] provided opportunity for his capture and execution. But this alone was no more than an annoyance. It was Jesus' association of imperialism with satanic rule and its near end that ultimately condemned him to the cross. Fearless, he went about freeing the bound and tortured Jews of Palestine from demonic forces, promising that God's intervention and justice were already present (Mark 5:1–20).

---

55. Perrin, *Rediscovering the Teachings*, 64; and Bultmann, *History of the Synoptic Tradition*, 162.

56. Using any means necessary, whether command of evil spirits, use of ointments, prayer, or by command—Jesus embraced any contemporary method necessary and expected by those he freed. See Luke 11:20.

57. His possession of the Spirit and ability to control and exorcise demons led to his being called "Son of God" in Judeo-pagan environments. Other parallels are noted later in this study. See Mark 5:7–8; and Luke 11:15–17.

58. Roman Law, *The Twelve Tables*, Crimes, Table VII.3 and 15, also Table VIII.9. See du Plessis, *Borkowski's Textbook on Roman Law*, 5–6, 29–30. In his discussion of the death sentence associated with magic under Roman law, Smith cites the commentaries of the early third-century Roman jurist Paulus: "It is the prevailing legal opinion that participant in the magical art should be subject to the extreme punishment, that is, either thrown to the beasts or crucified" (qtd. in Smith, *Jesus the Magician*, 75–76).

## EXORCISM AS A COUNTERMEASURE TO POSSESSION OF THE LAND[59]

Jesus' conflict was clearly not with Judaism, but like other contemporaries such as the Qumran community, was instead with those he saw in Jerusalem as possessed, corrupted apostates who were corrupting the law and tacitly rejecting the rule of God as sovereign king. This not only included the religious elite, wealthy aristocracy, and the leaders of the Sanhedrin, but also the high priests and their families.[60] As we have seen, Jesus clearly associated his exorcisms with the expulsion of demonic imperialism by God and the establishment of his kingdom.[61] Ultimately, Jesus' exorcisms and pronouncements directed at the elite led to a deadly confrontation. The elite aristocracy recognized the perilous risk posed by this illegal exorcist and vocal opponent as Jesus gathered other exorcists and followers to "invade" Jerusalem during the Passover (John 11:49–53).[62] The elite first countered this risk with warnings, then threats and attempted entrapment, and finally, Jesus' arrest and death.

This peasant exorcist adopted at his own peril the possibility of annihilation (for as a Jew, death under the permanent curse of crucifixion was tantamount to the destruction of body and soul).[63] He did so for the sake

---

59. See Crossan, *Historical Jesus*, 313–32; and Evans, "Jesus' Action in the Temple."

60. This included all the high priests and their families, particularly those appointed before 60 CE (e.g., the house of Annas and his five sons, as well as his son-in-law, Caiaphas, mentioned in the Gospels).

61. Consider, for example, the "binding of the strong man" (Matt 12:29); the exorcism of the Gerasene demon "Legion" (Luke 8:26–37), clearly an allusion to the Romans; the possession of Judas, an agent, informant, and assassin of the elite, which Jesus recognized; "What do you want Jesus of Nazareth, have you come to destroy us?" (Mark 1:21–28); "I have been sent to the lost sheep of Israel" (Mark 7:24–30; Luke 11:20); the establishment of the kingdom of God over the kingdom of Satan; and Jesus continuing to exorcise demons, spurring Herod to seek to kill him (Luke 13:31–32).

62. The only reason Jesus' exorcisms and miracles forced him into hiding was the elite's conclusion that he was their enemy, and therefore the enemy of the people under God's established rulers, the Romans. As a result, they sought his arrest, and indeed his life, at the festival as soon as possible. The Gospel of John reflects the impending danger for Jesus in the high priests' conclusion that he must die for the "people," since Jesus opposed the rule that God had established in the Roman occupation and the appointment of the elite over the people (John 11:49–53).

63. "Go tell that fox [Herod] that I will continue to cast out demons and heal today and tomorrow and third day I will accomplish my purpose" (Luke 13:32). Here, Jesus is referring to accomplishing his "purpose" of cleansing the land and displacing the enemies of God—that is, Herod and the elite, who are tacitly Romans, whom Jesus claims

of the king who was on the brink of arriving with mercy for the hungry and outcast, those who rejected apostasy and embraced God as their father. These children could bypass Jerusalem's authority and speak directly with God,[64] which may have implied suspension of the temple rites, and thus, the threat of treason and apostasy.[65] Jesus demanded that his adherents take perilous risks,[66] trusting that God would act to preserve them when he arrived fully with the kingdom. This can certainly be defined as a radical response to the perilous risk of apostasy.

## THE COUNTERMEASURES OF THE ELITE TO THE CHARISMATIC JESUS

It is in this historical environment of demonic possession that we find the confrontation of two entities in a common context of perilous risk, each attempting to cancel out the other. The Gospel of Mark documents the confrontation between Jesus and the religious elite (Mark 3:23–29). Here, Jesus announces that exorcisms are the indisputable "sign" that demonic possession of Judaism and the land was at an end.[67] Exorcisms, then, were the countermeasure to the perilous risk of pollution and apostasy introduced by God's opponents, the Jerusalem aristocracy and religious elite. It is they who embraced pagan rule, and thus, facilitated demonic possession of the land. The demons of Satan had flourished, and like the Roman occupiers they supported, the privileged elite had tortured and tormented the common Jews under their possession. In the elite's view, the dispossessed and

---

are affiliates of the demons that have invaded the land. Jesus brings their end on behalf of God as his exorcist.

64. Jesus teaches a simple prayer, not unlike other contemporary Jewish prayers, but with two very distinctive elements now embedded in the Lord's Prayer; namely, keeping one from apostasy (or demonic possession) and looking to the arrival of the "kingdom" already coming in power. This is the prayer of the exorcist Jesus.

65. "Take these stones down and in three days I will bring it into being" (John 2:19). The fullness of time, or the three days referenced by Jesus, reflects the end of the Temple occupied by the apostates and the direct access given by God to his new children who may address him as "*Abba*."

66. As an outlaw under Roman law, Jesus knew that if he were captured, his death by crucifixion would be the imminent punishment for a capital crime, just as it would be for those he authorized to also be exorcists: "Anyone who follows me must pick up his cross" (Mark 8:34).

67. See below for further discussion of Luke 11:20: "If I by the finger of God cast out demons, then the kingdom of God has come upon you."

helpless deserved their due as judged sinners, unlike the privileged elite and aristocracy themselves (Luke 18:9–14).[68] Like the Romans who were considered to occupy the land by the will of God, so too was it thought that the ill and dispossessed suffered because they must be sinners deserving of such punishment, even if it originated with their mother or father (John 9:3).

Not surprisingly, the culminating criticism of Jesus and his exorcisms as satanic came from the Jerusalem scribes. These scribes were supporters of the aristocracy and thus collaborators with foreign rule and Roman imperialism, including control over the priesthood, and by extension, the temple.[69] Ultimately, they publicly charged him with corruption and possession by the principal demon of Satan, Beelzebul, alleging that Satan had given him authority to control any spirit or demon to deceive the people. For the elite, support for Roman rule was required, since God set in place all authorities—even the brutal Roman occupiers. Therefore, they claimed that it was Jesus who was the possessed apostate:

> "Jesus was driving out a demon that was mute. When the demon left, the man who had been mute spoke, and the crowd was amazed. But some of them said, 'By Beelzebul, the prince of demons, he is driving out demons,' while others tested him by asking for a sign from heaven." (Luke 11:15; Matt 12:25–27; Mark 3:22–26)

Because the exorcisms are public events, the elite have been put in a position in which they must confront the indisputable evidence of various exorcisms seen by multiple witnesses (Mark 3:1–6).[70] They are forced to either publicly accept or reject Jesus' control of demons as originating from God, much like they were forced to choose when Jesus demanded their answer as to the source of John's authority, "Was John's baptism of God or from men?" (Mark 11:30). While they refused to answer Jesus' question, thereby avoiding public confrontation, Jesus' exorcisms gave them no quarter. Needing to address the source of his authority, they chose the most radical countermeasure available: Satan. In this way, Jesus was no longer a self-aggrandizing magician in the eyes of the elite; he was a blasphemer claiming the authority of God to contravene what the elite says God has

---

68. This is an accurate portrayal of Jesus' view of the fate of the elite (in this case, likely Herodian Pharisee, who opposed Jesus) and the fate of the dispossessed, the common Jews.

69. "Teachers of the law" (Mark 3:22).

70. See also Ehrman, *New Testament*, 263.

*Palestinian Judaism and Ecstatic Activity*

put in place. This would have been a remarkably inept association to the common Jew, who was outraged at the opulence and corruption of the Jerusalem elite: he drives out demons and frees the sick from conditions perceived to have been brought about not by misfortune or the judgment of God, but by evil agency that pursues the helpless and afflicts them.[71]

In answer to their charge, Jesus employs a *Mashal*, or parable, to defend the divine source of these miracles (Mark 3:23–29) and to implicitly warn that they are more than a sign; they are a countermeasure to the perilous risk brought about by elitist apostasy. It is the humble and repentant who now fill this role as God's children. Jesus' statement, "The first shall be last and the last first" (Matt 20:16),[72] thus resonates powerfully in this context as both a warning and eschatological statement; certainly his opponents would have understood this saying as such.

Jesus thus reverses this charge of apostasy with one of his most vehement warnings found in the New Testament, akin to Paul's curse on those who obstruct access to the gospel (Gal 1:8). That is, it is the elite who blaspheme the Holy Spirit of God by rejecting God's kingship and will:

> "So Jesus called them over to him and began to speak to them in parables: 'In fact, no one can enter a strong man's house without first tying him up. Then he can plunder the strong man's house. Truly I tell you, people can be forgiven all their sins and every slander they utter, but whoever blasphemes against the Holy Spirit will never be forgiven; they are guilty of an eternal sin.'" (Mark 3:27–30)[73]

The lower classes gladly accepted the exorcisms of a hero like Jesus who was able to command or negotiate evil spirits away. That is, they accepted him to have authority by the Spirit that possessed him or the Spirit given to him by God, whom he could call upon to act on his behalf. The elite accused Jesus of deception and profiteering from his magic, a typical

---

71. See the previous description of the accusations against Jesus as being Beelzebul's agent.

72. See also Mark 9:35, which gives credence to this statement as a political critique of the elite. Here, Jesus explains this statement to his disciples as the expectation that they not be like the elite, but rather embrace the eschatological reversal; this is how the children of the king are to behave towards each other. A similar statement is found in Matt 6:5, which is a critique of the Pharisees—that is, those who are complicit with the elite (i.e., the scribes), whose behavior Jesus warns will be judged for their arrogance.

73. Thus, those who accuse Jesus of being possessed by Beelzebul would themselves be in danger of possession by Beelzebul.

response from people in control who feared attack, particularly malevolent assault. Jesus designated his spirit as the "Holy Spirit," or the spirit sent by and of Yahweh, the Jewish God. Jesus' pointed warning was clear: he was not possessed by inferior spirits, such as those claimed by magicians or ecstatics or by those offered by pagan gods. Jesus was possessed—perhaps better described as saturated and filled—by the Holy Spirit of God, the most powerful of all forces to Jews. In the gospels, the Holy Spirit made other spirits flee or cower; they recognized this Spirit's authority to harm, cast them into lonely places, or destroy them, and so these lesser spirits obeyed Jesus' commands because the Holy Spirit was at his disposal, sometimes possessing him (as at baptism). When some magicians witnessed it as more powerful than their own, they tried to buy it, as in Acts 8:18. This underscores the pervasive belief in spirits available to dark magicians from gods or other malevolent forces. Therefore, for Jesus to warn his opponents about the perilous risk of blaspheming against the Holy Spirit by saying that Beelzebul possessed him was to warn that the Holy Spirit would not recognize or protect them against other spirits any longer—they would be rejected by it forever. The warning is ominous.

This saying confirms that the scribes of Jerusalem publicly linked Jesus' actions with demonic possession. His own family publicly said he was "mad," or possessed (Mark 3:21).[74] That his authority was demonic—that is, designed to deceive and convince the simple and poor to follow his blasphemous and dangerous teachings—is a charge later reflected in the Babylonian Talmud.[75] Jesus counters this charge by explaining that those who deny that it is the Holy Spirit of God that has possessed him will neither be protected nor freed from Satan, but instead will be cursed and separated from God, for it is they who are possessed.

It is in the charismatic tradition that we witness a classic example of the collision of countermeasures in which counter charges of perilous risk are validated as real, thereby confirming the indisputable historicity of these traditions. Jesus was indeed an exorcist of demons and maladies who

---

74. Morton Smith confirms this term denotes possession by evil (Smith, *Jesus the Magician*, 32–33).

75. As noted, the Babylonian Talmud includes the following: "On the eve of Passover they hanged Yeshu. And an announcer went out in front of him for forty days, saying: 'He is going to be stoned, because he practiced sorcery and enticed and led Israel astray. Anyone who knows anything in his favor, let him come and plead in his behalf.' But not having found anything in his favor, they hanged him on the eve of Passover" (*b. Sanh.* 43a).

uniquely linked his activity to the kingship of God and to the apostasy of the religious elite and Jerusalem aristocracy—a dangerous charge worthy of death. In Mark, qualitative risk analysis confirms that Jesus challenged and rejected the religious elite as true representatives of God based on their apostasy and complicit support of imperialism, thereby rousing their hatred of him (Mark 7:1–23). Interestingly, the charge follows Jesus' healing of a man with a withered hand in the synagogue on the Sabbath.[76] The accusation against Jesus came from *Pharisees who supported the Herodians*, that is, those who were also complicit with foreign rule and imperialism.[77] The objective of Jesus' opponents was to find a charge of sufficient severity to have him arrested for sedition. The aristocracy sought not just his silence; they sought his death as a dangerous magician and charlatan.[78]

## JESUS AND A NEW UNDERSTANDING OF EXORCISM IN ROMAN-OCCUPIED PALESTINE

There is something foreboding and powerful to be found in the traditions of Jesus' exorcisms and his ability to command the demons as compared to those of Eleazar, Choni, and Hanina. In the Gospel of Mark, Jesus is fearfully recognized as the Son of God (or a "son of a god" as heard by non-Jews) by the spirits he exorcises not just once, but repeatedly (Mark 1:23–28). This divine recognition, whether as a son of a god, the Son of God, or the son of David (or as an exorcist "greater" than exorcists who employ the incantations of Solomon), associates Jesus with something much more than a random, wandering exorcist. He portends cataclysmic change, which is both present and yet to fully come. In Jesus' case, the intimate connection between the miracle worker and God is extended to those exorcised and

---

76. For a description of this infirmity, please see the discussion in our analysis of Mark.

77. This will be discussed more thoroughly later; however, it is clear that the gospels expanded the conflict with the Pharisees, because they became opponents of the Christian communities of the Diaspora. The Pharisees were not Jesus' primary opponents during his own period of activity; rather, it was the scribes, Herodians, and other members of the Jewish aristocracy who were sympathetic with Rome (Smith, *Jesus the Magician*, 155).

78. This is clearly the implication of the Gospel of John's description of the raising of Lazarus. It is this event that sent Jesus' opponents back to Jerusalem to finalize the planning of his arrest and death through the paid assassin and infiltrator, Judas the Sicarii (the assassin or "dagger man").

the relentless overpowering of the most feared enemies of God. Indeed, it is Satan's demons who cry out in protest and anger as they are driven out to the wilderness or into pigs who drown themselves (Mark 5:1–20), reluctantly freeing the lowly, the innocent, and hopeless. Jesus demands that it be understood that it is only the power of God that can provide such miraculous freedom; it is the *euangelion*, the charismatic and transformative good news, which provides unbounded hope formerly unimaginable to the humble and vulnerable. Yet the scribes reject Jesus and publicly charge that he is in collusion with Beelzebul (Mark 5).

Instead of just popular miracle stories, the ecstatic traditions of Jesus were eschatological events of transformation from the kingdom of Satan to the kingdom of God—they were signs that the end of the age was inbreaking and the rule of God was now present: "For behold, the kingdom of God is [now] in your midst!" (Luke 17:21). This is the dramatic extension of Jesus' charismatic activity: the ultimate countermeasure to the pervasive expansion of the kingdom of Satan under imperialism and the Roman occupation supported by Jerusalem. Jesus therefore linked his exorcisms to the overthrow of the evil kingdom, not simply to individual cures or to his personal power in possessing the Spirit of God. God and judgment were coming on the elite fully with the arrival of the kingdom, and its inbreaking was already present. This went well beyond anything claimed by contemporary ecstatics, magicians, or sons of the gods.[79]

The eschatological transformation Jesus ascribes to his exorcisms reflects the historical context of his countermeasure to the perilous risk of demonic possession and apostasy of the land and Jerusalem. Consequently, the synoptic tradition regarding Jesus' exorcisms, where it is not centered on the person of Jesus but on the event of the kingdom, must be considered authentic and historically reliable. It is this that represents the central conflict of two entities that perceive each other as a perilous risk in a well-defined historical context. This conflict meets the test of qualitative risk analysis. As such, Jesus' exorcisms are completely unlike the "softened" miracle traditions attributed to Choni and Hanina, which have nothing to do with God entering history to expel demonic invasions or end the kingdom of Satan. This underscores why Jesus' charismatic activity is found not only in the earliest strata of the oral tradition, but in all strata. Exorcisms must be considered historical occasions in the short life of Jesus of Nazareth as he confronted evil and the Jerusalem elite. The central conflict, then,

---

79. Smith, *Jesus the Magician*, 130–39.

on which we must base our analysis and develop our use of qualitative risk analysis, is the Beelzebul controversy. It is to this controversy that we shall now turn.

# 4

# The Beelzebul Controversy
## Countermeasures to Perilous Risk

VIRTUALLY ALL NEW TESTAMENT scholars consider the Beelzebul controversy historical.[1] As such, it provides the core controversy wherein the countermeasures of Jesus and his opponents collide. We know it arose out of Jesus' opponents' indisputable belief that he commanded and expelled demons at will. Here we find what Jesus said about his authority, what his opponents countered with, and the perilous risks that each attempted to negate. The event reads as follows:

> "Now he was casting out a demon that was mute. When the demon had gone out, the mute man spoke, and the people marveled. But some [the scribes who came down from Jerusalem][2] of them said, 'He casts out demons by Beelzebul, the prince of demons,' while others, to test him, kept seeking from him a sign from heaven. But he, knowing their thoughts, said to them: 'Every kingdom divided against itself is laid waste, and a divided household falls. And if Satan also is divided against himself, how will his kingdom stand? For you say that I cast out demons by Beelzebul. And if I cast out demons by Beelzebul, by whom do your sons cast them out? Therefore they will be your judges. But if it is *by the finger of*

---

1. See the discussions in Koester, "History and Literature," 79; Ehrman, *New Testament*, 260–63; Horsley and Silberman, *Message and the Kingdom*, 49–53; Jeremias, *Proclamation of Jesus*, 91–92, 95; Vermès, *Jesus the Jew*, 53–82; Borg, *Jesus*, 126–28; and Patterson, *God of Jesus*, 72–73.

2. See Mark 3:22a.

*God* that I cast out demons, then the kingdom of God has come upon you. When a strong man, fully armed, guards his own palace, his goods are safe; but when one stronger than he attacks him and overcomes him, he takes away his armor in which he trusted and divides his spoil. Whoever is not with me is against me, and whoever does not gather with me scatters.'" (Luke 11:14–23, emphasis mine)

Clearly, the Beelzebul controversy represents the lightening rod charge against Jesus and reflects the perilous risk he represented to his opponents. Due to its coherence with our previous contextual analysis, it is indisputably historical[3] and meets all the criteria of qualitative risk analysis.[4] Besides the controversy having multiple-attestation (that is, it is found in all strata of primitive gospel sources and tradition),[5] it is unquestionably the point of historical conflict between Jesus and the Jerusalem elite over the source of his authority and the legitimacy of his claim to control or be possessed by God's Spirit. Charging that he is Satan's minion and is able to exorcise demons by calling on and being possessed instead by Beelzebul, the elite applied the ultimate countermeasure to the perilous risk of Jesus' growing popularity and influence among the peasants and disenfranchised. The concern that he might raise resistance, not unlike Herod's fear of John's influence, is understandable—particularly since Jesus made a claim to John's ministry (Luke 7:19–23) and, according to his enemies, claimed to have even taken control of John's spirit through magical power (Mark 6:16). In other words, the elite publicly accused Jesus of being a dark magician: he had used spells to conjure and raise the spirit of John (magicians raised the spirit, not the body of the dead) and had thereby taken John's power and authority as his own by means of his relationship with Beelzubul, prince of demons.[6] Only a deceptive conjurer and demon-possessed ecstatic, a "doer of evil" (the same accusation brought by the high priest to Pilate that Jesus was a dark magician),[7] would be able to perform the works attributed to Jesus.

---

3. We find direct correlations from anthropological studies, as previously described. See Lewis, *Ecstatic Religion*, 120–26, particularly Diagram 1.

4. See the previous chapters' analyses and the foregoing application of qualitative risk analysis to the tradition, combined with the tradition's multiple attestation in Mark and Q. This is the collision of countermeasure to negate the perilous risk perceived by two parties of the other in a similar context. It is the crux of historical conflict.

5. Crossan, *Historical Jesus*, 318–20.

6. Smith, *Jesus the Magician*, 98.

7. Ibid., 41.

In the context of first-century Palestine and contemporary beliefs about the control of demons, by naming Jesus as Beelzubul, the elite attempt to claim control over Jesus and his demon. This is not simply an attempt to label Jesus as a known magician, but to render his charismatic powers impotent.[8] Jesus, of course, did not end his successful public exorcisms, thereby refuting their charge of demonic possession. Instead, he countered by asserting a different source of his authority: "to know God" (Luke 10:22), which was to possess access to the Spirit and command demons by the "finger of God [*daktulo theou*]." It is this ability to command the Spirit of God as he willed that, as we have noted, he linked to the arrival of the kingdom of God. Moreover, he solicited and trained up to as many as seventy other exorcists and sent them out to invade all the villages and towns around Jerusalem to exorcise demons in his name (Luke 10:1–23). Jesus was at war with Satan.

There is something to this charge of Beelzebul-possession that resonated ominously with the early Christian community, thereby leading to the end of its trajectories in later gospels. Matthew and Luke drop the Beelzebul reference and this tradition completely. Clearly, the charge was disturbing to the early church because accusations continued to be leveled against the followers of Jesus (and the wandering charismatics who continued to exorcise in Jesus' name) that they practiced dark magic and demonic possession. In fact, Matthew and Luke attempt to clean up the tradition surrounding the nature of Jesus' exorcisms to obscure the charge that Jesus was possessed either by demons or Satan (or that subsequent charismatics who controlled demons in the name of Jesus were possessed by the evil spirit of the magician conjured from the dead). What Matt 10:24–25 does say about this controversy is quite interesting. Here, Jesus appears to warn his fellow exorcists that the elite will naturally accuse them of the same apostasy as agents of Satan:

> "A disciple is not above his teacher, nor a servant above his master; it is enough for the disciple to be like his teacher, and the servant like his master. If they have called the master of the house Beelzebul, how much more will they malign those of his household?" (Matt 10:24–25)[9]

---

8. To name the demon is the take control of it (Lewis, *Ecstatic Religion*, 123; Smith, *Jesus the Magician*, 57 and 77). Jesus did this repeatedly in his exorcisms when he commanded the demon to reveal its name (Mark 5:9).

9. Recall that Helmut Koester asserts, "Historians are on very thin ice if they try to recover the historical person of Jesus through a critical analysis of the sayings tradition. A person of past history can only be understood if the extant sources reveal the traditions

This saying likely comes from the secondary tradition, wherein charismatic itinerant preachers sent out by the Spirit replicated Jesus' itinerant activity as the exorcists of demons. It is more than a warning. The intent is clear. It is an affirmation by the risen Lord that those who level such accusations against Jesus or his exorcists *are themselves* the servants of Beelzebul, their master. It is a statement of reversal, a countermeasure that echoes back to Jesus' ministry. If this saying can be associated with Jesus' activity (such as sending his appointed exorcists into villages and towns of Galilee and Decapolis), it is his warning that those who oppose him do not recognize their own perilous state. Satan deceives them—the ultimate accusation against Jesus' opponents in the context of first-century Palestinian Judaism. Moreover, Satan will hinder them, and through possession,[10] will lead others to capture or kill them.

For this reason, Jesus orders his followers to escape Satan: "If they persecute you in one town, flee to the next" (Matt 10:23b). What is remarkable about this saying is that it is certainly historical. It comes from the conflict between perilous risks and directly from Jesus. It gives us a glimpse into his instructions to exorcists, including the twelve he personally chose and trained, as well as subsequent followers who continued ecstatic forms of ministry post-Easter by emulating his itinerant mission:[11] Flee! In other words, "Don't remain in that village, leave immediately, and continue to the next village to drive Satan out of the country and into the deserted places before he silences you!" When they leave, exorcists must exit dramatically. In protest, they are instructed to leave behind the evil that permeates that place. These exorcists must depart in silence, signaling the condemnation awaiting that town, and move on the next possessed village (Luke 9:5). Such a bold claim of authority was powerful, and based on the gospel tradition, was practiced frequently. The instructions were provided because both Jesus and his exorcists undoubtedly had failed to convince villages and towns that they were of God.

---

to which such a person belongs as well as the subsequent structures, practices and institutions of a community in which the memory of this person is preserved" (Koester, *Jesus to the Gospels*, 231). Matt 10:24–25 confirms Koester's thesis insofar as the practices of the community that preserved this saying included exorcists who, like the historical Jesus, were accused of being possessed by Beelzebul.

10. As in the case of Judas, by "entering his heart," (Luke 22:3).

11. This included exorcists and magicians not directly affiliated with Jesus or his ministry decades later (Mark 9:38; Act 8:18).

It is no wonder that Jesus' name continued to be employed for decades afterwards in the practices of charismatics and magicians.[12] This form of entry into a town or village was exactly what Paul practiced (Acts 13:51), although he reversed the order of proclamation in some towns (Jesus and the kingdom were proclaimed first, followed by exorcisms), while in other incursions he exactly mirrored Jesus' own practice of exorcism followed by paraenesis (Acts 16:16). In this activity, Jesus and Paul have many more similarities, as evidenced in the ritual practices that Paul assumed, including exorcism and eschatological meals. One of the most prominent was the format of Jesus' own itinerant pattern of entering a town and beginning an assault on foreign gods, demons, and Satan. Paul unquestionably adopted this form of attack not just because he was familiar with it, but because it was the way Jesus of Nazareth successfully exorcised. As Koester would suggest, Paul emulated the practices of the historical Jesus.[13]

Consequently, Beelzebul controversy is surrounded by historical elements and relevant sayings that point to its usefulness as a historical measure to challenge the validity of other controversy dialogues in the gospels. To assist in this effort, we can summarize its fundamental characteristics, which are coherent with the countermeasures taken by both Jesus and the elite to cancel the other out. Some of these elements we will explore later in more detail.

## Countermeasures of the Elite

Jesus is a known exorcist widely considered to be a dark magician. He has become an annoyance. The Jerusalem elite send representatives to publicly ridicule him in Galilee.[14] His authority and legitimacy are tersely rejected as satanic. The charge against him is blasphemy and deception, even outright possession by the prince of demons. Jesus' exorcisms, and therefore any sayings of his, are to be considered dangerous and deceptive. He is a blasphemer claiming the power of God, as are his fellow exorcists. Any who

---

12. Smith, *Jesus the Magician*, 62–64.

13. There are multiple examples suggested in Acts and in the authentic letters of Paul, but they are beyond the scope of this study. For further discussion on the continuity between Jesus of Nazareth and Paul, see Koester, *Jesus to the Gospels*, 218–23, 232.

14. Interestingly, this is exactly what happened to Paul when men sent by James came to Galatia to deconstruct his church, ridiculing him as a charlatan and false teacher. Is this the pattern that James witnessed firsthand, namely, the elite's challenge to his brother Jesus in sending emissaries to disrupt his mission?

follow him will suffer the same fate as he: death. Be warned, Jesus is to be avoided and rejected; don't be counted with him. Any who follow Jesus follow Satan, for the current order is that of God.

## The Implications

Jesus is an undisputed Galilean ecstatic and exorcist. He commands the demons and evil spirits. He has gained notoriety in Jerusalem as a deceiver possessed by Beelzebul. His followers include other exorcists.[15] Unlike his contemporaries (e.g., Choni or Hanina ben Dosa), Jesus associates his exorcisms with the complete overthrow of Satan's rule and demonic imperialism by God.

## Countermeasures of Jesus of Nazareth

Satan's kingdom has invaded and possessed the land, but this is now at an end. The undeniable evidence of God's inbreaking kingdom is seen in Jesus' successful exorcisms. He is the possessed servant of God, given authority over demons by the Spirit. By exorcising demons, the kingdom for God is reclaimed, village-by-village. By implication, those who resist this good news are the one's who are most deceived. The current order is at an end. Satan is being cast out, as are his minions. To deny the Spirit, Jesus commands, is to blaspheme.

In sum, the framework of the Beelzebul controversy and its historical elements are clear. They provide a set of comparative elements that allows for the reconstruction of the conflict of perilous risk between Jesus and his opponents. It is to this assessment we now turn.

---

15. See "your sons" in Luke 11:19.

# 5

# Reconstructing the Conflict of Perilous Risks

QUALITATIVE RISK ANALYSIS HAS been employed, and a historical risk context has been established in which to assess the activity of the exorcist, Jesus of Nazareth, and the response of Jerusalem elite in the context of Roman-occupied Palestine of the early first century. We have demonstrated that a perception of perilous risk is present, one that is real and threatening both to Jesus and the elite. It is now possible to analyze the conflict between Jesus and his opponents. Within this common historical context, in which each perceives the other as a perilous threat, we can recreate the countermeasures each employs to cancel the other out, and thereby isolate verifiable historical conflict. Using the Beelzebul controversy as a backdrop, qualitative risk analysis can now turn to the gospel sources to identify coherent countermeasures—whether in terms of actions, sayings, or events. The analysis of countermeasures to perilous risk will be iterative, moving from a broader view of the life situation of Jesus to the more specific techniques he employed to counter apostasy and demonic activity.

## QUALITATIVE RISK ANALYSIS AND JESUS OF NAZARETH

The following conclusions are suggested based on the foregoing evaluation of risk context and a new comparison of the gospel sources to it that is coherent with qualitative risk analysis.[1]

Jesus was a poor and oppressed Jewish peasant craftsman from a small village in Galilee (Mark 6:3). He spoke a distinct Galilean dialect that was often ridiculed in Jerusalem as that of an uneducated country bumpkin.[2] Having witnessed the oppression of the dispossessed and poor,[3] the expanding demonic possession of the land,[4] as well as the corruption and apostasy of the religious elite in Jerusalem,[5] he left his village and large family and traveled to the Jordan River at Aenon near Salim (a two-day walk from Jerusalem), taking up with John the Baptist in his call to repent from

---

1. For the purposes of this discussion, the contextual references from independent sources previously noted are not recounted here. Instead, references focus on other gospel traditions that begin to fall into a cohesive set of historical events based on them and the application of qualitative risk analysis. See also Koester, "History and Literature," 73–83; Jeremias, *Proclamation of Jesus*, 51–55, 85–94, 96–103; Bultmann, *Theology of the New Testament*, 1:3–29; and Crossan, *Historical Jesus*, 313–48.

2. The Talmud (*m. 'Erubin* 53b) describes ridiculing a Galilean in the Jerusalem marketplace for trying to buy *amar*: "You stupid Galilean, do you want something to ride on [*chamar*: a donkey]? Or something to drink [*hamar*: wine]? Or something for clothing [*amar*: wool]? Or something for sacrifice [*immar*: a lamb]?"

3. The oppression was felt in the local tax collectors, licensed by Rome, who were famous for their corruption, bribery, and pilfering from the local populace, all under the protection of Rome's elite. As we have confirmed, the primary function of the procurator was to enforce tax collection for the empire, a large portion of which was also given to Herod Antipas.

4. As discussed below, Jesus was familiar with demonic possession from his early years, having certainly witnessed possessions of the outcasts and dispossessed. Moreover, Jesus witnessed firsthand the brutality of Rome. In 4 BC, the Roman general Varus lined the road from Sepphoris to Galilee with two thousand crucified Jewish rebels (Josephus, *J.W.* 2:5.2; ibid., *Ant.* 17:10.10). Sepphoris, a Hellenized Roman city only a day's walk from Nazareth, was itself constructed with pagan temples and Roman opulence, and was certainly visited by the elite.

5. Ehrman, *New Testament*, 257–58. The Synoptics only record Jesus in Jerusalem once, but this cannot be accurate due to the common practice of taking pilgrimages to various festivals. John records three visits, which is more accurate, as is the description of Jesus going incognito at least once (John 2:13, 5:1, 12:12).

apostasy and prepare for the judgment of God.[6] Jesus publicly embraced John's message, putting his very life at risk.[7]

Prior to his arrival at John's camp, Jesus was already a known exorcist, ecstatic, and healer in the villages near Galilee (John 2:1–11). It is evident that Jesus had not followed the traditional pattern of the eldest son providing support by plying the family trade. Nor did he share the support he received for his exorcisms and charismatic healings (Mark 3:32).[8] Consequently, his family, including his mother, considered him "mad," denoting that he was possessed and had lost his mind to the demons and spirits he expelled (Mark 3:21).[9] Jesus then tacitly rejected his family and spurned them, moving into the countryside (Mark 3:31–35). He had been violently thrown out of his home village of Nazareth for blasphemy (Luke 4:29), thereby shaming his family. Escaping, Jesus, found residence in Capernaum, a fishing town of some size on the lake of Galilee, but without cost—likely in the home of someone he healed, probably the mother-in-law of a fisherman called Simon. Jesus soon gathered a small following, which included disenfranchised peasants and laborers, most of whom he trained to be exorcists. He provided for these five-to-twelve men through donations, meals hosted by those he had cured, or alms given by the curious. Jesus' band of exorcists was communal, carrying a "common bag" of money (Matt 8:14).[10] There were several women whom he had freed from multiple demons and spirits who also "provided of their means" for him, donating money for housing, food, and clothing (Luke 8:3).

Jesus' authority to exorcise and command evil spirits to heal the sick, lame, insane was feared by the villagers, but also welcomed by them—a trait of lower castes in need of protection.[11] They were desperate to find re-

---

6. Koester, *Jesus to the Gospels*, 237.

7. Ibid.

8. We can also consider Mark 3:32 as evidence that Joseph may have shunned Jesus.

9. Jesus acknowledges the return of demons back to those exorcised or onto the exorcist himself (Matt 12:45). The "strongman" is not bound, so he will "plunder" the house, meaning that the demon will turn on the exorcist (Luke 11:14–22). See Smith, *Jesus the Magician*, 32–33.

10. As an example of a witness, see Mark 2:15 on Levi the tax collector. Jesus' band carried a communal bag; Levi and other tax collectors who rebelled and deserted their appointed posts granted by Roman delegates most likely also donated to Jesus.

11. The evidence for this is overwhelming; see for example Mark 6:1–2, which presupposes that Jesus was already known as a charismatic and exorcist, for healing was a result of casting out evil, or demons.

*Reconstructing the Conflict of Perilous Risks*

lief and peace for their loved ones. Families cared for multiple generations and were responsible for their relatives' wellbeing no matter their plight. They were forbidden to cast them out, even if they wished. When illness, deformity, or insanity occurred, people were trapped with that circumstance, understanding only that some evil had come upon them in punishment for sin or wrongdoing, or else that they had fallen victim to capricious demons because they were weak and poor. To be clear, based on contextual analysis, most illnesses and afflictions—including the suffering of the mute, sick, or crippled—were understood to be the result of demonic possession or evil activity (Mark 9:14–29). Even at this early stage, many rejected Jesus, particularly the rich and religious leaders. For some, he was a considered a charlatan and profiteer. Many claimed he was possessed and dangerous. As a result, Jesus was an ominous local hero (Mark 6:1–2), considered close to God by the lower classes and to have his ear like other contemporary exorcists such as Hanina and Choni.[12] But more importantly, they believed he was greater than these figures, being fully possessed by the Spirit of God, an angel, or other divine spirit, as evidenced by his ability to negotiate with or control demons—demons who, to the terror of the locals, called Jesus by name and claimed he was "a son of a god" or even "the Son of God." Yet, unlike contemporaries who were considered ecstatics and sages, Jesus remained a reclusive in Galilee and was not known for his teachings.[13] He continued to leave Capernaum to avoid pressing crowds, often wandering off to the hills to meditate and pray, returning only days or weeks later (Mark 1:35; Luke 4:42, 5:16; Matt 14:13, 23). At this time, Jesus was not preaching.

All of this changed in his late twenties. Jesus learned of John's public rejection of the Jerusalem elite and his vehement charges regarding their corruption and apostasy. They were a "brood of vipers" possessed by demons, minions of Satan who were soon to be "cut down and thrown into the fire" in the wrath of God's coming judgment (Matt 3:7–10)[14] It was they who had led the land to be possessed. Their complicit support of Rome, their adoption of a foreign king, and their opulence and brutality were at

---

12. Vermès, *Jesus the Jew*, 69–80. See also John 11:41–42.

13. Again, the evidence for this is found in Mark 6:1–7, for those who heard him speak after he returned to Galilee were "astonished" at his teaching.

14. Matt 3:7 is certainly a more vehement recasting of Luke 3:7–8, but the statement by John concerning elitist claims to "children of Abraham" and privilege can only have originated with the aristocracy and elite. The soldiers referenced certainly weren't Romans, but rather the temple police, who are here confirmed as corrupt extortionists.

the heart of John's accusation.[15] John "commanded"[16] Jews to repudiate Jerusalem's corruption by accepting a mystic, spiritual baptism of union with God as king or his face judgment, for complacency meant siding with the apostate elite who were sure to receive the condemnation of God at any moment. Those baptized were to care for one another and to love members of the new community, the pure Israel. Consequently, John's baptism was tantamount to rebellion, and so the elite found him dangerous.[17] His public criticism of Herod Antipas for marriage to his brother's wife, Herodias (which was forbidden by Jewish law but acceptable in Hellenistic and Roman practice), went uncontested by the Jerusalem religious aristocracy. For John, this confirmed that the elite were apostates who must be rejected and warned of their impending doom. As such, John's was the classic prophetic call to repentance before the judgment of God. Indeed, Jesus recognized John as a prophet—one who would likely suffer violence for the kingdom of God (Mark 9:13; Matt 11:12; Luke 7:26). As a result of John's condemnation, the enraged tetrarch, perhaps the most dangerous imperialist aside from Pontus Pilate, sought to capture and silence him. Antipas held the authority to arrest and kill at will.[18] Likely at night, John is unceremoniously arrested, put in to chains, and taken to Herod's remote fortress, Machaerus. His followers scatter and offer no resistance. Interestingly, Jesus is also publicly challenged on the question of divorce, likely so that he too

---

15. John's activity of baptism implied Jerusalem's corruption, sin, and abandonment by God. Words ascribed to him included condemnation of the Sadducees, the temple elite, and Pharisees that supported the elite (likely Herodian Pharisees, as we shall see). Moreover, corruption is implied by the words against the temple police for their corruption and brutality and against the tax collectors, who were licensed by appointment—usually by Roman-selected representatives, often the aristocracy. Jerusalem elitism is also suggested by the presumed claim by the Sadducees that they are the "children of Abraham," and thus could act as they willed, perhaps also indicating their acceptance of Roman domination as the will of God (Luke 3:7–14).

16. Josephus, *Ant.* 18.5.2. See also Wasserstein, *Flavius Josephus*, 181–82.

17. Horsely and Silberman, *Message and the Kingdom*, 28–30. See Matt 14:5 and consider: "Herod, who feared lest the great influence John had over the people might put it into his power and inclination to raise a rebellion (for they seemed ready to do any thing he should advise,) thought it best, by putting him to death, to prevent any mischief he might cause, and not bring himself into difficulties, by sparing a man who might make him repent of it when it would be too late" (Josephus, *Ant.* 18:5).

18. "But Herod the tetrarch, who had been reproved by him [John] for Herodias, his brother's wife, and for all the evil things that Herod had done, added this to them all" (Luke 3:19–20).

may be arrested (Mark 10:2–12).[19] Most importantly, Jesus' affiliation with John, even though he stayed at a separate camp nearby, represented Jesus' public association with an enemy of the imperialists. As such, Jesus for the first time, accepted the perilous risk posed by Herodian, and thus, Roman retaliation and execution.

Before the arrest and immediately after his baptism by John, Jesus undergoes an ecstatic experience. The heavens opened and the Spirit of God came down upon him in the form of a dove and touched him, denoting that the divine Spirit possessed him. This language and image are found in contemporaneous literature, and represent the type of ecstatic experience expected for a charismatic like Jesus.[20] He hears a voice confirming that he is a son of God, or son of God. Both of these experiences are reported by other ecstatics and similarly described.[21] "Immediately," Jesus is "driven by the Spirit" into the dry and deserted hills of Judea, the barren wilderness, and began an aesthetic fast (Mark 1:12).[22] Demons were known to roam in deserts and deserted places such as the wilderness of Judea,[23] often having been expelled there by exorcists (Luke 11:24). Undoubtedly, Jesus expected to confront some of the demons he had cast out, given the historical context (Luke 11:24–26).[24] But ominously, it is not demons, but Satan himself who finds and confronts the young exorcist. Satan repeatedly attempts to possess Jesus or corrupt him during those unbearable days of hunger and thirst. This continues for over four weeks (Mark 1:12–13; Luke 4:1–13). In some of the most controversial passages in the New Testament, the gospels report that Jesus conversed with Satan (Mark 1:12; Luke 4:3–11). This is a remarkably shocking admission that would have terrorized and horrified any Palestinian Jew—frightening even other exorcists. In all of the Hebrew Bible, only God and Eve carry on a dialogue with Satan.[25] Jesus recounts Sa-

---

19. This question was clearly associated with the elite's attempt to charge Jesus with sedition against Herod, the charge for which John was arrested and murdered.

20. See Lewis, *Ecstatic Religion*, 53–57.

21. See Smith, *Jesus the Magician*, 96–108, 117, 121, 137.

22. Which sociologically mirrors, as we have seen, the experience of Shamans and other religious ecstatics.

23. See the discussion above on the casting out of the "queen of the demons" into the desert by Hanina ben Dosa.

24. Smith, *Jesus the Magician*, 104–106.

25. See Job 1:7, 9–12, 2:3–7; Genesis 3:14; Zechariah 3:1–2. Saul is allowed to be tormented by a spirit (1 Sam 16:14), while Satan speaks to the woman in Genesis, which leads to the fall.

tan's admission that he had infiltrated and possessed the "kingdoms of the world" and that its rulers "worship[ed] him" (Luke 4:5–6), the implication being that Jesus has been told by Satan that the Jerusalem elite and their patron, Rome, were possessed. Jesus must have shared this view with his followers, as it later defined the very nature of his confrontation with Satan and exorcisms. The jolting nature of this so-called "Satan tradition" in the wilderness confirms that Jesus was a known exorcist prior to his baptism.

Only Jesus could have shared this encounter. No one would have fabricated such a controversial story, particularly the early Christian community. The radical and controversial nature of the Satan tradition assures its historicity.[26] Knowledge of Jesus' dialogue with Satan, not just his exorcisms, led to later accusations of his possession and apostasy expressed in the Beelzebul controversy (Mark 3:22–27). Unlike Choni and Hanina, who commanded the demons to confirm their presence when they had vacated victims (e.g., a tipped-over bowl), Jesus spoke to the demons by name. For this reason, the *name* of Jesus was feared. His opponents (and later, even his family) assumed that because he was known to the demons, he must be possessed by them—a reasonable expectation given his contemporary setting. It was this desert encounter with Satan, not only his ecstatic experience at his baptism, that defined for Jesus' his purpose and mission: that he was an exorcist of *the one* God and possessed by the Holy Spirit, which was operative at his command. He was a liberator of those oppressed by evil and an enemy of all those who supported Satan's rule.

Jesus leaves the Jordan for Galilee after reconnecting with his band of exorcists. He rejects Satan, knowing that he will be tested in a "season" by every demonic power that can be sent his way and that his life is at perilous risk (Mark 3:5–6). He is a known compatriot of the radical prophet, John; he is an illegal exorcist and magician[27] thought to be empowered by Satan. Jesus is now at odds with the powerful elite, whom he perceives as supporters of demonic imperialism—it is the ultimate collision of perilous risks and countermeasures. He has "nowhere to lay his head" as he is pursued (Luke 9:58).

Soon thereafter, John is arrested and murdered by Herod Antipas. Jesus abandons baptism. To avoid John's fate, Jesus "withdrew" to Capernaum, far

---

26. Jesus chose the Twelve to be exorcists, and he concurrently claims that they confirmed the inbreaking kingdom of God: "And he appointed twelve to be with him, and to be sent out to preach and to have the authority to cast out demons" (Mark 3:14–15).

27. See Smith, *Jesus the Magician*, 75–76.

away from the Roman-controlled town of Tiberius on the lake to the south and from the grasp of the Jerusalem elite (Matthew 4:12; Mark 1:14–15; Luke 4:14–15).[28] Jesus is said to have "returned in the power of the Spirit" into Galilee (Luke 4:14), that is, the divine Spirit possessed him. John's arrest and death changed Jesus. He is reclusive no longer, but instead becomes aggressive and vocal. He enters synagogues on the Sabbath and begins to cleanse each by driving out its demons, thus taking back the land from Satan's control (Luke 4:14). Jesus announces that Satan's demonic rule over the land will be overcome by his charismatic actions through the "finger of God" (Luke 11:20). Thus, Jesus embraced exorcism as the ultimate countermeasure to repel evil and reclaim Israel. His exorcisms confirmed God's presence and judgment were imminent (Mark 1:1). Like John, he called on the people to reject Satan and to love and care for one another until the day of justice, to pray a simple country prayer requesting safety from ever returning to possession and apostasy, and to forgive each other as they had been forgiven for having embraced evil (Luke 11:2–4). Expelling demons accelerated the termination of Satan's rule. At great risk, Jesus announced that the elite would be displaced unless they accepted the presence of God's kingdom as already in their midst and accepted Jesus as God's legitimate agent.

To speed the overthrown of Satan, Jesus gathers, trains, and empowers multiple exorcists to join him in repelling demons to hasten the inbreaking of the kingdom of God (Luke 9:1). According to the earliest gospel tradition, Jesus selects the Twelve because they are either exorcists already or are willing to become exorcists:

> "And he went up into the hills and called to him those whom he desired: and they came to him. And he appointed twelve to be with him and to be sent out to preach and have authority to cast out demons." (Mark 3:13–19)

This explains the diversity of backgrounds of the Twelve and why they immediately left everything when Jesus called them to action. Each would be sent to cleanse the twelve tribes of Israel, thereby surrounding Jerusalem. There is no romantic ideal that should be applied to their mission. It was

---

28. The Maccabeans hated the Idumeans, Herod's family, and this hatred continued to permeate Galilee two centuries later. This was exacerbated by the crucifixion of thousands of Jews after the revolt of Judas the Galilean (Josephus, *Ant.* 18:1–10.23). The Jerusalem elite thought of the Galileans as country bumpkins with accents that betrayed their stupidity.

deadly, dangerous, and brutal—a war against Satan. These men were risking more than just their personal security and standing; they were risking being overwhelmed and tormented by the most feared enemy of their time. Some abandon him, thus the different names attached to the Twelve (Luke 9:62).[29] The Twelve were sent out into the villages "two by two" specifically to exorcise demons and to prepare each village for Jesus' arrival (Mark 6:7). Concurrent with each exorcism, they were tasked with announcing the end of Satan's rule and the entry of the kingdom of God, that it was "in their midst." Those villages that failed to receive them were given the sign of abandonment and doom: "kick the dust off your sandals" (Luke 9:5). Their decision to reject him was tantamount to acceptance of Satan, for Jesus came to "bring the sword" in the war on Satan (Matt 10:34). Initially, most of the exorcists were unsuccessful, but news of Jesus' success spread in the villages of Galilee and Palestine.

As Jesus arrived on the outskirts of most villages, he and his band were welcomed and sought out by dozens of the possessed and ill. No family struggling to care for a loved one who was suffering pain, illness, or mental anguish would hesitate to bring them to Jesus.[30] In their desperation to reach him, any means—whether by pushing through the crowds to simply touch him or pulling apart a roof to lower a paralyzed son down on a pallet—was justified. At other villages, he was told to leave. Jesus became well-known to the elite as a troublemaker,[31] and was soon identified as an outlaw to the Romans. His exorcisms were a capital crime, that of magic. To counter his expanded efforts, the elite publicly accuse him of empowerment by Beelzebul, prince of the demons.[32] Jesus counters that God alone is king and they are the corrupted apostates who even steal from widows.[33] He uses country stories from his experience in rural Galilee to tell popular *mashal*, or parables, in his attempt to communicate to the locals their hope and, through veiled tales, the impending doom of the elite. This controversy over the source of Jesus' authority marks the intersection of conflict and countermeasures to cancel out perilous risk. As such, qualitative risk

---

29. See also Matt 10:2–4; Mark 3:16–19; Luke 6:14–16.

30. See Lewis, *Ecstatic Religion*, 51–52; and Smith, *Jesus the Magician*, 9–10.

31. See Luke 9:7 regarding Herod Antipas.

32. Recall the Beelzebul controversy discussed above and see Luke 11:14–23 and Smith, *Jesus the Magician*, 32.

33. See Jesus' accusations, which mirror John's, in Mark 12:37b–40; Matt 23:1–36; and Luke 20:45–45.

analysis confirms the historicity of Jesus' exorcisms, his confrontation with the Jerusalem elite, and his proclamation to accept the inbreaking kingdom of God as already present. It also confirms that Jesus was considered a blasphemer, a threat, and a man who was marked to be crushed under Roman capital law if captured, particularly if he came to Jerusalem (Mark 14:1).

Jesus did not aspire to be a preacher. He only begins to articulate the meaning of his exorcisms in relation to the inbreaking kingdom of God after he exorcises. This brings us to those sayings Jesus employed at these exorcisms or charismatic events, whether spoken to the person freed of possession or to his opponents. Based on qualitative risk analysis, controversies that are related to the authority behind Jesus' exorcisms represent the most reliable and historically valid tradition about Jesus of Nazareth in the New Testament. Such a study can define what is most characteristic of his countermeasures to the perilous risk of apostasy and imperialism in these sayings. If a set of core sayings can be identified, then their central theme can create a cohesive framework on which to identify other similar sayings or events that can be recovered and confirmed as historically probable. By applying qualitative risk analysis to these sayings, we can approach the oral tradition with a new, deliberate, and objective methodology to reveal what is most characteristic of the young exorcist, Jesus. With that said, we now turn to the actions and patterns Jesus employed in his war on Satan, as well as the words spoken in his charismatic pronouncements and confrontation with the elite.

# 6

# Disarming the Strong Man
## Jesus' Attack on Satan and Demonic Imperialism

IN THIS CHAPTER WE will set the stage for a comprehensive analysis of Jesus' activity in his war on Satan. Qualitative risk analysis, combined with our many historical sources, allows for the recovery of those aspects of Jesus' itinerant mission that were most characteristic of his countermeasure to end the perilous risk of satanic apostasy and possession of the land. We begin with the historical context and then carefully move through his activity, illustrating the pattern of his exorcisms, sayings, and intentional actions to free synagogues surrounding Jerusalem from demonic control.

### RECLAIMING A POSSESSED LAND

In the context of countermeasures to perilous risk, qualitative risk analysis has confirmed that the young ecstatic and exorcist, Jesus of Galilee, engaged in reclaiming a possessed land from Satan after John the Baptist's capture and brutal murder. At great risk, John denounced the corruption of the Jerusalem religious elite and aristocracy by claiming they were possessed. As sympathizers with pagan Rome, these "vipers" embraced foreign rule and imperialism, thereby displacing God as king. They were therefore under the growing influence of Satan and his demons.

Countering this view were the Jerusalem elite. They held that God had established the power and authority of the Roman Empire, the *pax*

*Disarming the Strong Man*

*Romana*, as well as their own position as rulers of Palestine. Rome and the elite had been divinely appointed. Any opposition to this order resisted God and so must be crushed. Demonic possession signified punishment for sins against God or resulted from capricious demonic activity that deservedly tormented outcasts and the dispossessed. Men who claimed control over such demons were part of Satan's deceptive ruse. This meant that Beelzebul, the chief demon, or his minions possessed exorcists like Jesus, a charge common for ecstatics and charismatics even today.[1] As if this charge were not damning enough, Jesus' opponents also claimed he was charlatan, claiming that his exorcisms were for personal monetary gain.[2]

The corruption and brutality of the Romans in Palestine, particularly from 26–36 CE, has been thoroughly documented in our previous chapters. The religious aristocracy cooperated with the procurators in maintaining control.[3] Peasants who publicly opposed the established order as satanic (whether exorcists or not) or claimed, as Jesus did, that demonic expulsion was a sign that the current order was being overturned by God were guilty of advocating and practicing magic or sedition—both capital crimes under Roman law. As their primary countermeasure, the Jerusalem elite publicly accused both John and Jesus of being possessed and empowered by Satan (Luke 11:14–23, 7:31–35). Peasant activists, even those thought to be prophets or exorcist healers, were easy targets for Roman informants when accusations like this were made. Roman sympathizers could richly profit from betraying such men. It was only a matter of time until they were captured and killed. Whether it was one or thousands, death by sword or crucifixion awaited such men.

In occupied Palestine, spies were plentiful. Hunger, poverty, and desperation prevailed. Peasants such as Judas, as paid assassins and "daggermen," were quick to identify outliers like Jesus for silver and survival. Clearly, Judas knew of Jesus' reputation as an exorcist and follower of John long before he began his itinerant public ministry in Galilee.[4] While seen as a minor annoyance at first, Jesus was still considered potentially dangerous

---

1. See Lewis, *Ecstatic Religion*, 33–35.

2. This is why Paul is so careful to reject monetary support so that he is not charged as a magician and charlatan, one of society's despised.

3. Ehrman, *New Testament*, 257–58.

4. Ibid., 255.

To Be Near the Fire

as a magician. His value to these spies would increase if he spoke directly against Herod, taxation, the temple, or Rome.[5]

We have determined that Jesus, devastated by John's murder, began expelling demons in village after village. He associated the success of his charismatic activity with the displacement of the elite and the arrival of the kingdom of God, as well as the coming judgment of the current kingdom under the elite, Herod and Rome. This alone was seditious. Informants like Judas carefully infiltrated fringe groups as a devoted follower (or in the case of Jesus' band, as a fellow exorcist) to gain access to leaders, increasing the value of both their information and personal gain. When opportunity came and leaders were vulnerable to easy capture, they and their followers[6] were betrayed to imperialist agents and immediately imprisoned or killed. When it came to the Roman procurator Pontius Pilate, the response to Judas' information was either a premeditated ruse to draw out all possible followers[7] or an act of immediate and unmerciful cruelty (i.e., the brutal slashing of all present supporters, including the slaughter of men, women, and children as innocent bystanders). There was likely little remorse in the outcome for the informants—desperation for money and survival drove their actions.[8] As the Jewish apologist and historian, Josephus, confirms, the local folk considered the spies of Herod, the high priest, and Pontius Pilate as traitorous agents of apostate foreigners under the influence of Beelzebul.[9]

This is the historical context of Jesus' war on Satan after John's murder by those he believed under Satan's control, which is fully supported by the findings of qualitative risk analysis. The perilous risks Jesus faced daily were

---

5. Crossan, *Historical Jesus*, 313–18.

6. The record relating Saul of Tarsus' persecution of Jesus' followers, drawn from his own authentic letters, confirms that he used informants, then brutalized and arrested both men and women.

7. Pilates offer to release Jesus or Barabbas to draw out followers of either and then arrest, brutalize, or murder them. See previous discussion on Josephus, *Ant.* 18:60–62.

8. Sympathizing with the Romans for gain (and security) was the countermeasure these men chose to mitigate the perilous risk of hunger and poverty. Judas, one such informant, intentionally infiltrated the Twelve, the fellow exorcists chosen by Jesus to accompany him, according to the earliest tradition. Judas was paired with another of the Twelve and sent out to villages and towns to exorcise and announce the kingdom of God. Whether Judas exorcised will never be known, but just before his betrayal, Jesus acknowledged that Judas was not free of Satan, but was instead possessed by him. Judas kissed Jesus to identify him—a horrifying insult, but apropos for a heartless assassin.

9. John's identification of the elite and their minions as a "brood of vipers" can only be understood as agents of Satan.

*Disarming the Strong Man*

very real—Satan and his demons were still in control and assassins were on the hunt to destroy him. Jesus' countermeasures were shocking, dangerous, and coarse—whether publicly speaking with demons in the synagogue or driving them over the cliffs into the sea after they tried to stop him from entering a synagogue, he compounded those risks by announcing these events as evidence of the kingdom of God and the end of elitist imperialism. However effective Jesus' exorcisms may have been, they ended when he got to Jerusalem, the center of elitist power and Satan's control. Qualitative risk analysis asserts that successful countermeasures lead to a pattern of behavior that can be recovered. We can now reasonably test this premise by focusing on the traditions related to Jesus' activity as an exorcist.

## THE CONTEXT AND PATTERN FOR JESUS' RETURN TO EXORCISM AS A COUNTERMEASURE TO EVIL

Risk analysis has confirmed that Jesus abandoned baptizing with his band after the arrest and murder of John by Herod Antipas, a tetrarch of Galilee and Roman-appointed minion (Mark 1:39; Luke 4:11, 14–15; Matt 9:35).[10] He fled Judea, escaping Herod, "the fox" who was seeking other followers of John, and immediately returned to Galilee to resume exorcism (Luke 13:31–32). *Based on our analysis, Jesus then began a battle to overturn the demonic invasion of Israel and establish the kingdom of God in a pattern of itinerant ministry and exorcism of evil that was intended to encircle Jerusalem.*[11] Formerly a quiet and reclusive country exorcist who disappeared for days to be alone (Luke 5:16), Jesus became relentless after John's death, driving demons from every town and village that would allow him entry in his pursuit of Satan, but still seeking solitude when available.[12] The following is a reconstruction that is contextually coherent with the results of qualitative risk analysis and Jesus' countermeasures to perilous risk, as well as the pattern of his actions that are recoverable.

No longer reclusive and withdrawn (Luke 4:16–30), Jesus went to each village's synagogue, expelling demons and demanding a decision to repent as a witness to the intervening presence of God in their midst (Mark

10. Crossan, *Historical Jesus*, 313–14.

11. See Lewis, *Ecstatic Religion*, 88–89 for Lewis' discussion of the link between the oppression of the elite and possession as well as the reliance of lower castes on exorcists (as "masters of spirit") as a cultural phenomenon that crosses all cultural barriers.

12. Jesus is forbidden entry (Luke 9:51–56).

12:37–40; Luke 17:20–21). Those freed from Satan, the dispossessed and poor, were now the children of God, as were any who emulated their new, childlike innocence by embracing each other as the new family of the king. This repudiation of Satan—and with it, demonic imperialism—brought the kingdom of God into being.[13] Jesus employed simple country stories about fields, flowers, tilling land, wicked tenants and foreign owned vineyards of Galilee (Luke 20:9-19),14 and other familiar anecdotes that the elite and educated of the city were unable to decipher but the local folk could understand (Matt 13:34; Mark 4:34; Luke 8:10).[14] Many of these were spoken at or shortly after his exorcisms. He demanded a change in the view of sin[15] from the leaders of the synagogue who witnessed his exorcisms: namely, that illness, poverty, possession, or low status had nothing to do with wrongs committed by those afflicted. Such was the work of demonic oppression brought about by the apostasy of the elite and religious hypocrites. Because of his synagogue exorcisms, Jesus spoke as "one having authority, not like the Scribes [of Jerusalem]" (Mark 1:22). He demanded that mercy and forgiveness must predominate in preparation for the king's arrival, just as mercy had been shown to the possessed. Jesus asserts that the practice of mercy and forgiveness must displace the corrupt temple and its sacrifices (Matt 9:13). These dispossessed people were instead to be honored by the local synagogue as the victims of brutal occupation and demonic possession who had been freed by God, their father, who Jesus addressed as *Abba* (Mark 14:36).[16] Poverty itself would soon be ended, replaced by the justice and presence of God as king (Luke 6:20). The rich would weep and the poor would celebrate their restored status through their faith in Jesus' exorcisms and the certainty of God's impending entry (Luke 6:24–26). The rule of Satan, pagan domination, and possession were now ending.

13. Luke 8:15–17, 19–21; the healing of a woman on the Sabbath, Luke 13:10–17.

14. These *Mashal* were understood by other country folk and his fellow exorcists, the Twelve.

15. See Mark 9:41 on giving to the poor and good treatment, and also Luke 13:15 on freeing the possessed from bondage.

16. Pronounced *Abba*, or ab bah¢, with the accent on the later syllable, as Joachim Jeremias confirms. Paul confirms that Jesus used this term for God and continues affirming its use by the believers of the Way (Rom 8:15; Gal 4:6). Jesus also addresses God as *Abba* in his prayers (Matt 6:9). See Joachim Jeremias for the definitive study on Abba and the prayers of Jesus: "He spoke to God like a child to its father, simply, inwardly, confidently. Jesus' use of *Abba* in addressing God reveals the heart of his relationship with God" (Jeremias, *Prayers of Jesus*, 62). The extent to which Jeremias ascribes Jesus' use of *Abba* to his sole and unique place with God has been challenged.

Yet, despite his many exorcisms, it is evident that Jesus often failed to convince the synagogue leaders in villages and towns to accept the urgency of the crisis by embracing the kingdom and its democratized congregation of both clean and the impure, the former outcasts as the new "children of God" who must not "be offended."[17] For their rejection, Jesus warns that a fate worse than that of Sodom and Gomorrah will be theirs when the king arrives, acautioning them against an annihilation by fire[18]—something that Jesus' fellow exorcists, the Boanerges (Jacob and Yohanan), try to call down immediately. Even more ominous, Jesus warns that the evil spirits that he has exorcised will consider returning sevenfold to "that house" (Luke 11:24–26). This was a horrifying possibility, but still unpersuasive to some. When he is rejected, Jesus and his fellow exorcists shake the dust off their feet,[19] leaving these villages as a warning of their impending doom (Luke 9:5).

## THE PATTERN OF ATTACK ON SATAN

Qualitative risk analysis also suggests that in the context of successful countermeasures, Jesus employed a repetitive pattern to overcome the perilous risk of satanic occupation.[20] Extending his exorcisms beyond Capernaum, the village he adopted after being violently thrown out of Nazareth, he was intent on freeing all of Israel from demonic forces. Jesus engages a strategy of entering every synagogue in the vicinity, then expands to a broader circuit. A clear pattern of assault is evident in his effort to liberate Palestine, including Samaria, ending in the temple of Jerusalem. This would take months. Jesus begins his exorcisms in Galilee, then moves to Decapolis

17. The woes against Capernaum, Bethsaida, Korazin, and other cities clearly confirm his efforts were not successful in converting these towns and village synagogues to new behavior (Luke 10:13).

18. "But it shall be more tolerable in the judgment for Tyre and Sidon than for you. And you, Capernaum, will you be exalted to heaven? You shall be brought down to Hades. He who hears you hears me and he who rejects you rejects me, and he who rejects me rejects him who sent me" (Luke 10:14–16).

19. A practice of Paul and Barnabas at Antioch of Pisidia, where they were rejected and expelled by the Jews (Acts 13:51). Jewish tradition associated the dust of pagan and heathen towns and villages with pollution, full of the dust of the dead and impure. This kicking off of the dust is a well-known sign of impurity and death associated with that place. There is no peace for it, only pending doom, death, and judgment.

20. I. M. Lewis describes the social setting of the confrontation of exorcists with demonic control in Lewis, *Ecstatic Religion*, 33–34.

after a failed attempt to enter the Roman provincial capital of Gadara, then on to Judea beyond the Jordan, Samaria, and finally, having encircled the city, into Jerusalem, beginning in the temple.[21] The kingdom of God was not simply present in his activity and words; it was literally displacing the rule of Satan, whom Jesus' sees as falling like lightening (Luke 10:18). Consequently, in the earliest stratum of tradition, Jesus identified himself as the exorcist servant to Israel, sent to proclaim "justice [judgment] to the Gentiles" (Matt 12:18). The apostate would be warned, even given "hope," but would not stand in the end (Matt 12:16–21). Driven to speed the demise of demonic rule, Jesus selects and trains others exorcists to join him. They are to confront and expel demons, and with each successful expulsion, announce the inbreaking kingdom of God and his demand for justice and acceptance of outcasts. Jesus first chooses five-to-twelve followers as his apprentices (Mark 3:13–19), and then appoints as many as seventy, sending them out with varying degrees of success (Luke 10:1–20). His name is to be used during exorcisms,[22] which is consistent with other contemporary ecstatics, or divine men possessed by spirits or gods. Calling on the name of Jesus laid claim to the Spirit that possessed him.

Jesus' pattern of liberation is evident in the gospel narratives, as well as in non-canonical gospels.[23] The young exorcist intentionally bypasses the religious elite and, as noted, attempts to surround them with his authority and power. With God's presence having vacated the temple and Jerusalem, his Spirit and authority must be established in each synagogue. This will be evidenced by new practices of love and democratized acceptance of the outcasts and sinners. Those whose "ears and eyes are opened," having been freed from possession, abandon Jerusalem and look for the entry of God as king to reclaim his people (John 4:21; Luke 21:6). In the interim, each synagogue must practice the way of love, as only love is immune to evil. As Mark explains:

> "And he went throughout all of Galilee, preaching in their synagogues and casting out demons." (Mark 1:39)

---

21. See Matt 4:25, which explains why the order of Jesus ministry is lost and is jumbled in Mark. The original order of his ministry to free the land was displaced by paranesis and predictions of his death and resurrection.

22. See Smith, *Jesus the Magician*, 114 on the use of Jesus' name in exorcisms, a common practice.

23. Including the Gospel of Peter, the Gospel of the Hebrews, and the Gospel of the Ebionites, for example.

At each event, whether in controversy dialogues with his opponents or with those affected by the exorcism (including the demons themselves), Jesus linked each expulsion and healing to the inbreaking of the kingdom of God, and by implication, the displacement of the elite:

> "But if it is by the finger of God that I cast out demons, then the kingdom of God has come upon you." (Luke 11:20)

Critical and qualitative risk analyses have confirmed the historicity of Luke 11:20. Along with the context of countermeasures and the resulting clear pattern of attack, this saying provides a basis on which to compare other sayings of Jesus spoken during his exorcisms or in dialogue with those present at his exorcisms, including the demons he exorcised. Analysis may provide enough information to reconstruct the original proclamation of Jesus in the context of perilous risk and countermeasure to the rule of Satan. First, we must look to the social setting of Jesus' activity to analyze his sayings.

## THE SOCIAL SETTING OF JESUS' EXORCISMS AND THE NATURE OF JESUS' PROCLAMATION

The Synoptic Gospels confirm that when Jesus reenters Galilee after John's arrest, he comes "in the power of the Spirit," meaning that Jesus immediately returned to the practice of exorcising demons (Luke 4:14). The social setting of these events can be recovered. Jesus' practice was to enter a village synagogue as the exorcist of the kingdom of God:

> "And he went throughout all of Galilee, preaching in their synagogues and casting out demons." (Mark 1:39)

> ". . . and a report concerning him went out throughout all the surrounding country. And he taught in their synagogues being glorified by all." (Luke 4:14–15)

> ". . . proclaiming [preaching] the good news of God and saying, 'The time is fulfilled, and the kingdom of God is at hand; repent and believe in the good news.'" (Mark 1:14b–15)

These traditions are consistent with Luke 11:20, in which Jesus expels demons and then announces the inbreaking kingdom of God. The association is unmistakable. What is added here is that it was common practice for

Jesus to enter the synagogues of these villages to exorcise and teach.[24] His reputation as an exorcist provided him access to places of Jewish worship:[25]

> "And he came to Nazareth, where he had been brought up; and he went to the synagogue as his custom was on the Sabbath day." (Luke 4:16)

Jesus' teaching is now properly contextualized as the inbreaking of the kingdom of God. Often handed Scripture to read as part of the service (Luke 4:17–22), Jesus interpreted Jewish prophetic writings concerning the glorious coming day of Israel's reestablishment as now present: "Today this Scripture has been fulfilled in your hearing" (Luke 4:21). The primary passage Jesus requests to read from is Isa 61:1–2, for it specifically contextualizes his exorcisms as liberation from imperialism and oppression:

> "The Spirit of the Lord is upon me, because he has anointed me to preach good news to the poor . . . proclaim release to the captives and recover sight to the blind, to set at liberty those who are oppressed . . . to proclaim the acceptable year of the Lord." (Isa 61:1–2; Luke 4:18–19)

This passage should be associated with the core of Jesus' synagogue teachings. It is corroborated by an interesting encounter with followers of John the Baptist. Jesus was approached by disciples of the imprisoned John, for John sought clarification on whether Jesus would continue to battle apostasy: "Are you the one to come, [next after me]?"[26] Jesus reply is a definitive "Yes," and he again paraphrases Isa 61:1–2. Consistent with his exorcisms as efforts to free Israel from oppression, this tradition confirms that Jesus' countermeasure to demonic invasion and possession included reclaiming places of Jewish worship in the towns and villages of Galilee. They were to be set free of Jerusalem's influence (Mark 1:21–28). Conse-

---

24. The United Nations Educational Scientific and Cultural Organization (UNESCO) and the World Heritage Centre summarize numerous archaeological reports from Galilee in explaining, "The remains of as many as 50 different synagogues were identified in the Galilee, one of the most concentrated sites for synagogues in the world at that time. These early synagogues included Meron, Gush Halav, Navorin, Bar Am and Bet Alfa and Korazim, and Capernaum by the Sea of Galilee" (Permanent Delegation of Israel to UNESCO, "Early Synagogues in the Galilee," *UNESCO World Heritage Centre*, June 30, 2000, http://whc.unesco.org/en/tentativelists/1470/).

25. Which was "what we have heard you did at Capernaum" (Luke 4:23).

26. "The blind receive their sight, the lame walk, lepers are cleansed, and the deaf hear, the dead are raised up, the poor have good news preached to them" (Luke 7:18–23).

quently, this patterned practice of exorcism and healing at Sabbath gatherings reflects the historical *modus operandi* of the young Jesus. Examining Jesus' activity in the synagogue as a countermeasure to Satan's invasion and expulsion is now appropriate.

## THE GALILEAN SYNAGOGUE AS THE BATTLEGROUND OF JESUS' WAR: THE ENTRY AND ATTACK

Embedded in the various sources behind the Synoptic Gospels are multiple synagogue events related to Jesus' practice of exorcism and teaching. The context and social setting for Jesus' confrontation with Satan is his aggressive actions to overthrow demonic possession, thereby establishing the kingdom of God.[27] Jesus first begins this activity in the synagogues of Galilee, as the foundation of the emerging kingdom of God. This pattern has been established as coherent with the findings of qualitative risk analysis. It is clearly Jesus' countermeasure to the perilous risk of apostasy brought about by demonic imperialism and the corruption and possession of the Jerusalem elite. Examination of traditions associated specifically with this activity is therefore warranted.

### Entering the Synagogue

When Jesus enters the village or town synagogue, there is a recoverable pattern of his specific actions as countermeasures to demonic possession.

On the Sabbath, during worship, Jesus enters the village synagogue, whether invited or not (unless he is forbidden), to reclaim it for God. Jesus exorcises evil from the synagogue, commanding any demons present to make themselves known.[28] A demon then speaks, identifying Jesus as a "holy one" of God, the possessed servant exorcist. Jesus silences and then expels the demon in front of the congregation. Jesus declares the synagogue free and has prophetic Scripture read, usually from Isaiah. The kingdom of God is announced as present in their midst. Jesus demands forgiveness, mercy, and acceptance of the dispossessed. Jesus is then either accepted or rejected and threatened.

---

27. Lewis, *Ecstatic Religion*, 35.
28. Smith, *Jesus the Magician*, 128.

According to the evidence in the Synoptic Gospels and the problematic nature of these traditions themselves,[29] it is certain that Jesus spoke with demons. During the synagogue cleansings, Jesus is typically confronted. They speak to him directly, terrifying bystanders (Mark 1:27–28).

The tradition in Mark accurately reflects Jesus' practice of entering the synagogues of Galilee: "And immediately there was in the synagogue a man with an unclean spirit; and he [the demon] cried out, 'What have you to do with us, Jesus of Nazareth? Have you come to destroy us? I know that you are the *holy one*[30] of God'" (Mark 1:23–25).

Verbal confrontation with demons in the synagogues of Galilee was the norm (Luke 6:24–26). Demoniacs also attempt to intercept him before he enters significant villages and towns. As he approaches the town of Gadara, six miles southeast of Galilee across the Jordan, two demoniacs living among the Jewish tombs[31] confront Jesus. Gadara was the Roman provincial capital of Decapolis. Clearly, Jesus is assaulting this Roman stronghold, intending to expel its demons from the synagogue and announce the inbreaking kingdom of God to the Gentiles as well as to the Jews. They speak to him, saying, "Have you come here to torment us before the time . . . cast us out, and send us away into the herd of swine" (Matt 8:29).

The villagers are terrified and come out to the edge of the town to refuse Jesus entry, perhaps threatening him with stoning or violence. They order him and his band of exorcists to leave at once. Jesus fails to enter Gadara or cleanse the synagogue, and so moves on to the next village.

As noted in Mark, Jesus is identified as the "holy one." This is not to be understood as a messianic term, as the text (later translated into the Christological title, "Son of God") implies, but rather reflects the use of the term in Isaiah, the prophetic book most often quoted by Jesus during his synagogue cleansings. It reflects God's absolute separation from evil and implies that Jesus is the agent who, on behalf of God, expels evil as the "holy one" of God. Is it possible that Jesus is identified by the demons as the Messiah, the "Son of God"? Yes, but Jesus refuses to accept this designation during his ministry, thereby rejecting any messianic claim for himself, contrary to

---

29. Including later accusations, which are certainly historical, that Jesus spoke with demons because he was a minion of Satan.

30. Emphasis mine. Here, "holy one" is not a messianic term as implied by the text, which was later translated as "son of God."

31. The "desolate places" (Matt 12:43). See also Luke 8:29.

the retrospective attestation applied to this period by the generation who constituted the editors and authors of the Synoptic Gospels.[32] His refusal to accept any messianic claim is coherent with the conclusions of qualitative risk analysis: namely, that he was the servant of God who expelled evil and inaugurated the end of Satan's rule and the arrival of God as king. It is God who comes as king with his kingdom (Matt 12:15–21; Mark 3:7–12; Luke 6:17–19). Jesus is a chosen servant, a holy warrior of God (Matt 12:15).[33]

The confrontation with demons and evil possession typically continued into the evening following events in the synagogue. Jesus intentionally remains in the vicinity of the synagogue or in a nearby home, where he stays for food and rest. If the location of Jesus' temporary residence in Capernaum is accurate, he stayed in a modest peasant house only a short distance from the synagogue.[34] Jesus knows that he will be sought out, whether by demoniacs or by others who seek "healing" from evil spirits that infect or

---

32. Scholarship has confirmed that the Gospel of Mark was a source used by the editors of Matthew and Luke (along with a separate source: Q, or Quelle). Mark was not written by an eyewitness or by one of Jesus' twelve exorcists, and thus is not accurate as to the sequence or nature of events. Eusebius, reporting what Papias (60–130 CE) said he heard from John the Presbyter (perhaps John the apostle, but nonetheless an eyewitness to the apostolic period): "This also the presbyter [John] said: Mark, having become the interpreter of Peter, wrote down accurately, though *not indeed in order*, whatsoever he remembered of the things done or said by Christ. For he neither heard the Lord nor followed him, but afterward, as I said, he followed Peter, who adapted his teaching to the needs of his hearers, but with no intention of giving a connected account of the Lord's discourses, so that Mark committed no error while he thus wrote some things as he remembered them. For he was careful of one thing, not to omit any of the things which he had heard, and not to state any of them falsely" (Eusebius, *Hist. eccl.* 3:39.15). Likewise, Irenaeus says that Mark wrote his Gospel after the death of Cephas (Irenaeus, *Haer.* 3:1.1).

33. How does one explain the rapid rise of Christological titles post-Easter if Jesus never made a claim for himself? As we have demonstrated, the exorcist Jesus was certainly called "son of God," "Son of David," and "the Holy One of God," all titles applied to exorcists contemporary with Jesus. Consequently, the post-Easter community would have reapplied these titles to the risen Jesus (i.e., the Messiah to come), for they also carried messianic connotations.

34. There is much scholarship debating this location, but it is highly likely this was where Jesus resided while in Capernaum, for it certainly fits with the findings of qualitative risk analysis as to Jesus' *modus operandi* and his intent to remain near the cleansed synagogue while he continued to expel demons and exorcise evil spirits from the infirm. See Bible Archaeology Society, "The House of Peter: Jesus' Home in Capernaum?" *Biblical Archaeological Review*, March 29, 2011, http://www.biblicalarchaeology.org/daily/biblical-sites-places/biblical-archaeology-sites/the-house-of-peter-the-home-of-jesus-in-capernaum/.

possess their loved ones (Mark 1:32–34; Matt 8:16–17). Often, these people go to extraordinary measures to reach him. This allows him to also free the village or town from possession—apparently his normal practice before he moves on. In one case, which accurately describes the construction of a first-century home in Capernaum, villagers take apart the roofing above the room where Jesus is staying. They drop a pallet on which an infirm man is tied so that Jesus might exorcise the evil spirit from him (Mark 2:1–12). This can only be one of dozens of vivid memories associated with Jesus' exorcisms on warm spring or summer evenings. His inability to eat and sleep during these incursions due to the evening crowds led him to be considered "mad" (Mark 3:19b–22).

Jesus' appearance as an exorcist entering a town or village must be considered unique as well, drawn as it is from the descriptions attributed to him (Matt 10:7–9, 10a, 11–13; Luke 10:1–16). Jesus describes what an exorcist should do and wear. First, the pattern of entry is familiar: "Whenever you enter a town or village and they receive you . . . heal the sick [those possessed by evil spirits] in it and say to them 'The kingdom of God has come near to you,' . . . and eat what is put before you" (Luke 10:8a, 9–10, 8b). Next, he describes the distinctive physical appearance of the exorcist. When entering, no money is to be carried and no belt should be worn only a single tunic, the base garment that covered the loincloth.[35] Notice that no bag to carry supplies is included here, nor sandals (implying bare feet) or a walking staff (used for protection as well as balance—the sign of a traveler). There are to be no traditional greetings on the road, only silence in an obvious suspension of Jewish Palestinian custom of greeting, kissing, and blessing. This practice marks the entrant as a religious aesthetic, exorcist, or prophet separated from the local folk by what is clearly a noticeable and austere entry. When Jesus goes to the synagogue, he instructs other exorcists to find "who is worthy" (Matt 10:11–13) in the town first, likely a

---

35. According to findings in the Cave of Letters in the Nahal Hever, the tunic (*tunica* in Latin; *haluq* in Hebrew) was a linen or wool sleeved shirt that resembled a short nightshirt and was usually woven from two equal pieces sewn together at the selvage to leave holes for the arms and head. They may have been colored, depending on gender, and usually included a *calvi*, or vertical band of color, the width and color of which denoted authority or position. More than one tunic could be worn, which was particularly true for peasants who could not afford a more elaborate mantle. It was a simple piece of clothing worn over the loincloth. It was uncommon to wear a tunic alone, as a mantle was often worn over it with a leather belt. Anyone walking into a first-century village or town wearing such an outfit would have immediately been distinctive. Jesus' tunic was said to be woven without seam (John 19:23).

leader of the local synagogue who might offer hospitality, a Jewish tradition dating to the time of Abraham, who entertained angels unaware. Undoubtedly, Jesus also did so after his cleansing of the synagogue.[36] It is known that Jesus himself wore a tunic and a mantle with tassels or a fringe, for those who touched it were freed from possession by evil spirits and illness (Luke 6:19, 4:19; Mark 3:10, Matt 14:36).

## THE PATTERN OF JESUS' EXORCISM OF DEMONS AND SPIRITS

In most cases, it is reported that Jesus is able to expel the demons by the spoken word of his command, not just by touching or the use of special mixtures or other actions. In the case of the Gadarene demoniacs, Jesus simple says, "Go" (Mark 8:28).[37] However, for evil spirits that caused illness or death, Jesus sometimes worked privately with the victim and touched them or created a saliva ointment[38] to expel the spirit while pronouncing special words. Taking these infirm away from the village may have indicated that Jesus was concerned that his effort would not succeed, although Luke and Matthew remove these extra steps to eliminate such concern. However, from the standpoint of qualitative risk analysis, it is clear that Jesus also instructs the victim not to reenter the village once freed simply because he fears that the individual may be afflicted again more seriously, which appears to have been a common occurrence.[39] Regardless, it is evident that it was more typical for Jesus to work privately with those afflicted by an evil spirit to effect healings than is represented in the Synoptic Gospels:

> "And they brought to him a man who was deaf and had an impediment in his speech; and they besought him to lay his hand upon him. And taking him aside privately, he put his fingers into his ears, and he spat and touched his tongue; and looking up to heaven, he

---

36. Jesus was known to head to religious leaders' homes in each village to seek their traditional hospitality. Jairus, the "ruler of the synagogue," understood this and met Jesus on the way to the synagogue or to his home (Mark 5:35–43).

37. Jesus' command was also effective at a distance, as in the case of the centurion who seeks Jesus' assistance in Luke 7:1–10.

38. Saliva is mentioned by ancient authors as having been commonly used in cures by exorcists, healers, and even the emperor of Rome, Vespasian. According to Tacitus, Vespasian cured a blind man by spitting on his eyes and cheek. The cure worked, but only insofar as the man could see light (Tacitus, *Hist.*, 4.81).

39. See Jesus' concern noted above surrounding the return of the demon sevenfold.

sighed, and said to him, '*Ephphatha*,' that is, 'Be opened.'" (Mark 7:31–37)

"And they came to Bethsaida. And some people brought to him a blind man, and begged him to touch him. And he took the blind man by the hand, and led him out of the village; and when he had spat on his eyes and laid his hands upon him, he asked him, 'Do you see anything?' And he looked up and said 'I see men; they look like trees walking.' Then again he laid his hands upon his eyes; and he looked intently and was restored, and saw everything clearly. And he sent him away saying, 'Do not even enter the village.'" (Mark 8:22–26)

The most remarkable of Jesus' exorcisms—and most terrifying to villagers—was his ability to cast out death, usually from a young individual. Jesus' exorcised the evil spirit, in this case the disease of death, and recalled the person's spirit back to their body.[40] In ancient Judaism, death was spoken of as "sleep" that resulted from an evil infection that drove the person's spirit, or soul, away (or conversely, led to it being "carried away," sometimes by angels). Consequently, the body becomes lifeless without its soul. Death inhabited humanity after the sin of Adam and the fall; that is, death arose from evil, and its capricious power was released by the fall of man. This concept of death as an infection is the basis of Paul's argument in Romans, particularly Rom 5:12–14. Paul, like Jesus, understood this "sleep" not as a final death, but instead as a state in which one's body resided and from which one could be raised to life by the power of God. Jesus' reuniting of the spirit and body was the result of his driving out the evil infection and uniting the spirit and body again (1 Cor 15:51; 1 Thess 4:13–18). Nothing was more powerful or ominous in the ancient world. Such power over death and the ability to recall spirits to lifeless bodies thought to be "sleeping" was almost unheard of, except in Judaism by the prophets Elijah and Elisha[41] or reported attempts by pagans who were considered dark magicians. Jesus' actions would thus have either been revered or considered further evidence that he was connected to evil spirits he could conjure and control.

Jesus again employs personal contact and special words to expel death, thus overcoming the evil infection that rendered the body lifeless.

---

40. The synoptics primarily report young individuals, while John reports the resurrection of Lazarus, an adult man (John 11).

41. Elijah (1 Kgs 17:17–24) and Elisha (2 Kgs 4:32–37) each lie on the body of the dead boys repeatedly and pray to revive them.

In one instance, he takes with him into the inner room of a home lit with lamps only his fellow exorcists, Cephas, James, and John (meaning that this recollection must come from one of them):

> "And he said, 'The child is not dead but sleeping.' And they [those present] laughed at him. But he put them outside, and took the child's father and mother and those who were with him, and went in where the child was. Taking her by the hand he said to here, '*Talitha cumi*,' which means, 'Little girl, I say to you arise.' And immediately the girl got up and walked, for she was twelve years old." (Mark 5:39-42)

Here the gospel editor translates Jesus' words, but we find parallels to these words in other texts that were often used by ecstatics as a command to drive out evil.[42] Their meaning is now indecipherable. It is much more likely that the words of authority that Jesus used were familiar to other exorcists. In fact, there is every reason to believe that Jesus employed every technique that was both expected and familiar to contemporary Palestinian Judaism to perform exorcisms and overcome evil spirits, including those used by other ecstatics and magicians. In this case, the ruler of the synagogue's daughter is given freedom from the infection of death. That the "sleeping" dead could be raised was a common expectation, and in fact, was a prevalent belief in ancient Judaism, except among the Sadducees (Mark 6:16).[43] It certainly was the belief held by Jesus of Nazareth and Paul, a Pharisee of Tarsus. It is then no wonder that Jesus' fellow exorcists, Cephas and John, held this as a fact to be within the power of God, particularly since they had witnessed this very event in the villages of Palestine, and later followed Jesus' pattern of similarly raising the dead (Acts 9:36–43). Satan's power of death was being overcome by words and action in the exorcism of evil.

Did Jesus then raise the dead? Given that exorcism of death was coherent with the countermeasures Jesus took in destroying the occupation of Satan in Palestine, coupled with the historical context and beliefs of the time

---

42. Smith, *Jesus the Magician*, 95.

43. See also Dan 12:2 and Rabbinic literature such as *Sanh.* 90b and 91b: "From the Torah: for it is written: 'And the Lord said to Moses, Behold you shall sleep with your fathers; and this people will rise up' [Deuteronomy 31:16]. From the Prophets: as it is written: 'Your dead men shall live, together with my dead bodies shall they arise. Awake and sing, you that dwell in the dust; for your dew is as the dew of herbs, and the earth shall cast out its dead.' [Isaiah 26:19]; from the Writings: as it is written, 'And the roof of your mouth, like the best wine of my beloved, like the best wine, that goes down sweetly, causing the lips of those who are asleep to speak' [Song of Songs 7:9]" (*Sanh.* 90b).

that death was an infection of evil, there can be no doubt that he did raise those who had previously been thought dead. The most powerful of all signs that the kingdom of God and justice were inbreaking was now present.

The tactile aspect of Jesus' exorcism of evil is reinforced repeatedly in these texts. Jesus is most commonly surrounded by the infirm, particularly after his synagogue cleansings and retirement to a local home's hospitality, most likely the home of a ruler of the local synagogue.[44] Touching Jesus' garments or cloak, including the "fringe of his garment" would drive out evil spirits and stop Satan's torment (Luke 4:19, 6:17–19, 53–56, 8:25–33; Mark 3:10, 6:56; Matt 14:36). When this happens, Jesus reports that he feels "power had gone forth from him" (Mark 5:30), or in his own words, "Someone touched me; for I perceive that power has gone forth from me" to expel the spirit (Luke 8:40). To touch Jesus was to gain protection from malicious spirits and demons. It is for this reason that young women brought their children and infants to Jesus to touch him: to protect them from evil and illness, particularly given the high mortality rate among children in ancient Palestine (Mark 10:13–16). This is a moving scene, and one that is certainly coherent with the context, given Jesus' reputation. Other exorcists attempt to hold these women and children back, but Jesus stops them from doing so. This results in a saying that is completely coherent with Jesus' countermeasure to free Palestine from evil, and so is a reliable tradition. Thus, those who embrace his exorcisms as evidence of the kingdom and practice forgiveness and mercy are the children of God and those that reject him and influence the children to do so are doomed:

> "Let the children come to me, do not hinder them; for to such belongs the kingdom of God." (Mark 10:14b; Luke 18:15–17)

> "Whoever causes one of these little ones who believe in me to stumble [or sin], it would be better for him if a great millstone were hung round his neck and he were thrown into the sea." (Mark 9:42)

When Jesus or his exorcists are successful in cleansing a synagogue, he acknowledges that the exorcist has attained special standing with God, assuring the exorcists that they will be resurrected to life in the kingdom when it arrives: "rejoice that your names are written in heaven" (Luke 10:20b). In a clear Semitism, Jesus equates the expulsion of demons and spirits with

---

44. Jesus was likely heading to the home of the Jairus, head of the synagogue. Jairus knew of Jesus' common practice of entering the synagogue to exorcise and teach and meets him on his way there (Mark 5:21–43).

treading on "serpents and scorpions, and over all the power of the enemy ... and nothing shall hurt you" (Luke 10:19). Jesus's band of exorcists has begun to overthrow Satan, and Jesus declares this to be so at each event, saying, "I saw Satan fall like lightening from heaven" (Luke 10:18). Given these traditions and their coherence with the context of countermeasures and established pattern, we can now examine other sayings of Jesus' associated with his synagogue cleansings.

## RELATED SAYINGS OF JESUS, COHERENT WITH HIS SYNAGOGUE CLEANSINGS

As noted, the words of demons are remarkably well preserved because they reflect the confrontation of Jesus and Satan in the setting of the synagogue, which is virtually unique in all of Jewish literature. Such traditions reinforce Jesus' practice of cleansing synagogues of evil, then restoring it and its congregation to the kingdom of God. Jesus can expel demons by commanding them to vacate their victims:

> "That evening they brought to him many who were possessed with demons; and he cast out the spirits with a word, and healed all who were sick." (Matt 8:16)

The demons identify Jesus as the exorcist of God, the "holy one," and the opponent of Satan in front of terrified witnesses. Some demons identify themselves by name, including the demon known as "Legion" (Luke 8:26–39; Mark 5:1–20). While the text identifies Legion as a demon, the name is also a clear reference to Roman occupation, designating Roman occupation as the work of Satan. Reportedly, Jesus is always able to silence and then expel such demons.

Yet, despite these public encounters with demons, Jesus is rejected by most of the religious elite and even many local Jews, leading to the charge that he is either the agent of or possessed by Beelzebul. This controversy underscores the basis of Jesus' conflict with religious opponents who considered him mad and possessed. As such, by employing qualitative risk analysis and utilizing the context of the Beelzebul controversy as our basis, we can analyze the controversy traditions and assess their reliability as to the countermeasures of Jesus.

## CONTROVERSY STORIES AND THE COUNTERMEASURES OF JESUS: CONFLICT WITH AGENTS OF SATAN

The Beelzebul controversy incorporates sayings that are coherent with the countermeasures of Jesus to end satanic rule through his exorcisms. Consequently, this controversy provides a reliable litmus test by which to measure the historical content and validity of other controversy dialogues in the Synoptic Gospels.

For example, another saying of Jesus related to Beelzebul controversy is found in Matt 10:24–25. Here Jesus appears to warn his fellow exorcists that the elite will naturally accuse them of the same apostasy, of being agents of Satan:

> "A disciple is not above his teacher, nor a servant above his master; it is enough for the disciple to be like his teacher, and the servant like his master. If they have called the master of the house Beelzebul, how much more will they malign those of his household." (Matt 10:24–25)

This saying is more than a warning. It is an affirmation that those who accuse Jesus are themselves the servants of their master, Beelzebul. It is a statement of reversal, showing that his opponents do not recognize their state, for Satan deceives them. For this reason, Jesus' followers will suffer and be persecuted: "If they persecute you in one town, flee to the next " (Matt 10:23b).

Clearly, the Beelzebul controversy is surrounded by historical elements and relevant sayings that point to its usefulness as a historical measure in testing the validity of other controversy dialogues in the gospels. The framework of the Beelzebul controversy and its historical elements are clear. They provide a set of comparative elements by which we can assess other controversy dialogues in the Synoptic Gospels. We will now apply these results to the Synoptic Gospels.

7

# The Risk Context of the Controversy Dialogues
## The Collision of Countermeasures to Perilous Risk

WE BEGIN BY DEVELOPING the context of the controversy dialogues in the Synoptic Gospels. In Mark, Jesus engages in several controversies with the religious elite—the scribes, the Sadducees, the Jerusalem aristocracy, Herodians, and the temple leadership. Also included are vicious disputes with certain Pharisees, but primarily those who were sympathetic with the Herodians,[1] as we know of Paul's own description of his vehement and violent opposition of the Way (Gal 1:13–14).[2] Jesus also answers questions from others within the Pharisaic party. He appeals to them to accept the imminent entry of God evidenced in his exorcisms—the violent arrival of the kingdom. It must be remembered that originally, the Pharisees also rebelled against imperialistic assimilation (Indeed, this rebellion was at the root of Pharisaic formation a century-and-a-half before Jesus.[3]) as the for-

---

1. The historical evidence for a party within the Pharisees is certain, as Mark 12:13 confirms.

2. Also see Acts 7:57–58, 8:1–3, 9:1–2; 1 Cor 15:9; and especially Acts 22:2b–5, which is certainly one of the most accurate portrayals of the vehemence and violence associated with Paul's persecution.

3. Finkelstein, *Pharisees*, 1:73–81. The rebellion against the Seleucid tyrant, Antiochus Epiphanes (160–146 CE) by the Maccabees was founded on an attempt to assimilate Judaism into Hellenism, which resulted in the pollution of the temple through the sacrifice of a pig on its altar. Overall, an interesting correlation exists between Jesus'

mation of the synagogue and oral tradition, as well as schools of training by leading sages.[4] These are all a formidable and laudable tribute to this resistance in the rich history of Judaism. Jesus is most often affiliated with the Pharisees. Indeed, Paul's own adaptation of his Pharisaic heritage and the new view of the law it offered is also a tribute and testament to the vitality of first-century Pharisaism. Paul never says he has abandoned his Pharisaic roots, only counted his former belief in meriting righteousness as baseless before God. Nonetheless, based on Paul's own attempt to destroy followers of Jesus, it is clear that certain Pharisees affiliated with the Jerusalem elite and Herodians rejected Jesus and challenged him publicly. Therefore, we must be cautious to separate Jesus' confrontations with the elite from those with the Pharisees who ought out Jesus to debate with him, but remained receptive to dialogue with him. We begin with an overview of the dialogues in their present form.

## THE TWO COLLECTIONS IN MARK

The author or editor of Mark incorporates two separate collections of controversy dialogues (Mark 2:1–3:6, 11:27–12:44) that are likely taken from a more primitive source, either oral or written. That Jewish witnesses of the first generation stood behind the oral traditions absorbed in the Gospel of Mark seems almost incontrovertible. The use of the "historical present" in the Greek narrative, that is, the use of the present rather than the past tense to describe Jesus' activity, underscores the vitality of these oral stories as they were relayed to new believers. The intentional use of this tense betrays an oral background.[5] Indeed, this is exactly the way oral traditions would have been presented in order to draw listeners into the immediacy of the events. Moreover, the number of Aramaisms is striking, and when combined with the use of the historical present, the certainty with which the traditions can be traced to the first generation is significantly strengthened. Here are just a few of the words used:

---

purification of the temple and his pronouncement of God's arrival as king in order to eliminate the apostasy of the temple elite who had acceded to foreign imperialism. For Jesus, this purification was totally reliant on God's action in history, not on any army he might raise!

4. Most notably Beit Hillel and Beth Shammai (ca. 50 BCE to 30 CE).

5. This tense change may indicate that oral traditions were quickly brought into the compiled written narrative without editing due to an need for a document to explain the shocking crisis at hand: the impending destruction of Jerusalem.

## The Risk Context of the Controversy Dialogues

- *Boangerges*: "Sons of Thunder" (Mark 3:17)
- *talitha cum*: "Little girl, get up" (Mark 5:41)
- *Corban*: "Offering to God" (Mark 7:11)
- *ephphatha*: "Be opened" (Mark 7:34)
- *rabbi*: "Teacher," or "lord" (Mark 9:5)
- *Bartimaeus*: "Son of Timaeus" (Mark 10:46)
- *rabbouni*: "My teacher," or "my lord" (Mark 10:51)
- *hosanna*: "Cry to God in praise" (Mark 11:9)
- *abba*: "Dad," or "Papa" (Mark 14:36)
- *Golgotha*: "The place of the skull" (Mark 15:22)
- *eloi eloi lema sabachthani*: "My God, my God, why have you forsaken [or 'forgotten'] me?" (Mark 15:34)

Virtually all of these Aramaic words embedded in the oral tradition captured by the Gospel of Mark are omitted or transliterated in the Gospels of Matthew and Luke. Along with other elements, this confirms the priority of Mark and that it was used as one of their narrative sources.

In two notable cases, the words must have come from those standing with Jesus, i.e., present at the raising of a seemingly dead little girl and at the death of Jesus on the cross when he spoke one of the most controversial sayings, the cry from the cross. We cannot discount the women who accompanied Jesus that are named in Mark—Mary of Magdala; Mary, the mother of James and Joses; and Salome, for example—all of whom must be *counted as apostles* just as Paul does in regard to Junia in Rom 16:7. Only a witness would be bold enough to recount the original opposition even Jesus' family had to him and his ministry. Likewise, only a witness could relate how the disciples themselves failed to understand Jesus' significance (Mark 8:32, 8:18–19, 6:52, 4:40, 4:13) or describe Jesus' emotional responses in specific situations, such as his displeasure (Mark 1:43), deep sighs (Mark 8:12), or his love (Mark 10:21). Consequently, we find in Mark evidence of primacy in the oral tradition that suggests a foundation in witnesses. Granted, these traditions were kept by the community for specific needs and were likely amended and expanded by early Christian prophets under inspiration of the Spirit and risen Lord, but nonetheless, the evidence of original witnesses behind these traditions is strong.

To Be Near the Fire

The patterning of events in each unit also suggests an origin in oral tradition. Many have an oral mnemonic quality, which betrays a consistent structural pattern that builds to a climaxing statement, and also include compelling visual elements—both of which assist in memorization and oral presentation (i.e., oral rhythm and embellishment). Consistent with the conflict of perilous risks, each dialogue reports a confrontation over the source of Jesus' authority, whether his authority to exorcise demons or to render a victim free of the illnesses, deformities, or incapacities presumed to be a result of some sin on the part of the victim or the victim's family. In other cases, Jesus is authorized to abrogate the law or Jewish practices. The dialogue ends with a saying of Jesus' that terminates the argument by asserting, if not proving, his claim of authority to reject scribes' elitist control. Interestingly, in each controversy Jesus associates his authority with the Spirit possessing him, which originates from the God of Israel (i.e., God's authority, endowed power, or the Holy Spirit of God that possesses him or is available for him to direct at his command). He thereby counters any charge that he is a charlatan, a magician, or otherwise possessed by Satan or controlled by demons by asserting the authority of God and his Spirit. For example, when Jesus exorcises a demon or spirit, he does so by telling the victim that they are "forgiven," that is, that the possessed person is released from death or the power of Satan—an authority that can only be granted by God. Jesus is immediately (and understandably) charged with blasphemy, a charge worthy of immediate execution. Jesus is accused of being under the control of the blasphemer himself. Consequently, like in the Beelzebul controversy, the controversy dialogues accurately reflect the collision of perilous risks and countermeasures, and so must be evaluated in terms of their contribution in terms of understanding the historical life situation of Jesus' ministry to free the land from possession in a war on Satan. In particular, Jesus' controversy dialogues resulting from his exorcisms may have the highest claim to authenticity, for they capture both this conflict of risk as well as his claim that they confirm the arrival of the kingdom of God, displacing the kingdom of Satan and "binding the strongman" (Matt 12:27–29).

## CONTROVERSY DIALOGUES AND THE AUTHORITY TO ACT AS GOD

The origin of these controversies must have come from the synagogue activity of Jesus, which includes his exorcisms and subsequent proclamation of the inbreaking kingdom of God. Yet, their collection and inclusion in Mark certainly reflect their necessity for meeting contemporary issues, a conclusion based on their retention in the oral tradition for thirty years until the production of the Gospel of Mark itself (ca. 68–70 CE). By the time these units are incorporated into Mark, the early Jewish-Hellenistic church was encountering strong opposition from the Pharisaic-influenced synagogues of the Diaspora, from which the churches were partially formed and drew adherents.[6] As evidenced in Paul's letters (ca. 50–60 CE), local synagogue leaders and members violently persecuted the followers of Jesus for blasphemy (some of whom they stoned without opposition from local authorities), and even threatened or practiced excommunication,[7] creating intense controversy and social disruption surrounding those expelled. Before his ecstatic experience on the road to Damascus, Paul himself participated in a violent persecution of Jesus' followers in Palestine for at least two years under his Hebrew name, Saul. Undoubtedly, he leveled the same charges at exorcists who continued to practice using Jesus' name. Paul pursued the followers of Jesus to the very towns and villages that Jesus himself had visited, and his actions were brutal (Gal 1:13–14) rather than simply vehement disputes, as he himself admits. For example, he participated in the stoning and murder of Stephen. He arrested both men and women as he went from synagogue to synagogue, covering over a 150-mile radius while carrying letters of authorization from Jerusalem's high priest. Paul made certain that those who were expelled lost everything: social position, safety as a protected member of an ethnic community, and the livelihood of their trade, even imprisoning men and women in Jerusalem. The basis of this rejection of these "Jesus-followers" was not simply that Jesus was a crucified criminal, a dangerous political embarrassment, or a possessed minion of Satan, but also fundamentally lay in how Jesus willingly abrogated or

---

6. Accordingly, by 50 CE, we know that Paul located a synagogue in every major metropolis where he taught, lived, and was expelled. The synagogue in Corinth was able to raise a riot against Paul, but their reputation as troublemakers led Gallio (51–52 CE) to dismiss them out of hand.

7. The punishment described was given for blasphemy, which in turn implied excommunication (2 Cor 11:24).

dismissed Jewish rituals and practices, including Sabbath restrictions and dietary rules *by claiming the rights of God*. This implied that he might claim the authority to relax or suspend the payment of temple taxes or the payment of imperial taxes. Jesus thereby asserted equal standing with God, a blasphemous contradiction of the *Shema* and the fundamental tenets of the Judaism. This made Jesus a serious threat to the religious elite.

## OUR TASK

As a result, the controversy dialogues within these two collections may reveal the very complex and layered accusations leveled against Jesus during his ministry: that he was a possessed deceiver who instigated resistance and the dissolution of Jewish practices. His opponents would accuse him of a litany of evil practices, for might not this Galilean exorcist and magician, who was possessed by Beelzebul, demonstrate his apostasy by degrading the Sabbath and ignoring table fellowship restrictions? Would his growing influence then the end of tax payments? Our challenge is to determine whether the controversy dialogues in Mark contain characteristics that can be traced back into the life setting of Jesus and the countermeasures he employed in his conflict with the Jerusalem elite; indeed, controversies that were similar to the Beelzebul debate.

We begin with a brief analysis of the units as they stand in Mark. Within each there are separate dialogues. A pattern is evident. They move from the controversy itself—usually over Jesus' authority to abrogate Sabbath practices or exorcise authority believed to be God's alone— to a saying of Jesus, which is always the capstone of the controversy. Jesus' authority to act in the stead of God or relax religious practices is then asserted. The purpose of these dialogues is clear: the community can employ the saying to defend its own relaxation of standards under the authority of the risen Lord, Jesus Christ. Since both units (Mark 2:1–3:6 and 11:27–12:44) were incorporated into Mark after the death of Cephas, Paul, and other first-generation witnesses, and because the destruction of Jerusalem was imminent (which was the catalysts in the formation of the first Gospel), retention of these sayings was critical.[8] This implies that these units had circulated orally from community to community for twenty to thirty years until they reached this final form.

---

8. See the discussion above on the formation of Mark, which was similar to crisis that led to the formation of the sources comprising the traditions of John.

*The Risk Context of the Controversy Dialogues*

That there are several individual dialogues within each unit reflects the multiple challenges faced by the *ecclesiae* (i.e., churches) of the Diaspora. Most were formed by itinerate missionaries out of Jewish communities and synagogues. Based on Paul's own experience, there was intense, often violent opposition from the existing leadership. Consequently, the controversy dialogues are vibrant evidence of social and religious conflict, which is valuable in tracing the history of the formation of these communities in the Hellenistic-Roman milieu. These dialogues reflect the character of the intense local Jewish opposition to the nascent *ecclesiae* as well as the response of the followers of Jesus, who always resorted to a saying of Jesus as risen Lord. Such sayings were unassailable by opponents. In the vernacular of qualitative risk analysis, here we witness the countermeasures to risk by conflicting parties, especially the perilous risk to the *ecclesia* that threatened its survival. Using findings from our analysis of the Beelzebul controversy and our work in qualitative risk analysis, it is possible to recover the original setting of some of Jesus' sayings, although in others the original setting has been lost. As such, it is appropriate to examine the controversy dialogues and ascertain what they may reveal about Jesus' activity and sayings adopted by the early church.

## THE CONTROVERSY DIALOGUES: UNIT 1, MARK 2:1–3:6

In the first controversy dialogue of Unit 1, Mark 2:1–12, "the teachers of the law" are with Jesus one evening, sitting (or reclining during a meal) in the largest room of a village home in Capernaum. Several days earlier, Jesus had completed his cleansing of the local synagogue, exorcising a demon from the congregation to signify its freedom from Satan's possession (Mark 1:23–26). It had been reclaimed for the kingdom of God, so long as it accepted outcasts and welcomed them as children of God. Capernaum seems to have initially complied with this demand, based on the crowds that gathered. As was his custom, Jesus continued to exorcise demons and drive out evil spirits that evening after the synagogue encounter, particularly after sunset, when the Sabbath ended. In this case in Capernaum, he was invited to a home nearby local synagogue. His exorcisms and "healings," or driving out evil spirits, continued well into the next morning.

Capernaum was likely the first success among Jesus' Galilean synagogue cleansings, although it did not last, for he later cursed the town for its unbelief (Luke 10:15). He had miserably failed in his attempt to cleanse the village synagogue his father and family attended in Nazareth, and as a result he was thrown out of town and nearly killed. This may be the reason Joseph is never mentioned again—he disowned Jesus. Jesus may have already been successful in Magdala[9] or other villages, but his itinerant travels beyond Galilee began after he had settled in Capernaum. Indeed, he seems to have chosen Capernaum as his home base. He may have done so because the town was located a relatively safe distance from imperially-controlled Sepphoris[10] and Tiberias, the Roman capital of Galilee built by Antipas.[11] Capernaum had no stationed Roman garrison.[12] Also, Jesus found other willing or trainable exorcists there to enlist in his war on Satan. Ultimately the home where he stays is inundated with the sick, the deformed, and possessed. Desperate for rest, Jesus escapes into the countryside for days at a time. After a long search, he is found and agrees to return to Capernaum. There, "teachers of the law," undoubtedly scribes from Jerusalem, are waiting.[13] Using informants, they have tracked Jesus to this home. Taking

---

9. Likely Magdala Nunayya on the shore of Galilee, where Jesus landed (Mark 8:1–3). A stone with a menorah carved on it was found in the later period synagogue, which, like the Capernaum synagogue, was likely build over the first-century site.

10. Sepphoris (also known as Tzippori in Hebrew) was destroyed by the Roman governor Varus after a rebellion that followed the death of Herod around 4 BCE. Herod Antipas began rebuilding the city in 1 CE. It was a completely Hellenized Roman city thereafter, but due to its proximity to Nazareth (3.7 miles) and his role as a carpenter's apprentice, Jesus would have worked there. In Sepphoris, Jesus would have been vulnerable to Herod's spies and control.

11. Built in 14 CE (with construction continuing for several years thereafter), the city was not kosher, having been located on an old cemetery.

12. Luke 7:1–6 mentions a centurion's slave who was ill in Capernaum, and that this centurion had donated the funds to build a synagogue. This tradition has a remarkably strong claim to authenticity. The centurion had learned of Jesus via the synagogue he built for the Jews in another village, one that Jesus had cleansed by driving out evil spirits. Having heard of Jesus the exorcist through this synagogue event, the centurion seeks out his assistance to help one of his important slaves who has fallen ill. The centurion did not live in Capernaum, since no Roman garrison was stationed near Galilee until the second century (Safrai, "Roman Army in Galilee," 103–114). However, Roman soldiers did patrol the area and the Via Maris. If this centurion had retired from the army, then he may have chosen to reside near Galilee, Tiberias, or a town in the Decapolis.

13. Luke 5:21 is careful to distinguish between "teachers of the Law" and Pharisees. The *grammateis*, or scribes, were a literate, educated class made up of the wealthy order of Jerusalem. Some also identified with the Pharisees' grassroots movement to reinvigorate the Law into contemporary practices and customs. Nonetheless, they were the lawyers who rigorously protected the Law from abuse or blasphemous practices, particularly by peasant exorcists who rejected Jerusalem.

advantage of the Jewish tradition of hospitality shown to travelers,[14] they are admitted and fed. Whether simply curious about his growing notoriety or intent on finding grounds to have him arrested, they are certainly there to assess the risk he poses to maintaining the peace, particularly since he announces the nearness of the kingdom of God (and thus, the end of the current order) at each of his exorcisms.

Having pushed through the crowds that surrounded the home, these scribes are shown to the largest of the rooms, one that likely served for family dining and Sabbath gatherings. The scribes, a few of Jesus' fellow exorcists, and perhaps some family would have been present. According to Mark 1:29–31, this may have taken place in the home of Simon, a fellow exorcist who had formerly partnered with the sons of Zebedee in a small, imperially-licensed fishing business.[15] Jesus, who was already renowned for his exorcisms, had invited this young man to become a "fisher of men" (Mark 1:17), i.e., an exorcist who would rescue the possessed from Satan. Simon, who Jesus renamed as Cephas,[16] lived with his wife and extended family, which included his mother-in-law. Jesus had cured her of a fever, meaning he had exorcised an evil spirit (Mark 1:21).[17]

The next events in Mark 2:4 strongly suggest a Galilean eyewitness was present. Desperate to reach the exorcist Jesus, four men carry a paralyzed male to the entrance of the home, but they are unable to push through the crowds. They tie the *teknon*, a young man or child, to a pallet and climb to the roof, pulling him up about twelve feet with rope. They find the edge of the roofing and begin tearing it up by hand in order to make a hole large enough for them to drop him through.[18] They break up the clay and

---

14. Again, based on Abraham's entertaining angels unaware (Gen 18:2) and the custom still in place today in many cultures of the Middle East (Heb 13:2).

15. The route passed Capernaum and the western shore of Galilee. The dried fish could have traveled from Galilee to Damascus to the north, or to Ashdod and Jaffa to the south, then on to merchant ships to other destinations. Simon may have been suffering financially, catching and drying fish such as carp or *musht* (talapia) for trade. The gospels themselves report several unsuccessful attempts to collect sufficient catch. Merchants who passed Capernaum via the Via Maris purchased these fish, and Romans considered the dried fish of Galilee a delicacy.

16. Meaning "the rock." Jesus seems to have given names to his exorcists—in this case, the rock on which Satan's power would be broken.

17. It is reported in Mark 1:21 that the fever left her "immediately," evidencing that it was an expulsion.

18. Unhewn crossbeams were laid atop the basalt support walls. Across these beams were branches and saplings for cross-support. Specially prepared clay was packed on top

separate the branches underneath. This description of dismantling (literally "digging") accurately portrays structures found in Galilee and Palestine, and certainly in Capernaum. Aside from the accuracy of the description, breaking up the roof offers a striking visual, making this memorable event excellent for oral lore; it is a visceral image that gives the tradition mnemonic quality. One can only imagine the crumbling clay falling into the room as the stunned guests watch the branches and saplings separated by hand overhead. The accuracy of the description suggests that this event indeed dates to the activity of Jesus. There are other elements that support this conclusion as well.

Next, Mark 2:5–12 provides one of the most haunting and human descriptions in the New Testament of the young exorcist, Jesus. To begin with, Jesus is oblivious to the damage being done above him, intent as he is on the vision of the boy tied to the bier as it is lowered to him. Jesus witnessed these desperate men's determination to free their friend or relative of evil. Unlike the scribes present, Jesus is not concerned about touching this boy or becoming ritually unclean. It is likely that Jesus was also called to help lower the pallet to the floor and untie the young man. He addresses him diminutively, reassuringly speaking to him as "son." The scene accurately reflects the extreme juxtaposition of angst (the terror of possession) and hope (radical actions to reach this exorcist, or "holy man") in first-century Palestine. As we have established, peasant Jews lived in a world of harmful demons and evil spirits. This desperate action by families of the sick and infirm is indicative of the extreme measures that would be taken to rescue the helpless. Without hesitation, Jesus speaks to those present, chiding them.

Contrary to expectations, Jesus contends that sin did not bring on the paralysis (Mark 2:9). It is instead due to the capricious nature of the demons that possess and ravage the land, tormenting the weak, outcasts, and dispossessed. He says, "Which is easier: to say to this paralyzed young man, 'Your sins are forgiven,' or to say, 'Get up, take your mat, and walk?'" (Mark 2:9). Jesus is indifferent to whatever supposed sin may have occurred, if any. Nothing needs to be forgiven; Satan alone needs to be bound and cast out. The infection of the land brought about by the apostasy of Jerusalem had led to the innocent being possessed and prophets being killed. Jesus is at war with Satan and his demons. He demands that the healed man walk in front of everyone, carrying his pallet to demonstrate that even the most terrifying of infirmities, demonic paralysis, has been overcome.

---

of the branches to make a water-resistant surface.

*The Risk Context of the Controversy Dialogues*

The helplessness, depression, and lingering death arising from paralysis brought on by forced occupation of evil was a parallel to the evil infection of imperial occupation and the corruption of the temple establishment.[19] Jesus clears a path for the man in front of the scribes of Jerusalem, ignoring their objections and charges of blasphemy.

These scribes' remarkable lack of awe and compassion at the expulsion of evil betrays their intent: to find fault with Jesus so as to bring an accusation against him back to the elite. Consequently, this exorcism and controversy dialogue is a debate over Jesus' authority. Jesus' saying over the controversy is finally presented: "But I want you to know that the Son of Man has the authority on earth to forgive sins" (Mark 2:10).

## TESTING THE VERACITY OF MARK 2:1–12 USING QUALITATIVE RISK ANALYSIS

We have already suggested that a number of features in this controversy are coherent with the conflict of countermeasures. Applying the structural elements of the Beelzebul controversy to this dialogue shows that there are enough similarities to suggest its reliability as originating in the ministry of Jesus. Recounting these structural elements, we find the following.

Jesus is an undisputed Galilean exorcist. He has gained notoriety in Jerusalem and is confronted by "teachers of the law," the scribes from Jerusalem, or the Pharisees together with the Herodians, followers of Antipas who track Jesus to entrap him (Mark 3:6). Their objective: to bring credible witnesses to testify that Jesus made a seditious statement or action by speaking out against taxation or condemning the Herodian regime.[20] They come to Jesus' center of charismatic activity, Capernaum. Jesus has been conducting synagogue cleansings and has returned. In the evenings, he is surrounded by the ill and possessed. As is his custom, he is engaged in freeing a possessed land by casting out demons until morning. Jesus has denounced Satan by expelling him in front of the congregation. Satan's kingdom is thus at an end, the undeniable evidence of which is brought to each community by Jesus' exorcisms to usher in God's inbreaking kingdom. As in the Beelzebul controversy, the objection from the elite is that

---

19. Evans, "Jesus' Action in the Temple."

20. Matt 17:24–27 details this event in Capernaum. Tax collectors, agents of imperialism, ask if Jesus is planning on paying the required the "two-drachma" tax. Again, he is questioned in the temple (Mark 12:14) by Pharisees sympathetic to the Herodians.

Jesus cannot forgive sins, and that by doing so he speaks blasphemy, and so must himself be of Satan. The question raised here is over Jesus' authority to cast out demons and make pronouncements concerning the kingdom of God, which threatens to displace the imperial kingdom and rule of the elite. This controversy dialogue mirrors the fundamental tenets of the Beelzebul controversy.

Consistent with other controversy dialogues, Jesus concludes the event with a saying of authority. In this case, we must be cautious. His saying references "the Son of Man." But here the term "Son of Man" is not intended as a title. Instead, it is a familiar and contemporary circumlocution for "I."[21] Thus, it is not a reference to the apocalyptic Son of Man or to any other divine or messianic figure. If this is understood as a circumlocution, Jesus is affirming that his exorcisms obliterate the power of Satan. He is authorized to exorcise evil and make pronouncements. Of course, from the perspective of the post-Easter community, Jesus was referring to himself as the coming Son of Man, the judge and Messiah of God. However, in its original qualitative risk setting, Jesus cites his exorcisms as evidence for the inbreaking of the kingdom of God and its transformative impact on those who embrace the arrival of God as king. Consequently, this controversy is coherent with the findings of qualitative risk analysis and is coherent with Jesus' activity.

## Unit 1, Mark 2:13–17

The next dialogue, Mark 2:13–17, presents a conflict between Jesus and certain Pharisees who are respectfully identified as "teachers of the law." What is interesting is that they do not seek to entrap Jesus. But when Jesus requests an invitation to share table fellowship with a local tax collector—considered to be the most repugnant and corrupt of Jews—they are indignant, asking his followers: "Why does he eat with tax collectors and sinners?" (Mark 2:16). If these men were scholars sympathetic to the Pharisaic view of the law, a view that Jesus also mirrors at times,[22] then they were

---

21. See Black and Vermès, *Aramaic Approach to the Gospels*, 310–30; and Vermès, *Jesus the Jew*, 188–91.

22. Jesus' commandment on loving one's neighbor reflects the teachings of contemporary Pharisaic sages, such as that of Hillel (110 BCE–10 CE): "That which is hateful to you, do not do to your fellow. That is the whole Torah; the rest is the explanation; go and learn" (*b. Šabb.* 31a), while his prohibition against divorce is similar to the teachings of Shammai (50 BCE—30 CE).

*grammateis* who were intrigued by Jesus as an exorcist, but even more so by his proclamation of God's near arrival. These "teachers of the law" were perhaps like others who "secretly" followed Jesus for fear of retribution and "... looked for the kingdom of God."[23] Free of the influence of the temple elite and priestly aristocracy,[24] their dispute with Jesus was not about a seditious act or comment, but about the company he kept. Why would the proclaimer of the kingdom consort with a tax collector? This must also be our question.

Despite their objections, Jesus publicly defends his non-kosher table fellowship with the worst of all social outcasts and "sinners" in Palestine. Tax collectors were imperially licensed to collect taxes from Jews on behalf of Herod and the Romans. They were notoriously corrupt in their assessments, using their position to enrich themselves. Backed by the military power of Roman garrisons and the temple police, tax collectors were known to be ruthless, even murderous extortionists.[25] They were hated as traitors and, as complicit participants in foreign imperialism and pagan military occupation, they were considered lost—or better—dead to God.[26] Of all apostate Jews, certainly Jesus would condemn the tax collectors just as he did the elite. But Jesus does just the opposite. Not only does he invite himself to an evening meal at a well-known tax collector's home (in a breach of countless Pharisaic ritual and purity restrictions) to eat with this reviled figure and his friends (thus consorting with enemies of Judaism), he also invites this man, Levi (otherwise known as Alphaeus), to become his friend and fellow advocate on behalf of God as king, since he repents his apostasy. This tradition captures one of Jesus' most aggressive countermeasures. His attack on demonic imperialism includes this attempt to turn tax collectors

---

23. Much like Joseph of Arimathea, a Pharisee and member of the Sanhedrin (Mark 15:43).

24. Jeremias, *Jerusalem in the Time*, 254–55. For a helpful discussion on the complicity of the scribes with the temple elite, see ibid., 233–45.

25. Consider, "But Joseph took with him two thousand foot soldiers from the king, for he desired he might have some assistance, in order to force such as were refractory in the cities to pay. And borrowing of the king's friends at Alexandria five hundred talents, he made haste back into Syria. And when he was at Askelon, and demanded the taxes of the people of Askelon, they refused to pay anything, and affronted him also; upon which he seized upon about twenty of the principal men, and slew them, and gathered what they had together, and sent it all to the king, and informed him what he had done" (Josephus, *Ant.* 12:180).

26. For a helpful discussion on the hated position of tax collector, see Jeremias, *Jerusalem in the Time*, 32, 56, 124–125, 303–5.

against the regime. Failure to collect taxes would result in Roman retribution against the elite, their displacement, and their end. These teachers do not understand this plan. They only see Jesus' actions as impure.

One can only imagine the other such "sinners" at the table. If this was a dinner meal, consider the scene: Jesus, exorcist of evil spirits and demons, proclaimer of the kingdom of God, and harsh critic of imperialism and apostasy, reclines on a comfortable couch, eating tainted and unholy foods next to his host, a Jewish traitor—the most offensive place Jesus could publicly take. Because of all the problematic issues and risks associated with this event, there can be no doubt whatsoever that this tradition finds its origin in the life situation of Jesus' perilous mission. It is a shocking, radical act fraught with perilous risks for Jesus and his disciples, and yet, it clearly stands as testament to the mercy granted to those who reject imperialism and embrace God as king and father. For Jesus to turn tax collectors against the Jerusalem elite and imperialism is to undermine evil. Jesus is invading the kingdom of Satan. He seeks to end the expansion of corruption and oppression that falls upon the dispossessed and those rendered powerless by merciless taxation.[27] Jesus infiltrates the inner circle of the most powerful people seduced by imperialism. Jesus therefore risks rejection by those who follow him as well as those whom he is desperate to free. This is the perilous nature of Jesus' risk-taking and countermeasures in his war on Satan, and it could easily result in his death.

To their objection, Jesus responds in a form similar to Talmudic disputation,[28] not in anger. He asserts that he frees "sinners" from Satan's control, not only the "righteous" (Mark 2:17), for there is no limitation to God's mercy—implying that even hated traitors can be redeemed. His listeners are horrified. Jesus' use of the word "righteous" implies that he considers these people to also be "teachers of the law" and children of God. Yet, if Jesus' listeners reject his claim that God calls even the worst of "sinners," they also deny the arrival of the kingdom of God evidenced by his exorcism of demons and evil spirits. This is the *euangelion*, the good news.

What is often lost on many commentators is the fact that, in the context of qualitative risk analysis, the tax collectors who turned to Jesus also risked everything—revenge, retribution, stoning, and death. For them, it was the most perilous possible risk. Consequently, this controversy has

---

27. See Horsley, *Spiral of Violence*, 312–17.

28. These disputes debated the truth of the Law and its purpose, often related to contextual settings.

every claim to historicity solely on the basis of the perilous risks present. Indeed, of all the controversy dialogues in the two units analyzed, this tradition has the highest claim to reflect the controversial situation of conflict and perilous risk.

## Unit 1, Mark 2:18–24

In the next dialogue, Mark 2:18–24, "some men" question and then reject Jesus because he and his disciples do not follow the Pharisaic practice of fasting twice weekly on the second and fifth day of the week (Matt 9:14; Luke 18:12). By inference from the context of the passage, this was also the practice followed by John's disciples. We must not go too far in our suppositions, however. Certainly, Jesus did fast on the Day of Atonement, a precept of the law (Lev 16:31).

So who are the "some"? Ascribing the origin of this controversy dialogue simply to the Pharisees would be quite problematic, so Mark does not do so. The Pharisees invite Jesus to meals (Luke 11:37, 14:1)[29] and some accept him as a reformer (including members of the Jewish ruling council, the Sanhedrin, albeit secretly by most). It is clear, based on this and other traditions noted, that the Pharisees' as a whole did not reject Jesus outright, but many[30] did *resist* his radical proclamation, leading to vocal encounters and healthy dispute. The incorporation of opposition from the Pharisees only came later, when Christian communities of the Diaspora fell into conflict with synagogues after the destruction of Jerusalem.[31] It is the gospel editors who begin to emphasize the confrontation with the Pharisees to provide instruction and guidance to the community, thereby displacing Jesus' contemporary opponents. It is noteworthy that Pharisees were also sympathetic to Paul when on trial (Acts 23:9). As a result, the author or editor of Mark did not characterize this as a confrontation with the Pharisees; therefore, the tradition must reflect an event from Jesus' ministry.

Who, then, were those who questioned Jesus? From the perspective of qualitative risk analysis, the question would be posed as follows: What would be the most applicable origin of this controversy in which perilous risk would be evidenced? In other words, what setting betrays a qualitative

29. Acts 15:5 reports that there were certainly Christian Pharisees.

30. That is, other than Pharisees who supported the Herodians in seeking to destroy Jesus.

31. Smith, *Jesus the Magician*, 155.

risk context where perilous risk is evident? The only group mentioned for which significant risk was being experienced, and for whom Jesus' actions would create significant dissonance and perilous risk, would be the *disciples of John*. At this time, John is still in prison, having not yet been murdered by Herod (Mark 6:14), and while some of his followers obviously do not know of John's attestation on behalf of Jesus (Mark 1:7–8), many of John's closest disciples had left to follow him.[32] Clearly, this tradition records a nascent, but critical schism developing between the two camps, wherein those who have turned from John to Jesus are being identified as too radical. Moreover, those who had hoped that Jesus was John's successor have become disenchanted. The tradition of John sending followers to question Jesus about his mission is certainly reliable and reflects not only doubt, but also disappointment (Luke 7:18–20). Indeed, Jesus abandoned baptism. John's followers, already operating under fear and distress, are forced to criticize Jesus and those who have turned to him. All hope may be lost. Thus, since it is unlikely that the "some men" were Pharisees, and since they were certainly not scribes, they must be John's disciples, echoing John's own doubts about Jesus. Consequently, Mark softened the source of the question as being from "some men" because the tradition was still useful to the community, which may have included followers of John in the Diaspora. For example, Apollos, a follower of John, knew the traditions about Jesus, but still remained loyal to John.[33]

Jesus' reply, that fasting cannot be possible when the joy of celebration is present, is an allusion to the arrival of the kingdom of God. He compares it to another visual and memorable scene of joy and celebration of life from Palestine: the arrival of the Jewish bridegroom to his wedding. A seven-day feast follows the ceremony and consummation of the marriage. Since the kingdom has not yet arrived, Jesus may be alluding only to the coming of the bridegroom with his wedding party at night to his bride's home. As he approached, there was celebration and a shout announcing his arrival. The expectation was for the union to then take place, followed by a multiday feast. The idea of a fast was impossible. It was perhaps the penultimate cultural celebration of Jesus' time, outside of religious festivals.

---

32. Including Andrew, certainly (John 1:35–42).

33. The statement that he knew only "the baptism of John" would indicate he had experienced that baptism, and despite the events surrounding Jesus, Apollos continued in an understanding of being within the Baptist's teachings and call to repentance (Acts 18:24–28).

While we cannot deny a Palestinian setting, it is clear that the saying also served the purposes of the *ecclesiae* in conflict with Jewish communities of the Diaspora. Mark 2:17–20 serves to explain why the early followers of Jesus, and later in the *ecclesiae* of the Diaspora, did not follow the Jewish practice of fasting. Based on the problematic nature of the saying in its historical context and the perilous risk it reveals between the followers of John and Jesus the exorcist, this saying has a strong claim to an origin in the activity of Jesus.

## Unit 1, Mark 2:23–28

In Mark 2:23–28, while walking through the fields, hungry and fleeing from Herod, Jesus and his disciples quickly pick the "heads of grain," or *staxus*, off the stalks for food. They do this on the Sabbath. Jesus does not care if it is a serious breach of Jewish practice or whether they are seen. The *staxus* would have been the sparse stalks remaining after the field had been harvested in late May or early June; Jesus and his disciples are picking through what's left. Thus, Jesus' and his followers take only the leftovers, otherwise they would be accused of theft. This tradition quite remarkably demonstrates the impoverished nature of Jesus' ministry while on the move, a historical fact that is often overlooked. Indeed, poverty was rampant, and few Palestinian Jews would have had enough food or means to assist Jesus and his fellow exorcists. Moreover, many would not want to risk doing so, particularly since Herod's spies were attempting to track Jesus. Supporting Jesus on the run could cost someone his or her life (Luke 13:31).

From the outset, qualitative risk analysis would confirm the validity of this tradition, as it is evidence of three perilous risks: for Jews who might aid Jesus, for Jesus and his followers who are starving, and also for those whom Jesus challenges to accept his proclamation but who will be excluded from the celebration if they do not. Jesus was in grave danger (Luke 9:58). Given the serious contextual situation, it must not escape us that in Mark 2:24 the Pharisees who confront Jesus *do not inform on him*, though they do challenge his breach of Sabbath restrictions.

After witnessing Jesus' actions in the field, the Pharisees denounce his breach of the Sabbath (*Shabbot*) restrictions on work, which can be understood in Rabbinic thinking as actively creating or controlling one's environment on the day of rest (just as God rested from his creative activity on the

Sabbath, so should all Hebrews).³⁴ In his defense, Jesus cites King David's demand of Abiathar (it was actually Ahimelek, the father of Abiathar) to allow him to eat the priest's consecrated shewbread, which was forbidden unless he was "clean"; that is, unless he and his men had abstained from women during their military mission, which they had (1 Sam 21:6). The fact that the author or editor of Mark did not correct this error is evidence of the raw form of this oral tradition, and perhaps of the urgent nature of its absorption in this unit in the formation of the gospel. We do not know whether Jesus himself made the incorrect ascription to Abiathar. But clearly, like Jesus and his followers, David and his men were also starving.

Here, the tradition in Matthew is expanded, which is usually an indication of a later form, but in this case a saying is included that is wholly consistent with Jesus' condemnation of the temple elite. On the basis of qualitative risk analysis, we may conclude that this saying was most likely part of the original oral form. Mark either shortened or was not familiar with it. Jesus says, "I tell you that something [or someone] greater than the temple is here" (Matt 12:6). This statement is fraught with perilous risk. Both blasphemous and seditious, it would result in a violent response if the elite were present. In Mark, Jesus responds with far less controversy:

> "The Sabbath was made for man, not man for the Sabbath. I [*bar nasha*, or 'son of man,' which in this case is surely a circumlocution for 'I,' as we have determined before]³⁵ am Lord of the Sabbath." (Mark 2:28)

The only direct parallel for this statement in ancient Judaism is found in a statement by Simon ben Menasya (180 CE) "The Sabbath is delivered to you and you are not delivered to the Sabbath,"³⁶ but its origin may be Mark. Nonetheless, we must not simply gloss over this term "Lord of the Sabbath," and the statement in Matthew would imply that Lord of the Sabbath was a title. Did Mark also understand "Lord of the Sabbath" as such? Some scholars have attempted to associate the "Lord of the Sabbath" with the title, "Lord of the Armies," or "Hosts of God." If this was Jesus' intended use, he would be making a militant claim by associating himself with Da-

---

34. In Hebrew, the word for work is *melahka*, signifying creative action (Gen 2).

35. For an extensive and helpful discussion on Jesus' form of speaking and his use of divine passives and circumlocutions, see Jeremias, *Proclamation of Jesus*, 9–11. Also see his discussion of Jesus' use of antithetic parallelism in passages such as Mark 2:27 in ibid., 14–19.

36. Ibid., 18 n. 3.

vid, which also could be understood as a messianic claim. It is possible that Jesus could have employed this terminology to indicate he is at war with Satan as Lord of the Sabbath. It is more likely that Jesus employs a circumlocution of humility, which is characteristic of his emphasis on humility before God as king and father and typical of his way of speaking, even during his exorcisms of demons—he silences them and forbids them to even speak of his being a "holy one" of God. This would also suggest that Jesus' statement in Matt 12:6 emphasizes not himself, not "someone," but rather the kingdom that was inbreaking: "something" greater is here.

Consequently, Jesus' saying in Mark is characteristic of his criticism of other Rabbinic Halakhah on the Sabbath, and the over-reaching restrictions placed on its practice in the Jewish oral tradition.[37] Jesus' pronouncement here is not an innocuous statement. Indeed, it is a remarkably troubling statement to the Pharisees, negating the most basic of practices of both the oral Torah and their view of the law. On the basis of qualitative risk analysis, this statement—particularly his devaluation of the temple—therefore creates a perilous risk for Jesus and his followers, who were already on the run. This event certainly arises from Jesus' ministry at one of its most critical moments. Jesus claims authority to abrogate the Sabbath. This creates perilous risk and, as a countermeasure to charges of apostasy, provides the overarching response that "something greater is here." In other words, the one who announces the kingdom of God and overthrow of Satan is with you, possessed by or possessing the Spirit of God. By implication, God no longer occupies the temple.

## Unit 1, Mark 3:1–6

The last dialogue in this unit is Jesus' cure of the man with the "withered hand" (Mark 3:1–6). This man could not use his hand. In the context of first-century Palestine, such an affliction was assumed to result from an evil spirit. The condition may have been infantile paralysis or poliomyelitis, which is a viral disease usually contracted through polluted water and often affects children such as those in ancient Palestine. It is an incurable, lifelong, debilitating disease—one that would have resulted in this man being cast out as impure. The contemporary conclusion would have been that he was suffering for his own sins or some sin committed by his family.

---

37. Ibid., 208–214.

Jesus intentionally expels the evil spirit while the congregation is gathered in the synagogue—as such, this is a Sabbath cleansing. We are not told which synagogue. It is not on the shore of Galilee, so it was not Capernaum.[38] Mark 3:7 would suggest that following this event, Jesus retreated to Galilee, having been threatened. What is clear is that Jesus had been tracked to this synagogue. Some of those present were "looking for a reason to accuse him," indicating that they sought to bring charges of sedition or blasphemy, which were both punishable by death (Mark 3:2). It is they who decide to go to the Herodians[39] as spies to assist in a plot to murder Jesus, for they "sought to destroy him" (Mark 3:6).[40] The characteristics and elements of this dialogue are coherent with the Beelzebul controversy and the charges brought against Jesus, and so this tradition should be considered reliable as arising from the ministry of Jesus.

## THE CONTROVERSY DIALOGUES OF UNIT 2, MARK 11:27–12:40

The next collection is Mark 11:27–12:40, another compilation of individual controversy dialogues that had circulated orally. It includes many of Jesus' most vehement and dangerous clashes with the elite. Unlike the previous unit, in which the elite or their agents seek out Jesus in the countryside and villages, here we find Jesus in Jerusalem. He has entered the city and the temple after having successfully cleansed as many of the surrounding synagogues as would accept him or his exorcists. Jesus now confronts satanic influence and possession at its core, where apostasy had taken hold through demonic imperialism and the influence of foreign gods. The conflict in

---

38. Jesus began teaching and debating in this synagogue early in his ministry (Mark 1:21).

39. As noted, the Herodians were a separate party of Jews who publicly supported Herod the Great, and his son, Herod Antipas, who succeeded him as tetrarch of Galilee and Perea from 4 BCE to 39 CE. Since the Herods supported and were empowered by Rome, they were complicit in accepting and profiting from power gained through foreign domination over the Jews (For example, Antipas' built his capital on the Sea of Galilee, naming it Tiberias in honor of his patron, the Roman Emperor.) and thus represented the elitists whom Jesus radically condemned for apostasy, thereby risking his own life.

40. Some interpreters go too far in translating *pos ton apolesosin*, meaning "destroy," as "to kill." The term is likely a derivative of the Hebrew word, *abaddon*, meaning "the destroyer." The term does denote that this group of Pharisees, which were politically sympathetic to the Herodians, clearly understood that Jesus and his band of followers would be silenced or scattered, or that they wanted Jesus crucified.

## The Risk Context of the Controversy Dialogues

Jerusalem creates perilous risk, both for Jesus and for the elite. His opponents attempt to lure him into publicly opposing Roman taxation (a capital offense), erring on the nature of the resurrection (a religious attack on his integrity), misquoting the *Shema* (a basis for blasphemy as an agent of Beelzebul), rejecting the Davidic messiah (since the elite would be justified by the Messiah), and announcing that the Jerusalem scribes are possessed. As a collection, these attempts at entrapment define the breadth and nature of the perilous crisis perceived by each and the countermeasures each employs to cancel the other out.

As in the previous section, each dialogue ends with a pronouncement by Jesus. The unit also includes the *Mashal* of the wicked husbandman, which punctuates the harsh criticism Jesus levels at the chief priests, scribes, and elders.[41] In these dialogues, the conflict rapidly escalates beyond accusations that Jesus is an agent of Beelzebul. The elite repeatedly and publicly confront Jesus by demanding proof of his authority. In this return to Jerusalem, Jesus invades the temple itself and drives out the profiteering moneychangers, naming them agents of Satan.[42] This is an exorcism. The elite are infuriated. Jesus claims unparalleled authority. He identifies Satan's agents as those people approved by the elite. He refuses the exchange of foreign coin for temple currency. The elite counter with the accusation that he is possessed. Jesus further intensifies the conflict. Resurrection and hope are no longer found in the temple (Mark 15:29);[43] they are found only in embracing God as king (Mark 11:22–26), which negates the privilege of the corrupt and apostate to rule. A closer examination is warranted.

---

41. The scribes in the second temple period (prior to 70 CE and the destruction of the temple) included many who were also priests or headed the temple police, so they were certainly complicit with the elite (Jeremias, *Jerusalem in the Time*, 233–43).

42. And likely also for his entry into Jerusalem, which was publicly acknowledged as the entry of a prophet, if not a messiah (Mark 11:1–11).

43. Jesus claims that the temple could be restored in three days after having driven out Satan, not physically destroyed and rebuilt. John 4:21–23 quotes Jesus as denying that the temple has relevance anymore for the worship of God. The kingdom of God was already present (Luke 17:21).

## Unit 2, Mark 11:27–33

In Mark 11:27–33, Jesus enters the temple and is confronted by the chief priests,[44] the leading scribes, and elders.[45] That is, virtually all of the key members of the Jerusalem leadership who have tracked and tried to entrap him in a seditious comment or act. This tradition may have intentionally conflated all of Jesus' opponents into one scene for polemic purposes. Nonetheless, it is certain that Jesus was confronted in the temple by authorities sent by these men.[46] Remarkably, this young Galilean exorcist and peasant is portrayed as confidently facing off against the most powerful men in Judaism—men who could crush him and men he believed were under Satan's control. Given these risks, Jesus here displays his confidence in the delivery of God, but perhaps more immediately, his confidence that he can protect himself by calling on the memory of John, the popular prophet murdered by Herod. Jesus ignores his opponents' questions on the source of his authority to exorcise demons and redirects a question at them, one that is fraught with perilous risks for both himself and for the Jerusalem elite: "Was the baptism of John from heaven or from men?" (Mark 11:30). With his question, Jesus publicly links his ministry and legitimacy to that of John and challenges imperialism and the Herodian regime. It is a radical, brilliant, and bold move—one that immediately creates political and religious risks on both sides of the conflict.

If the elite answered for John, then Jesus could demand an accounting: Why they did not embrace and support him (just as they should support Jesus)? If they answered against John, they would be endorsing Herod's brutal decision to behead him (a mere eighteen-to-twenty-four months prior to this controversy).[47] The chief priests and elders understand the risks and dangers present, surrounded as they are by the Passover crowds witnessing this confrontation. John the Baptist was widely regarded as a prophet by the common folk, even sixty years after his death.[48] John was

---

44. The plural here must implicitly include both Annas, the former high priest and father-in-law to Caiaphas, and the current high priest. According to the Gospel of John, Jesus was taken to both.

45. Here understood to be members of the Sanhedrin, both lay and religious, and perhaps also the *Nasi*, the head of the council, and the *Av Bet Din*, the head of the court that tried religious matters.

46. See the example found in John 7:45.

47. Herod was hated (Josephus, *Ant.*, 18:109–115).

48. The authenticity of the report found in Josephus, *Ant.*, 18:109 is almost universally

popularly held to be a prophet of God, and his beheading by Antipas was considered murder. Josephus confirms that Herod's motivation was fear of John's popularity, as the crowds would "do anything he said."[49] Antipas understood John's activity to be a perilous political risk to his own authority if he did not act. Antipas could have been deposed by the Romans, much like his brother, Archelaus, had been in 6 CE.[50] Indeed, Herod's position was tenuous. Only six years later, he was exiled to Gaul on the strength of his nephew Agrippa's mere accusation that he was an enemy of the new Roman Emperor, Caligula. The Romans, particularly Pontius Pilate, would have responded violently if Herod had not arrested and imprisoned John.[51] Thus, for the chief priests, scribes, and elders to publicly reject John would most certainly have resulted in riots.

It is clear that Jesus had anticipated the question and considered it pedestrian. As we have discussed, he had already responded to the Beelzebul controversy while cleansing the synagogues of Galilee and Palestine. Whether these men believed that their status would intimidate and silence a simple country exorcist, or whether they decided to put the question to him bluntly in order to publicly entrap him as they had John, the result was disastrous. Jesus turns the question of authority back on them: Are *they* legitimate? He holds up John as the standard by which to measure that legitimacy. They look foolish, unprepared, even simple-minded. Having been cornered by someone they had considered to be an uneducated country bumpkin, a magician who consorted with the dregs of society, and a charlatan who took meals and support from outcasts and even women, they could only remain silent. Jesus' question created real, perilous risk for the elite. They were now facing the risk of popular judgment as to their complicity with Antipas. By reversing the question of authority and invoking the question of John's baptism (i.e., legitimacy), Jesus willfully and radically escalated the conflict to deadly levels. Powerless to act against Jesus, his opponents attempt to quietly withdraw. Jesus is now an undisputedly perilous risk to the elite. But he is not done with them.

---

accepted as authentic by scholars.

49. Ibid., 18.5.2.

50. According to Josephus, the brutality of Archelaus is legendary (ibid., 17:6).

51. Josephus reports that Pontius Pilatus was the Roman procurator for ten years—no insignificant amount of time in one of the most volatile and rebellious Roman provinces in the known world. This testifies to his ability, ruthlessness, and effectiveness in maintaining control. Josephus relates Pilate's brutal treatment of the Jews in the riot over the aqueduct he built using sacred money and the murder of the rebels (ibid., 18:60–62).

To Be Near the Fire

## Unit 2, A Mashal,[52] Mark 12:1–12

Jesus continues his assault. He tells a parable, or *Mashal*, speaking loudly enough to be heard by the growing crowd (Mark 12:1–12). This *Mashal* is drawn from the life situation in Palestine, where wealthy absentee owners of vineyards let out the land to tenant farmers in return for a share of the crop. The description of the vineyard, with its hedge,[53] winepress, and watchtower,[54] accurately reflects archaeological remains from the Roman period. Although the tenant farmers were supposed to care for the land, reap its benefits, and honor their obligations to the owner, they become so corrupted by evil that they ultimately kill the legitimate heir, thinking the owner will never come. This *Mashal* of the wicked tenants is found in all of the Synoptic Gospels as well as the Gospel of Thomas.[55] On the surface, it appears to be a country story recounted by a so-called "hick." However, once again, it is anything but. Employing thinly veiled language, the parable is a high-risk condemnation of the elite as evil murderers—those facing the wrath of God. It accuses the elite of not just rejecting God, but goes further to suggest that, like their forefathers who murdered the prophets, they were also complicit in John's death for remaining silent and allowing Herod to act. Jesus is merciless—and fearless—in this public criticism of the elite. The *Mashal* again links his ministry to John's, but also to the prophets. Jesus also expands John's role: John was more than a prophet; he was a "son of God." Jesus thereby accuses the Jerusalem elite of seeking the death of the son of the husbandman, the "cornerstone" of the emerging kingdom of God (Mark 12:10). To be clear, in the original life setting, and consistent with the perilous risk evident in the event, the "son" in the *Mashal* is not Jesus, but rather John the Baptist. This becomes evident when Jesus poses another question: "What then will the owner do?" (Mark 12:9). They should have never been party to the murder of John; thus, they must respond by

---

52. Analysis has shown that that the human response to warnings is significantly heightened when such warnings are presented in the form of "vivid, affect-laden scenarios and anecdotes," such as parables or *Mashal* (Slovic et al., "Risk as Analysis," 12).

53. The hedge was most likely a ditch, with the dirt creating a bank on which stones and thistles were placed to keep out animal and thieves.

54. Stone watchtowers were occupied by watchmen in the spring to fall, from ten to twenty feet and could incorporate a small residence below, sometimes large enough for the watchman's family. More common towers were simple stone structures on which the watchman sat under the shade of a simply covered canopy of branches or leaves. Several have been found in Palestine dating to the Roman period.

55. For example, see the sayings in *Gos. Thom.* 65–66.

agreeing with Jesus' assessment. They thereby publicly accuse themselves. Jesus' confrontation with the elite is finished.

The perilous risks evidenced for both Jesus and the elite collide in this controversy dialogue, marking it as indisputably coherent with the activity and understanding of Jesus of Nazareth. Not only are elements of the Beelzebul controversy present, the controversy also extends to a new, urgent, and dangerous level. Interestingly, this tradition is largely free from later elaboration of Christian prophets or the community of Mark.[56] From the moment Jesus spoke this *Mashal* until the night of his betrayal by the elite's paid assassin, he set in motion his own capture and death.

That this unit remained intact in the oral tradition until it was absorbed into Mark is confirmation that it provided the Palestinian community with a response to the harsh criticism from the Jewish religious elite as to the source of Jesus' authority, as well as validation that the ministry of Jesus was prophetic and complimentary with that of John's. Since Mark was composed about the time of the destruction of Jerusalem in 70 CE, the Herodians, temple elite, Sadducees, and Essenes had all been exterminated by the Romans or taken into slavery. How, then, was this tradition employed outside of Palestine? In this case, this unit may have had an alternate purpose. It may have helped gained sympathy from those Pharisees who would acknowledge that the elite had indeed received their justice at the hands of the Romans. Thus, the tradition was likely employed as an apologetic, one that the Pharisees of the Diaspora would embrace.

## Unit 2, Mark 12:13–40

The remaining controversy dialogues in this unit, Mark 12:13–40, represent an array of poignant sayings of Jesus that provide the community with powerful responses to opposition, including accusations of being enemies of Rome. And yet, virtually all of these dialogues can be shown—through an application of qualitative risk and comparison with the characteristics of the Beelzebul controversy—to have originated in the life setting of Jesus' ministry. For example, with regard to the intense eschatological aspect of Jesus' preaching concerning God's coming intervention in history,[57] the elite

56. It is possible that the "cornerstone" that was rejected was added to the context, although this does fit the context of Jesus' reply.

57. That is, the inbreaking of God in history as evidenced by Jesus' proclamation, his forgiveness of sins, and the miracles he performed, which overwhelmed all of God's enemies.

hoped that his radical elevation of the poor and outcasts, combined with Jesus' expectation of God's imminent arrival as king (i.e., that God's justice and judgment on the apostate was near), would lead Jesus to publicly reject the legitimacy of foreign rule through a repudiation of Roman taxation. If Jesus did so, he would free Jews from the obligation to pay Caesar's tribute (an act of rebellion), or proclaim a Jubilee Year.[58] With this hope in mind, Jesus' opponents craft a question to elicit his public rejection of taxation so as to accuse him of sedition. It was a maliciously clever plan, contextually coherent with the perilous risk Jesus represented to the elite's political control, particularly during the Passover, when Jerusalem was filled with enormous crowds of pilgrims. Only a public charge of sedition would justify Jesus' immediate arrest by the temple police (who reported to Caiaphas, the high priest) and a public execution under Roman law.

This question of taxation drove to the very heart of Roman occupation. This was the primary directive and military responsibility of Roman procurators in Palestine,[59] including Valerius Gratus (14–25 CE) and Pontius Pilate (25–37 CE); namely, to collect taxes and tribute to Rome while crushing any resistance, and so keep the peace. The political elite—those who supported the high priest, including the Sadducees, Jerusalem aristocracy, and Pharisees who were sympathetic with the Herodians—then launched their plot. They approached Jesus among the crowds, likely near the temple. They first patronized him, saying that he taught "accurately" the Way of God. Then they posed the question, "Is it acceptable to pay the imperial tax to Caesar?" (Mark 12:14). Jesus requests a silver *denarius* and says,[60] "Render to Caesar the things which are Caesar's and to God the

---

58. The Jubilee Year was the Jewish custom, not practiced in Jesus' lifetime, by which forgiveness of all debt and obligations was granted such that wealth was somewhat redistributed every fiftieth year. For Jesus to call for a Jubilee Year would have amounted to social upheaval unheard of in Palestine for generations.

59. Pilate was the fifth procurator appointed to Judea and is characterized as a governor. There were over a dozen types of procurators, but Pilate's role is clearly broader insofar as he demonstrates the authority of a governor.

60. Jesus asks for a denarius because it had the image of Caesar on it; the denarius was used for the Roman "poll tax," which was levied on all non-citizens of Rome, including the Jews of Palestine. It was due annually for all mature males under sixty-five and had to be paid in Roman coinage to local Jewish tax collectors appointed or licensed by the local Roman authorities. If Jesus' opponents, who intentionally handed him a denarius, could get him to reject payment of the imperial poll tax, then Jesus was a rebel—just as Judas (also known as Yehuda) the Galilean had been in 6 BCE, having raised a rebellion against the Romans in response to taxation.

things that are God's" (Mark 12:17). He understands their trap and knows the kingdom is imminent; taxation is nothing compared to submission to the coming rule of God as expressed in humility, forgiveness, and love of one's brother, which overcomes evil and the possibility of satanic possession. Indeed, the practice of love and forgiveness, which is the essence of the law, frees one from the possibility of evil.[61]

Having failed in their attempt, the Jerusalem elite ended their public effort to catch Jesus out in a seditious statement. "They were amazed at him," for Jesus' answer neutralized any possible charge against him or his followers (Mark 12:17). Qualitative risks analysis confirms that this controversy dialogue rests squarely in the historical context of the collision of perilous risks for both Jesus and the elite that were engendered by Jesus' radical, eschatological proclamation of the king's arrival.

Jesus' reply was useful in the life situation of the early communities. In the Diaspora, followers of Jesus, both Jew and Gentile, were at great risk. They embraced as their Lord and Savior (the same titles that were applied to Caesar) a crucified Roman criminal who had been condemned as a traitor and rebel. But, by not rejecting taxation as suggested by the Jewish elite, the followers of Jesus could claim that he was not a rebel. Instead, he was crucified on the false accusations of the elite and aristocracy, the same rulers who raised rebellion against Rome and fostered the destruction of Jerusalem and their homeland. Thus, both Rome and Jesus were the innocent victims of the seditious Jewish aristocracy. This tradition was the penultimate evidence presented by the early Christian community as to the innocence of Jesus and the culpability of the Jewish aristocracy who were annihilated by Rome in the Jewish war. In fact, Paul repeats this very argument in his letter to the Roman *ecclesia* (Rom 13:1–7).

Indeed, in the context of perilous risk, there could be no more important saying of Jesus for the community than this, since it offset ever-growing accusations of rebellion and sedition even as it confirmed the Christian community's public commitment to paying tribute to Rome, all based on this saying of its "Lord."[62] Of Jesus' many sayings in Mark, this specific state-

---

61. The Lord's Prayer makes this association clear; forgiveness of others justifies the plea to keep oneself from apostasy with God's help and protection.

62. It is likely that this saying was used also as an admonition to other believers who had fervent eschatological expectations of the imminent arrival of Jesus as Messiah and God as King and wanted to forgo payment of taxes or to cease working and look to communal support, as in Jerusalem. In this case, the saying was retained and used as a "church order" saying—that is, a saying used to instruct and keep the assembly from

ment served the nascent community of the Way as it expanded into Hellenistic-Roman metropolises, many of which were either garrisoned with Roman soldiers or filled with retired Roman citizens and veterans, such as the Roman provincial capital of Ephesus or the re-colonized Corinth, as well as Rome itself. When word spread[63] that the followers of Jesus served as their Lord a Jew who had been crucified as a Roman criminal, that they prayed for his return as Messiah—the Jewish leader to reestablish the independence of Israel and the kingdom of God—their loyalty to the empire and to Caesar as divine protector was called into question.[64] Of course, this suspicion ultimately led to the interrogation of Christians as to their loyalty to Nero, Domitian, and later, Trajan.[65] Christian refusal to repudiate Jesus by sacrificing to the deity and genius of the emperor resulted in a legally sanctioned execution of Christians during Trajan's reign, chillingly recorded in letters of Pliny the Younger, who served as the *legatus Augusti*, or Roman imperial governor, of Bithynia and Pontus (110 CE). Until such legally sanctioned persecutions took hold, the community was armed with sayings of Jesus either to face off with Jewish opponents or to reassure local rulers and magistrates of their quiet, peaceful, and taxpaying lives.[66] Consequently, the early communities must have frequently employed this saying to confirm that they were not rebellious, that they paid their taxes, and that they were quietly living as working citizens, freemen, servants, and slaves in a community of love, mercy, forgiveness, and peace—not as a band of rebels.

---

coming under persecution or scrutiny of Roman officials.

63. Most likely by local Pharisaic Jews trying to reverse the expansion of Christianity. See the discussion below on Paul's opponents in Galatia.

64. The letters of Pliny the Younger to the Emperor Trajan regarding the arrest, condemnation, and execution of Christians based on their refusal to provide oblation, or sacrificial honoring, to the cult of the Emperor testify to this very fact (Pliny the Younger, *Ep. Tra.*, X.96–97).

65. The persecution is generally held to have taken place around 111–113 CE.

66. The saying surrounding payment of taxes also raises an important eschatological question. In Mark, Jesus is presented as the eschatological prophet of God bringing the good news, but also the impending intervention of God as king. Given this, why would the community be concerned with paying taxes and retaining this tradition? It is quite evident that the saying fits an intense eschatological situation, just as the destruction of Jerusalem and the uncertainty of the event about to unfold underscores the separation of believers of the Way from the rebels in Jerusalem, who had stopped paying taxes long before and ousted the Romans from the city. Believers were leaving the city to escape destruction but continued to pay of taxes, always waiting for the arrival of God as king.

*The Risk Context of the Controversy Dialogues*

## Unit 2, Mark 12:18–37

Also included in this unit are three other controversy dialogues, each representing an integral part of the core message, and all of which may be traced to the life situation of the ministry of Jesus. These include the question about the resurrection (Mark 12:18–27), the great commandment testing Jesus' understanding of the *Shema* (Mark 12:28–34), and the question about David's son and the Messiah (Mark 12:35–37). These controversy dialogues are prompted by questions from some Pharisees sympathetic to the Herodians or Sadducees, with the exception of Jesus' discussion of David's son. The dialogues conclude with a moving scene and comparison of human and divine love: the arrogance and corruption of the elite is contrasted against the demand for complete surrender to God as portrayed by a poor widow who engenders God's mercy.

## Mark 12:18–27

The original setting of this tradition about the resurrection (Mark 12:18–27) can only have found its origin in the ministry of Jesus—in the era before the destruction of Jerusalem and the annihilation of the temple. We know this because this question comes from the Sadducees, the religious sect associated with the temple, the priesthood and high priesthood, as well as with the religious festivals—that is, the cultural fabric of the people of Israel that brought thousands of pilgrims to Jerusalem every year to find atonement and solace with God through sacrifice and celebration at his temple. The Sadducees rejected the resurrection of the dead, and knowing that Jesus was not only expecting, but also publicly proclaiming the general resurrection soon, their desire was not only to embarrass him, but to fully discredit him. This is an ancient controversy in Judaism that predated the ministry of Jesus by centuries. As a proponent of the resurrection of the dead, Jesus' popular recognition afforded the Sadducees and the elite the opportunity to make a bold point by undermining the legitimacy of this uneducated, itinerant, Galilean, exorcist. By assuming that their interpretation of the law invalidated the possibility of a resurrection, the Sadducees employ their literalist interpretative method of exegesis to pose a question drawn from the law relating to familial responsibility for widows. Before we address their question, it is important to understand why they rejected resurrection of the dead.

The Sadducees held that God's desire was for righteousness through maintenance of ritual practice in temple worship as prescribed by the law, payment of tithe taxes to maintain the social fiber of Israel (including its priestly families and religious elite), observance of religious festivals, and, by implication, reverence for their claim to prescriptive social standing as the ruling theocratic authority over Israel. Righteousness would be rewarded with blessings and favor, but reflected one's proper reverence and service to God for the gift of life and the blessing of being his people of the law. At the time of Jesus' ministry, the aristocrats were very wealthy, occupying the upper-tier of society. To maintain their standing, they cooperated with the Romans to control the country, providing assurance that peace would be maintained and that all rebels would be silenced or surrendered to Roman authorities.[67] If the powerful and influential Sadducees and high priest could find Jesus guilty of false interpretations and rejection of the law, they could discredit and arrest him on charges of blasphemy. The implication of this dialogue is that Jesus had become influential enough to become a threat. This, then, represents the Sadducees' countermeasure to silence Jesus, and so fits the test of qualitative risk analysis.

The Sadducees raise the question of what happens to a childless widow who is taken in by her dead husband's brother, which was an expectation of the Jewish law (Deut 25:5). And what if this was to happen again and again, for a total of seven times? "Therefore, in the resurrection when they rise, whose wife will she be, for all seven had her as his wife" (Mark 12:23). The question is posed from the Sadducees' literalist point of view—there is no answer, and therefore, there is no resurrection of the dead. But Jesus rejects their assumption and corrects them:

> "You are mistaken, for you do not know the Scriptures or the power of God. For when they rise from the dead they neither marry nor are given in marriage, but are like the angels in heaven." (Mark 12:25)

The Sadducees are caught in their own literalist trap. They could not reject the existence of angels, for the activity and presence of angels were thoroughly documented in Scripture. If the risen ones were like angels, then resurrection was valid.

---

67. According to Josephus, the Zealots hated the priestly families and elite. During their partisan control of Jerusalem during the siege of Vespasian and Titus, the Zealots robbed, beat, and killed the elite, rejecting their claims of authority and rule.

*The Risk Context of the Controversy Dialogues*

Jesus turns to the real issue raised by the Sadducees: the resurrection of the dead. Understanding that the Sadducees were literalists in their interpretive exegesis of Scripture, he brushes away their question and then answers with a question that uses their own exegetical methodology: "Have you not read in the book of Moses, in the burning bush passage, how God spoke to him saying, 'I AM the God of Abraham, the God of Isaac, and the God of Jacob?'" (Mark 12:26). Jesus' question forces their literalist interpretation of Scripture to a contrary conclusion: that resurrection is valid since God is the God of these men, that God speaks about them in the present tense, that they are living, and are therefore resurrected. The Sadducees are silenced.

Given this setting and historical context, why would the community have retained this controversy dialogue? How did it fit their life setting in the first century? As we have seen, the Gospel of Mark was likely compiled shortly after Cephas' death between approximately 65 and 67 CE, during the persecution of Nero. Jerusalem was then moving towards rebellion, just as the Roman army under Vespasian was forming in Syria. The religious elite and Jewish aristocracy were still in control of the city, which of course included the Sadducees, the temple, and the priestly elite and aristocracy. Radicals within eventually took control of the city and later turned on the elite. Given this perilous context, this saying must have not only had a setting in the ministry of Jesus,[68] but also in the life situation of the Jerusalem church, whose membership included some of the most influential witnesses to the ministry and resurrection of Jesus. The saying certainly would have served this community in its controversies with the Sadducees and priestly elite before the rebellion engaged the Romans. But, since many of the traditions in Mark seem to have circulated outside of Palestine and Jerusalem, what can we conclude about the saying and its use in the Hellenistic Roman milieu? How would this saying have served these nascent communities as well?

To begin, the concept of bodily resurrection was generally considered repugnant in Hellenistic-Roman society, although there are notable

---

68. There is little doubt of this, since the Sadducees had been obliterated after the destruction of Jerusalem in 70 CE. This controversy has its historical setting in the period when Jesus was in Jerusalem (ca. 28–30 CE) during the height of power of the religious elite, particularly the Sadducees, priestly families, aristocracy, and Herodians. This is a religious debate between Jesus (who not only proclaimed the resurrection of the dead, but was also known to have brought men and children back to life) and the priestly elite who rejected this claim, and therefore both Jesus and John the Baptist.

exceptions.[69] Resurrection and control of a dead person's spirit was considered possible through magic. More commonly, resurrection was portrayed as otherworldly. In Greek literature from Plato's time forward, death was considered an event of the soul, since the concept was that the human was made up of both body and soul, and the body died. In many mystery cults, death was a transformation of the initiate into a new life united to a deity—a rebirth or awaking, but one that took place while living in the flesh.[70] In other cases, death and resurrection were a means of transportation to another world or place, not a reconstitution in this world. As such, this question as to the use of the saying outside of Palestine still seems to have been a Jewish interpretive issue, not a Hellenistic one. Consequently, it is tempting to place the setting in which this saying was most commonly repeated and used in early Christian preaching in the local synagogue. This is where believers and missionaries appealed to Jews to reject the elitism of the Sadducees and priestly aristocracy and instead embrace the perilous proximity of God's near judgment and mercy, which ensured the participation of the humble and righteous in the general resurrection of the dead. In the resurrection, those risen are "like the angels in heaven" (Mark 12:25).

This would have resonated with the Diaspora synagogue, where Jesus' would have been perceived as being correct—the resurrection of the dead was a scriptural fact that even the Sadducees and priestly aristocracy could not deny. If Jerusalem was, in fact, still standing, the saying would have been most useful in the missionary preaching and teaching in the Jewish synagogue. After the destruction of Jerusalem, the saying may have been employed in debates about the legitimacy of the resurrection of the dead with Hellenists, but it is just as likely that it lost its effectiveness in

---

69. The response of the Greeks to Paul's preaching in Acts 17:32 is generally an accurate reflection of contemporary view of resurrection by most Greeks: only Dionysius the Areopagite and a woman who was also present, Damaris (and a few others with them), wanted to hear more from Paul. However, it is clear that there were many examples of Greeks and Romans (and their gods) who were said to have been raised from the dead in bodily form (Pliny the Elder, *Nat.*, 29:1.3). However, I do not think this was the prevalent view as the first-century document, Acts of the Apostles, reflects the controversy over the Christian claim to bodily resurrection (Acts 17:32). See Celsus, *On Medicine*, 2:6.15; and Herodotus, *Hist.*, 4:94–96 for a list of those who had supposedly returned from the dead only to die again.

70. Examples can be cited from literature, from Attis to Osiris and the cults that formed around them, but the direct parallels to the development of Christianity seem strained to me. Pausanias was my first encounter with the cult practices, and although he writes after the assemblage of the Acts of the Apostles, there is no doubt that these cults likely predated Christianity (Plutarch, *Is. Os.*, pts. 1–5).

life situations facing the nascent community and had simply been retained as another example of the brilliance of the Lord's teachings during controversial times. As such, the most appropriate life setting was during the pre-temple destruction period, about the time the Gospel of Mark was compiled, thereby confirming the compositional date of Mark.

## Mark 12:28–34

The next dialogue concerns what is commonly termed "the golden rule," but is actually a conflation of the fundamental themes of Judaism; namely, the central prayer of Judaism—the *Shema*[71] given by Moses in his expansion of the first commandment—and the Great Commandment of the Law to love one's neighbor (united in Mark 12:28–34).[72] Jesus' unification of these themes into his response is an extension of the dialogue with the scribe who was listening to Jesus' response on the resurrection. The scribe, or in Hebrew, *sofer*, steps forward.[73] Jesus' answer appears to have impressed him—that is, Jesus' use of literalist scriptural interpretation, the interpretative method of the Sadducees, to silence the Sadducees on the matter of the resurrection of the dead. It is important to recall that the scribes, these *grammateis*, or students of Scripture, were considered legal experts as lawyers of God's law whose status was designated by special robes and garb.[74] Ordination came after years of study from childhood to young adulthood, followed by working under a master to develop knowledge and expertise, and was not usually achieved before age forty. Tthe ordained scribe (a *hakam*) was able to judge religious and ritual matters as well as criminal and civil matters to earn the title of Rabbi.[75] As such, some scribes, particularly from the trades, become famous as respected interpreters who provided

---

71. *Shema* is Hebrew for "hear."

72. "Do not seek revenge on your neighbor, but love your neighbor as yourself. I am the Lord" (Lev 19:18).

73. The scribe learned his trade from family, where the tradition, literacy, and expertise were handed down father to son (1 Chron 2:5). They were experts in copying Torah scrolls and writing decrees of divorce, or *sofer setam*. They were typically poorly paid, but their employment was usually associated with political rulers and sometimes with the rich. As such, their clothing may not have been of the finest cloth, but the "flowing robes" would have indicated that of these robes were long with more prominent tassels on the ends.

74. See Mark 12:38 for an accurate description of the robes worn.

75. See Jeremias, *Jerusalem in the Time*, 236.

insight and application of the law to contemporary settings. This includes Shammai, who was a carpenter, Hillel, who was a day laborer, and also Paul, who was a tentmaker. Yet, this is not the background of Jesus' interrogator.

The scribe asks Jesus to provide the first and greatest commandment in the law of Moses. Jesus cites a portion of the central prayer of Israel, "Hear oh Israel, the Lord our God, the Lord is one,"[76] saying, "And you shall love the Lord your God with all your heart, with all your soul, with your entire mind, and with all your strength, this is the first and great commandment" (Mark 12:30). Jesus' response provided the pure definition of the faith of Israel in God alone, which would have comfortably fit in with any of the Jewish religious sects contemporaneous with Jesus. But then Jesus expands his answer to the scribe's question by adding a critically important statement: "And the second *is this*,"[77] that is, on the same level and of equal importance: "You shall love your neighbor as yourself" (Mark 12:31). Jesus is the first in contemporaneous Judaism or Jewish literature to equate *these two commandments* as the summary of the law *and* as the pure expression of the love of God, his will, and his nature as merciful king. Jesus establishes that love for God is only fully expressed when one loves one's neighbor, which is also defined succinctly by Paul when he unites them into the central place of the gospel of love, the love of *Abba*.[78] This is the behavior of the children of God, the repentant of the king who recognize the overwhelming mercy they have received and now must extend it to others, thereby participating in the inbreaking kingdom of God that is to fully arrive soon.

It is in this critically important dialogue that Jesus drives to the heart of his radical and socially transformative gospel proclamation on behalf of God as king—the command to love others stands as justification and mercy for the repentant and frees the practitioner from apostasy, evil, and possession. To love God completely is to love the neighbor, and in doing so, find

---

76. This is part of the *Shema*, the most important prayer of Jewish religion (Deut 6:5), which is repeated in worship to this day.

77. Emphasis mine. Matt 22:39 adds the statement, "and the second is like it," or equal to it, and so is explicit in stating what Mark intends to imply.

78. In Gal 5:14, Paul goes further and says that loving the neighbor is by itself the summary of the whole law, and summarizes not only the law, but also the gospel of "the more excellent Way" in 1 Cor 13. Rabbi Akiba (50–135 CE) also agreed with this summary in *Sipra* 89b. Rabbi Hillel (110 BCE—10 CE) stated the same in the negative form, "That which is hateful to you, do not do to your fellow," (*b. Šabb.* 31a), adding, "That is the whole Torah; the rest is the explanation; go and learn." But Jesus links loving God completely with the love of the neighbor as an active commandment, not a legalistic entreaty, for this was the thrust of his entire gospel.

*The Risk Context of the Controversy Dialogues*

safety from Satan's control. God's authority and power for each individual within the new community of God is thus democratized, for it bypasses the authority and control of the Jerusalem elite by extending mercy to all social strata, especially outcasts—those without hope or access to God. Jesus then displaces the rigorous ritual of the *Halakhah*, the sacrificial requirements of the temple elite that drew its authority from the interpretive prowess of the scribes. He makes God's mercy and forgiveness available to all. Satan is deposed as ruler. Loving others as one has been loved makes the child of the king the fulfiller of the whole law—almost an inconceivable possibility to the hopeless, the outcasts, and the "sinners" to whom Jesus proclaimed the gospel. There is nothing the elite, who are under the influence of Satan, can do to forestall this radical proclamation. Thus, the perilous risk Jesus creates for the elite[79] by negating their authority over the people and putting their autonomy under the Romans at risk during Passover week leaves the elite with no effective public countermeasure. This ultimately leads Jesus' opponents into clandestine attempts to silence him, which succeed.[80] Consequently, qualitative risk analysis confirms that this controversy dialogue unquestionably originated in the life setting of Jesus' ministry.

## SUMMARY

Since the results of qualitative risk analysis confirm the historical reliability of the exorcism and related controversy dialogues, particularly in the conflict of countermeasures to competing perilous risks, we can rely on these traditions as a rich source for identifying and isolating other sayings of Jesus that are coherent and consistent within this context, including the

---

79. He confounds all the leading elite religious leaders of his time: the scribes, the Sadducees, the priestly elite, and the Herodians, as well as the Pharisees that supported the Herodians.

80. It is also apparent that Jesus' linkage of these two commandments *was radical in its eschatological emphasis* on the nearness of God's rule. This represented a threat to the religious elite because it (1) democratized justification in the law to a simple, yet accessible command to fulfill the entire law by loving one's neighbor according to the king's command; (2) claimed that God was only present to the individual believer (*sans* elitist control); and (3) the eschatological inbreaking of the kingdom of God had commenced through it. Consequently, Jesus brought into being a radical new interpretation of the law that forced active love into the heart of the repentant individual by trusting his nearness and mercy in following the call to repent and command to love. For Jesus, only in this way could one truly love God with all one's heart, soul, mind, and strength. Indeed, this was the only valid way to embrace God's true will and nature as the king.

*Mashal*. Before doing so, it will be helpful to recap this tradition as recorded in the sources of the Synoptic Gospels.

When assessing the gospel tradition using qualitative risk analysis, it is clear that in Jesus' demand to recognize God as king we find the origin of the deadly crisis and the perilous risk that provoked this Galilean exorcist's radical countermeasures and urgent proclamation on behalf of God; namely, the devastating apostasy and pollution of Judaism, the high priesthood, and the temple by the Jerusalem aristocracy and religious elite who embraced demonic imperialism and pagan influence. Jesus criticized contemporary Jewish practices to varying degrees, but the focus of his vehement verbal assault, criticisms, and dire warnings of impending doom and judgment were directed almost exclusively at Jerusalem's wealthy Jewish aristocracy, the high priest and priestly family, the Herodians, scribes, and Sadducees (including Caiaphas), particularly at those members of the elite who had embraced or tacitly supported Roman imperialism and foreign kingship over Israel, its priesthood, and the temple. This conflict is reflected in the controversy dialogues.

Demanding immediate repentance and supported by charismatic wonders, Jesus declared the end of demonic imperialism. The king approached and would displace the authority the old elite to end their heresy. The new elite people of God were the humble believers who had embraced his call to repent and prepare for the entry of the king and his kingdom with the general resurrection. This eschatological reversal (i.e., overturning of the social and religious order) had begun, and those who embraced Jesus' *euangelion*—the good news of joy, forgiveness, and acceptance—would be received by God as their king, and moreover, as their loving *Abba*. Theirs was a place of honor in the kingdom of God. As such, we find Jesus only incidentally criticized by the Pharisees, the common laymen and religious reformists whose membership also included priests.[81] They were ritual purists, but legal liberals in comparison to other sects, and were rigorous in the practice of the oral Torah, *Halakhah*. When Jesus did harshly criticize them, we find that his focus was primarily on those Pharisees who publicly supported the imperialists and those who conspired with the Herodians[82]

---

81. Josephus, *Life*, 1–2. See also Jeremias, *Jerusalem in the Time*, 256–58. Jeremias confirms that a large numbers of priests were Pharisees and provides a list of the more prominent adherents, including Jose ben Joezer, R. Zadoq, Josephus, and Joezer. Indeed, priests were active in the Pharisaic movement at the time of Jesus.

82. Examples include Mark 12:38–40; Luke 4:33–37; Mark 3:1–6; Luke 13:10–13; and Luke 14:1–6.

*The Risk Context of the Controversy Dialogues*

in plotting to silence him. Proof that Jesus centered his protests, condemnation, and call for radical repentance on the elite is found in his inclusive support of all other religious sects, all social strata (including the social outcasts and sinners), and even the inclusion of women into the circle of his closest followers. Moreover, he included the religious, violent rebels, the Zealots (perhaps related to the Sicarii, according to Josephus; one of Jesus' own disciples, Simon, was a Zealot). Finally, Jesus' rejection of the apocalyptic eschatology is clearly evident in his severe criticism of *bar nasha*, or the Son of Man apocalyptic tradition. He also criticizes other popular messianic expectations, including the expectation of a Davidic messiah. He does so primarily because the elite had appropriated this imagery and attempted to justify their authority by appealing to future messianic vindication.

As evidenced in the Jesus tradition through an application of qualitative risk analysis, and as confirmed by independent Jewish and Roman historians,[83] it is clearly the elite who promoted and profited from foreign kingship and imperialism by embracing corruption and bribery[84] in accepting as their patron and king the pagan emperor of Rome. Jesus identified his exorcisms as evidence of demonic possession of Israel. Hungry, poor, and disenfranchised, he called those like him to prepare for the king to vindicate them by ending apostasy. His message to join in his rejection of the elite was not only coherent, but also punctuated by proof after proof that God was acting with him to expel these enemies. He often publicly called on Jews to abandon Jerusalem's authority and instead embrace the rule of God and the impending arrival of the new kingdom. Indeed, the kingdom was already inbreaking and present, displacing the rule of the elite. Social standing and even gender restrictions were suspended by Jesus—all disenfranchised people were welcomed as the true children of God. This is why Jesus was supported financially by the women who fed and followed him,

---

83. The complicit acceptance of imperialism by the Jewish aristocracy is well documented, and this political association with the Romans and the corruption of the aristocracy is described thoroughly in Evans, "Jesus' Action in the Temple"; Horsley, "High Priests"; and ibid., *Spiral of Violence*. Evans provides what I consider to be the very best assemblage of evidence of the corruption and complicit apostasy of the Jewish aristocracy and religious elite.

84. See multiple historical sources outside the New Testament, especially: the Dead Sea Scrolls, including 4Q162 pIsa$^b$; Josephus, *J.W.*, 4.5.2 on the pollution of the temple; ibid., 2.17.6 on the evidence of oppression in the burning of the temple records; ibid., *Ant.*, 20.8.5 on assassination and murder in the temple; ibid., 9.4 on the acceptance of bribes; and ibid., 18.1.1 on cooperation with Roman imperialists. See also Jeremias, *Jerusalem in the Time*, 49; and Chilton, *Temple of Jesus*, 107–111.

which raised further controversies, and why he attracted tax collectors and outcasts. To the Jerusalem elite, who likely barely knew he existed until he came to Jerusalem at the Passover, Jesus represented a real and perilous risk, but one they were used to crushing mercilessly.

Consequently, what Jesus understood as the malignant apostasy of the elite (Luke 20:47)[85] led him to publicly confront the most powerful forces of his time, for after surrounding Jerusalem via synagogue cleansing, he would ultimately confront the elite in the defiled temple at the Passover festival in Jerusalem. Neither Rome nor the Jerusalem hegemony acted alone in this confrontation, but rather as the result of their complicity with the apostate influence of the demonic powers that possessed them (Luke 22:3).[86] In every charismatic act and confrontation, Jesus was the victor (Luke 11:20).[87] Reasserting God as king,[88] Jesus repeatedly demonstrated the overthrow and end of these demonic forces and announced the inbreaking kingdom of God. The elite and all those who "sinned against God" must urgently and humbly repent now and become like children, or face justice.[89] The

---

85. This Scripture shows that for Jesus, the corruption and greed engendered by the influence of apostasy led the religious elite to "devour" the property of widows through legal technicality, evidencing the malicious abandonment of God's rule and law. As we will soon learn, the perilous risk of apostasy was more than a human act; for Jesus, apostasy was complicit with the influence of Satan. Also, it is critical to understand that Jesus is not indicting Judaism, but rather the specific Jewish aristocracy and religious elite of Jerusalem who embraced foreign rule. These heretics were appointed or enabled by the Romans in Palestine, and this included those Pharisees sympathetic to the Romans who are identified in Matthew, Luke, and Mark as associated with the Herodians.

86. These powers influenced the actions of the apostate, even among Jesus' closest disciples. This is a tradition that was formed very early, and in that context, reflects the confrontation Jesus had with the forces of evil: "I saw Satan fall like lightning from heaven" (Luke 10:18).

87. Luke 11:20 constitutes an undisputed saying of Jesus that is accepted as authentic by even the most critical of scholars. Our application of qualitative risk analysis will expand the implication of this saying by placing it in the context of confrontation and countermeasures over the perilous risk of apostasy and imperialism to provide remarkable corroboration as to the core message of Jesus, the radical son of *Abba*.

88. In Luke 18:16, God as king is associated with the kingdom of the new children of God, which is made up of the repentant and childlike who abandon apostasy and imperialism and is available even to the elite.

89. Matthew 18:16: "But if anyone causes one of these little ones who believe in me to sin, it would be better for him to have a large millstone hung around his neck and to be drowned in the depths of the sea." This may also be the original context for Jesus' sayings in Luke 12:5 referring to God: "But I will show you whom you should fear: Fear him who, after your body has been killed, has authority to throw you into hell. Yes, I tell

poor, humble, and meek had nothing to fear.[90] The social outcasts, the sick, and the despised were welcomed into forgiveness and acceptance—literally to God's table when he arrived—if they too repented (Luke 14:12–24). Thus, Jesus radically democratized access to salvation and elevated even the fringes of society to equal status, all to the outrage and socially destabilizing fear of the Jerusalem elite, who themselves were under the influence of Satan. Repentance would not stop the intervention of God into history—it was too late.

Qualitative risk analysis also confirms that Jesus claimed an unassailable authority in his demands based on his unique access to and relationship with God. Not only was he the herald of the king, he was *the* exorcist of God, a "holy one," possessed by the Holy Spirit. As a chosen son, he was intimate with God, as his public address to him as *Abba*, or dear father, confirms. Jesus thereby displaced the authority of the elite with the kingly authority and fatherhood of God (rather than his own, as Jesus was not asserting equality with God or the Spirit, but instead the sovereignty of God as king). The high priest was rejected. As assurance of his authority and his unique relationship to God, Jesus cited the provision of his charismatic powers to disable all apostates and overthrow Satan, who was "falling like lightening" (Luke 10:18). Imperialism and apostasy were doomed, and the rule of God was emerging. Jesus stood at the center of the conflict as a representative of the king—the old age of prophetic warnings, which included the activity of the murdered prophet John the Baptist, was coming to a close just as the new age of the kingly rule of God, defined by the violence toward God's enemies who opposed it,[91] was already becoming present (Matt 11:12).

Now, set in the context of this confrontation, we can identify which of Jesus' public acts, exorcisms, sayings, and controversy dialogues are countermeasures to the perilous risk and corruption of God's temple and people under the domination and influence of Satan. Jesus' saying, "Repent, for the kingdom of heaven is at hand" (Matt 3:2, 4:17; Mark 1:15) is an urgent demand that reflects this confrontation, not a call from a street corner preacher. Individual units of gospel tradition, as well as general groups of sayings, have been successfully analyzed using qualitative risk analysis to identify

you, fear him."

90. See the antitheses of Matt 5:3–10.

91. For example, the murder of John the Baptist, Jesus' fellow baptizer and radical, by Herod Antipas, who was complicit with and subject to the authority of Rome.

the original setting and form of each saying or event. This has allowed for recovery of the core of Jesus' message and the radicalism expressed in his sayings and countermeasures prior to their further adaptation in the life setting and needs of the church during the period of oral circulation. The historical significance and life setting of these events and sayings can be elucidated and even rediscovered, providing confirmation as to the historicity and reliability of the tradition in a new light, as well as insight into what was characteristic of Jesus. Thus, a core of the Jesus tradition that is clearly from the days of his ministry can be recovered with confidence.

More specifically, in Mark we meet a young, formerly reclusive Galilean exorcist who performs a wide variety of exorcisms and cleansings.[92] In Mark he is at war with Satan, carefully encircling Jerusalem by freeing local villages and synagogues from demonic influence and possession. Jesus is usually successful in driving out evil spirits in healings; at least eleven instances are noted, all of which are directed at the powerless and helpless—that is, the countless outcasts designated as "sinners" by the religious elite and their counterparts. If we include the exorcisms (and resurrection as an exorcism of the disease of death) attributed to Jesus, the total charismatic events climb to fourteen (Mark 1:23, 1:30, 1:32, 1:40, 2:3, 3:1, 5:1, 5:22, 5:25, 7:24, 7:31, 8:22, 9:17, 10:46). There is little doubt that these events elevated Jesus of Nazareth to notoriety—a stature among Palestinian Jews that can only be described as awe mixed with fear, particularly among the common folk (Mark 1:28). For Jesus, these events confirm the nature of God, his mercy as king, and the limitlessness of his love. The healings in Mark are only effective in response to complete trust that God is the king who is imminent. Trusting in the good news of God intervening in history and responding to this good news by recommitting to God alone as king makes one a repentant child, safe from the impending justice to be delivered on the apostate and possessed, and worthy of his mercy (Mark 2:5). This is consistent with the significant use of *pistis*, or "faith," and "belief," or *pistuo* in the gospel of Mark (Mark 1:15, 2:5, 4:40, 5:34, 36, 9:23–24, 42,

---

92. Peter Kirby quotes Andrew Bernhard in explaining, "The following reconstruction of the hypothetical source employed by the author of the fourth gospel is derived from the analysis found in Robert Fortna's *The Fourth Gospel and Its Predecessor*" (Kirby, "Signs Gospel"). This reconstruction identifies twenty-four "signs," or miracles, that made up the original gospel of the "beloved disciple": Mark 1:6–7, 19–49, 2:1–11, 2:12a, 4:46b–54, 21:1–14, 6:1–14, 6:15–25, 11:1–45, 9:1–8, 5:2–9, 11:47–53, 2:14–19, 12:37–40, 12:1–8, 12:12–15, 18:1–11, 18:12–27, 18:28–19:16a, 19:16b–37, 19:38–42, 20:1–10, 20:11–18, 20:19–22, 20:30–31ab. See Funk and Hoover, *Five Gospels*, 322–29, 471–533; Fortna, *Gospel of Signs*; and ibid., *Fourth Gospel*, 19.

*The Risk Context of the Controversy Dialogues*

10:52, 11:22–23, 31, 13:21, 15:32, 16:13–17). In the last days of imperialism and apostasy, the eschatological power of faith and belief provide the way to salvation and resurrection when the king arrives. Jesus' repudiation of imperialism as demonic and insistence on its near end is thereby validated in his exorcisms. Therefore, Jesus the exorcist is historically coherent with the findings of qualitative risk analysis. His charismatic events signal the end of the opponents of God and are the affirming countermeasure to all apostate forces against the king.

Consequently, the exorcisms and public expulsion of evil spirits in synagogues are not only repugnant to the elite, but are also dangerous to their stability and control in the countryside. Ultimately, when they learn of Jesus' exorcisms and cleansing of synagogues, his criticism of imperialism, and his announcement of its overthrow under the emerging kingdom of God, the elite send agents as paid informants to track him. Under orders, they are to entrap him into making a seditious comments in front of witnesses, a capital offense (Mark 12:13). This is the social setting of many of the controversy dialogues. While the offense expressed by these agents is that Jesus' exorcisms are performed on the Sabbath (and in synagogues) in an affront to the strict application of Sabbath restrictions of the law and oral Torah, or *Shebikhtav*, the true issue is Jesus giving aid and social standing to the outcasts and announcing the end the current order. Jesus asserts that it is outcasts and now the *freed possessed* who are "first" to be accepted by the king (Matt 21:31). They sit in the place of honor at God's banquet and are destined for resurrection in the emerging kingdom of God as proof that Jerusalem's authority has been vacated. The elite have no authority to judge under the law or condemn the lower social classes and outcasts. Indeed, the elite are wicked. They have embraced satanic pagan religion and a king who rejects God as sovereign. The land is possessed. The last prophet, John, has been murdered. Jesus has abandoned being reclusive and gone to war to defeat Satan. Based on qualitative risk analysis of the setting in which Jesus performs these exorcisms, they reflect the original historical context. They are intentional acts of defiance of elitist power and authority as demonic as a means of publicly demonstrating their displacement and impotence. Thus, both the exorcisms and controversy dialogues are only fully coherent when placed in this setting of conflict between real and perilous risks.

It is unlikely that a later editor would construct confrontational exorcisms and controversy dialogues such as these, particularly using the outcasts of society to confront the authority and power of the elite, if they had not actually occurred. By performing these exorcisms and publicly defending them, Jesus of Nazareth demonstrated the overthrow of the perilous risk of apostasy while concurrently creating a perilous risk to his own life. According to Jesus, the Jerusalem elite no longer had authority to disenfranchise and prejudicially condemn lower social classes of Palestinian Jews. Indeed, the eschatological reversal of these individuals' standing—both social and religious—becomes the powerful charismatic sign as to the nature of God's kingship. Trust in God's kingship yields unmerited mercy.[93] Jesus' opponents counter by claiming that Jesus' charismatic activity must be associated with Satan, a charge that is often repeated (Mark 3:22–29). Consequently, Jesus' exorcisms represented a perilous risk. The validity of this conclusion is confirmed by the infiltration of his inner followers by an assassin, followed by his betrayal, execution, and death.

Fundamentally, we find in this risk-driven conflict between this peasant exorcist and the powerful elite a glimpse into the mythological setting that both had embraced by accusing each other of being possessed by demons. For the Jerusalem aristocracy and religious elite, Roman power and rule was the will of God, and it was their duty to honor and accept his will and defend it from rebels and opponents. For Jesus, the will of God as king was to expel apostates who were complicit with corrupt foreign practices and brutal repression—it was time for a divine rebellion. As such, qualitative risk analysis confirms that the Galilean exorcist, Jesus of Nazareth, was a radical and dangerous Jew in the eyes of the elite, and one who should be crushed.

---

93. For example, see the healing of paralytics and the forgiveness of sins in Mark 2:1–2. Here, Jesus shows mercy for the faith of the loving family and friends of a paralytic man who could not reach Jesus where he was teaching in the large private room of a home in Capernaum, so they climbed atop and took apart the roof of the room, leading to charges of blasphemy by the Jewish elite present. See also the examples of the man with the withered hand (Mark 3:1–6), the healing of the woman who was bleeding (Mark 5:25–34), the raising of Jairus' daughter (Mark 5:22–24), the healing of a deaf man (Mark 7:31–37), the healing of the blind man (Mark 8:22–26), and the healing of Bartimaeus (Mark 10:46–52).

# 8

# Jesus' Exorcisms and the Risk Context of His Mashal

JESUS' EXORCISMS WERE A blatant countermeasure to perilous risk. They represent his village-by-village struggle to reclaim a possessed land from Satan and demonic imperialism. After encircling Jerusalem, expelling demons from every village and town synagogue that would allow him access (we know he was stopped or expelled from at least three), Jesus does what John the Baptist would not do. He enters the city both he and John considered possessed, corrupted, and evil: Jerusalem. His *modus operandi* in cleansing synagogues is now all too familiar to us. Indeed, the discernable pattern we detected in previous chapters through our application of qualitative risk analysis has uncovered the following historical conflict and countermeasures behind Jesus' war on Satan.

Jesus and a small band of fellow exorcists attempt to enter a village and its synagogue on the Sabbath during services. If successful, he immediately commands all demons present to speak out or for all those afflicted by evil spirits (e.g., the infirm, physically disfigured or chronically ill) to step forward, or he brings an afflicted person into the congregational meeting on his own volition. His command is usually effective (not so in Nazareth, however). Demons announce themselves by identifying, then naming Jesus, often using the Judea-pagan title "son of a god," "son of God," or "master [of spirits]," which are titles found in contemporary sources applied to charismatics, divine men, and magicians.[1] Jesus demands the name of the demon to take control of it, then negotiates its departure, or he summarily casts it out using various means familiar to his contemporaries, whether a salve made of his saliva, ritual washing, touch or grasp, or simply a terse command to "Come out," or "Go." Usually, the religious leaders present (particularly the scribes or Pharisees affiliated with the Herodians, or those paid to track Jesus sent by the Jerusalem elite) verbally abuse or challenge Jesus. Since he speaks with demons they decide he is possessed by the chief demon, Beelzebul. Violence sometimes erupts. In one case, Jesus' opponents attempt to stone him for blasphemy. Jesus warns that to reject him is to reject the Holy Spirit at his command, given by God, or to deny that he has access to authority and power over demons by his possession of God's Spirit and power, the "finger of God."

However, what is distinctly different about Jesus' exorcisms, as opposed to contemporary charismatics and *magoi*, is that he provides an eschatological interpretation of the event. He claims his exorcism confirms the literal presence of the inbreaking kingdom of God, which by implication displaces the kingdom of Satan. Jesus demands a decision of those present to acknowledge the event as such, as well as his legitimacy and the divine source of the good news. He calls on them to reject apostasy, recommit like a child, and enter into the adoption of the king. To do so, they must accept, feed, and clothe the outcast and disenfranchised, and even share table fellowship with them, or face exclusion from the kingdom when it arrives. If rejected, Jesus warns that their judgment has been set because they side with Satan. We see this pattern in the Beelzebul controversy (Mark 11:14–23)[2] and also clearly evidenced in the cure of the man with the withered hand, (Mark 3:1–4:29), the Gerasene demoniac (Mark 5:1–6:21), the man with dropsy (Mark 14:1–35), and others. In many cases, other traditions have been inserted into this framework by Mark, but the pattern is evident and is fully coherent with qualitative risk analysis' findings surrounding the conflict of perilous risks between Jesus and the elite, or those who he considers "blind" and possessed by Satan.[3]

---

1. Our foregoing analyses and presentation of contemporary sources—including the studies of I. M. Lewis, Morton Smith, Geza Vermès, Helmut Koester, Norman Perrin, Joachim Jeremias, Bart D. Ehrman, E. P. Sanders, and many others—supports this conclusion.

2. Mark 11:14–23 constitutes the most certain confirmation of this pattern in its historical form.

3. The pattern includes exorcism, accusation, kingdom, rejection and warning,

This pattern occurs as Jesus encircles Jerusalem. It is also evident in his incursion into Jerusalem. In Mark 11:15–19, Jesus enters into the temple courtyard and "looks around," clearly to determine the location of demonic possession. His visit confirms that the temple is possessed. Demonic corruption is evident in the temple itself by the blatant profiteering of the elite. The next day, Jesus enters the temple and physically drives out the moneychangers, overturning tables and whipping those present. Licensed by the elite to extract fees from the thousands of helpless pilgrims who must exchange their money into temple silver during the Passover festival, these moneychangers are expelled by Jesus.[4] Today, we read of the tables being overturned as the only example of Jesus being physically violent, although he is brutally violent to the demons and verbally assaults his opponents. However, our use of qualitative risk analysis and analysis of contemporary charismatic actions confirms that the overturning of tables was more than an attempt to temporarily disrupt commerce. *Overturning tables and objects was a clear sign that demons have been expelled and have obeyed a command to depart*[5]. Consequently, Jesus expels the demons that possess the temple and its precincts. In other words, he expels "the den of thieves" (Mark 11:17), a term applied to demonic possession. Thus, the cleansing of the temple was akin to Jesus' cleansing of synagogues by expelling Satan and his demons. Given this understanding, we should look for other elements that make up the pattern of Jesus' exorcisms, which constituted a very public and dangerous countermeasure, since from this point, the elite sought to destroy Jesus.

In the temple event and as the last week of his life unfolds, we then see the discernable pattern of Jesus' synagogue cleansings emerge. Jesus exorcises (Mark 11:15–17). The religious leaders challenge his authority and

---

and a *Mashal* or demand, all of which are evidenced in the parable of the Man with the Withered Hand: Mark 3:1–8 (exorcism), 3:20–22 (accusation), 3:23–30 (kingdom), 3:31–35 (rejection and warning), 4:1–34 (*Mashal* or demand). Likewise in the exorcism of the Gerasene demoniac, Legion: Mark 51–13 (exorcism), 5:14–17 (rejection), 5:18–20 (kingdom and warning), 5:13 (*Mashal*); as well as the parable of the Man with Edema: Luke 14:1–6 (exorcism), 14:2–3 (accusation and rejection), 14:12–14 (kingdom), 14:5, 1–11 (*Mashal* or demand).

4. See also Ehrman, *New Testament*, 240, especially "The Temple as an Incident as an Enacted Parable," which also supports the historicity of the event and that it had specific significance for Jesus.

5. Josephus, *Ant.*, 8:45–48. Josephus describes the activity of Eleazar the exorcist, explaining that when Eleazar's exorcisms was successful, a cup or basin of water would be overturned by the fleeing demon.

then reject him (Mark 11:27–33). He counters and presents the kingdom (and indeed, warns against their rejection of it in Mark 11:32–33), describes those who have violently suffered for it (e.g., John, the afflicted, and the dispossessed), *and then offers a Mashal* with a warning and demand to accept him or be judged (Mark 12:1–12). Opponents attack him repeatedly in an attempt to silence him, and failing that, seek to capture him using informants or spies. In Jerusalem, Jesus provides more warnings and *Mashal*. Interestingly, when the elite fully reject him, Jesus makes his public prediction that the temple will be destroyed and then restored in "three days," a Semitism for the divine fullness of time, presumably meaning when the kingdom arrives.[6] It is evident as the week progresses that Jesus recognized he had failed to liberate Jerusalem, expel its demons, or return it to God's control—Jerusalem and the Temple were doomed. At the communal meal, he anticipates capture and death, recognizing Judas as a paid informant and assassin of the elite.

It is in this context that we can detect a pattern of how Jesus employs the *Mashal* in his village incursions and cleansings, thereby confronting the perilous risk of possession. They appear to have a specific placement and purpose, and it is this patterning that we must now explore.

## THE USE OF MASHAL IN THE SYNAGOGUE AND TEMPLE CLEANSINGS

In the context of Jesus' village exorcisms and confrontations with the elite, qualitative risk analysis has identified a number of sayings that can be reliably ascribed to Jesus. These include sayings during and after his exorcisms and controversy dialogues, and in one previously analyzed instance, a *Mashal*, or parable.[7] As our analysis of the pattern of Jesus' exorcisms has shown, we should expect the *Mashal* as a weapon in his attempt to drive Satan out of towns and villages. As such, we should also be able to evaluate sayings attributable to him from his incursion into Jerusalem as well. In other words, the *Mashal* are employed as part of his ritual cleansing of the synagogue and Temple. This is their original setting, although this does not preclude their use elsewhere.

---

6. Jeremias, *Parables of Jesus*, 108–109, 187 n. 65.

7. *Mashal* in Hebrew, *Mathla* in Aramaic; see the previous discussion on binding the strongman (Mark 3:23).

Based on a review of the Synoptic gospels, the *Mashal* was one of Jesus' most prolific forms of eschatological communication, typifying the crisis and judgment facing the possessed and those under Satan's influence. It is likely that most of these were originally associated with Jesus' exorcisms and charismatic events, or expansions of parables spoken in that setting. Those parables that emphasize the overthrow of Satan and epitomize the conflict of perilous risks, (e.g., the Wicked Tenants), are fair game for analysis in either the synagogue or Temple setting. It is to the *Mashal* we now turn in order to examine their coherence with the countermeasures of Jesus.

## THE PARABLES AS COUNTERMEASURES TO PERILOUS RISK AND APOSTASY

We must use a source that helps us recover the most original form the *Mashal* Jesus' employed in his conflict with opponents. Any study that acknowledges the importance of Rudolf Bultmann's *History of the Synoptic Tradition*[8] also cites the works of the German Near Eastern and New Testament scholar, Joachim Jeremias, primarily in relation to his analysis of the parables of Jesus.[9] Jeremias' role as Professor of New Testament at the University of Gottingen positioned him squarely in the center of the swirling controversy over the reliability of the Jesus tradition during the last century. Butlmann's application of *formgeschichte*, or form criticism, to the Synoptic gospels resulted in his conclusion that the sayings of the historical Jesus were inaccessible. That is, Jesus' own words were no longer recoverable.[10]

---

8. Bultmann's students included Hans Jonas, Ernst Kasemann, James M. Robinson, Gunther Bornkamm, and my own teacher and friend, Helmut Koester, all of whom made significant contributions to New Testament studies. Bultmann also engendered dozens of books in response to his scholarship, many of which were critical reactions that ranged from outright dismissal to more proper engagement with the ideas expressed in his *History of the Synoptic Tradition*. Regardless, Bultmann's scholarship has stood the test of time and continues to exert an influence through his students and their students.

9. See Jeremias, *Central Message of the New Testament*; ibid., *Eucharistic Words of Jesus*; ibid., *Prayers of Jesus*; ibid., *Rediscovering the Parables*; ibid., *Jerusalem in the Time*; ibid., *Parables of Jesus*; ibid., *Proclamation of Jesus*.

10. As Bultmann says in his introduction: "For the most part, the history of the tradition is obscure, though there is one small part which we can observe in our sources, how Marcan material is treated as it is adapted by Matthew and Luke . . . we may still discern a certain regularity in the way Matthew and Luke use Mark. In the case of Q admittedly, we are dependent upon a reconstruction from Matthew and Luke; but even

Jeremias' research on the parables of Jesus was comprehensive in providing contemporary analysis of Jewish and Semitic sources, supplemented as it was by other forms of critical research. From the plethora of reactions to Jeremias, including those by Bultmann's students,[11] he was either highly regarded or wholly rejected and criticized as being too enthusiastic in ascribing multiple synoptic sayings to the *ipsissima vox* of Jesus. Because Jeremias' work on the parables is widely considered as a watershed study, we will use it as a foundational tool to recover what is possibly the earliest form of a parable, then provide an application of qualitative risk analysis to a select group, and ultimately evaluate what they suggest about the conflict of perilous risks. However, there are some cautions to be discussed before we begin this process.

A concise presentation of Jeremias' work is found in a translation by Norman Perrin of the University of Chicago, *The Problem of the Historical Jesus*. Jeremias clearly did not agree with Rudolf Bultmann, or for that matter, with many of the ardent form critics. He tacitly rejected Bultmann's assertion that the historical Jesus was inaccessible through analysis of the sayings tradition. On the contrary, for Jeremias, a remarkable amount of reliable material was not only evident, but was significant and revealing about the ministry, mission, proclamation, and eschatology of Jesus of Nazareth in its contemporary setting, all of which could be recovered using different criteria. He agreed that the Synoptic Gospels certainly did contain the church's kerygma (that is, a refocusing on the proclamation of Jesus as the Christ), but were able to do so because sayings, stories, and parables were founded on historical material that often originated with Jesus

---

here it is possible on occasion, by comparing Matthew and Luke to recognize what laws governed the development of material from Q to Matthew and Luke. If we are able to detect any such laws, we may assume that they were operative on the traditional material even before it was given its form in Mark and Q, and in this way we can infer back to an earlier stage of the tradition than appears in our sources . . . The aim of form criticism is to determine the original form of a piece of narrative, a dominical saying or a parable. In the process we learn to distinguish secondary additions and forms, and these in turn lead to important results for the history of the tradition . . . There are analogies at hand both for the form and history of the tradition. For the former we may take especially the sayings and stories of Rabbis, but also Hellenistic stories, and for both there are the traditions of the proverbs, anecdotes, and folktales. Fairy stories are instructive in many respects and in some way folk songs are even more so, because the characteristics of primitive storytelling are more firmly preserved in their set form" (Bultmann, *History of the Synoptic Tradition*, 6).

11. Most notably, Helmut Koester. See Koester, *Jesus to the Gospels*, 14–15, particularly 81, 84–85, 276–77.

himself. Jeremias completely rejected the idea that Jesus of Nazareth was "lost to history," or that the sayings of Jesus could rarely reveal much about his original message.[12] Consequently, while Jeremias praised the benefits of *formgeschichte* and the fruitfulness of the method's rendering of the history of the tradition and its development, it was Jeremias' opinion that the Jesus of history was the basis of these traditions themselves. Thus, Jeremias was making a claim as to the historical reliability of the gospel tradition that was radically different from Bultmann's: that there was a very discernable link between Jesus' preaching and demands and the proclamation of the church, which carried on his message reliably. Our work in applying qualitative risk analysis also supports this conclusion—again, based on core historical facts accepted by virtually all scholars, including form critics.

## THE PARABLES OF JESUS—GENERAL ANALYSIS AS TO THEIR HISTORICITY

In *The Parables of Jesus*, Jeremias focuses on what he considers the most unique and distinctly creative productions of Jesus, namely, his *Mashal*, or parables. Simply stated, Jeremias confidently asserts that the essence of the proclamation of Jesus is contained in them. While this is laudable, our interest lies in perilous risk and countermeasures to negate those risks. As we have demonstrated, only in the conflict of perilous risk between two entities who attempt to cancel each other out can we find historical conflict, which in this case is Jesus' effort to rid the land of demons and the kingdom of Satan before the arrival of God. Qualitative risk analysis will help us confirm whether this assertion is valid. Is the parable coherent with the

---

12. "Authentic," at least in my reading, designates for Bultmann that a saying is reliably associated with the "historical Jesus," namely, Jesus of Nazareth during his ministry, although this is not the function of form criticism. The saying or tradition must be free of any theological enhancement betraying the needs of the community, embellishment, or redaction by early believers, either at the primary (Palestinian) or secondary (Hellenistic) level of the transmission of the tradition. For Bultmann and most form critics, the historical Jesus is considered lost. Since it is virtually impossible that any saying or tradition was not retained and then circulated by the church, thereby receiving its influence (i.e., it reflected Jesus through its own eyes), or that it reflected Jesus' Jewish setting, Bultmann finds it virtually impossible that any saying can be ascribed to the historical Jesus, but only to the transmission history of the church as it passed from its Palestinian to Hellenistic setting (or arose in the Hellenistic setting, thereby making it impossible to have originated with Jesus). See Marshall, *New Testament Interpretation*, 153–64, for an articulation of objections to Bultmann's radical conclusions on the "laws of transmission."

conflict and countermeasures employed by Jesus in his confrontation with the Jerusalem elite?

Jeremias' own conclusion as to historicity of parables is based on his analysis of oral forms, Aramaisms or Semitisms, and comparison with contemporary literature and stories Jesus used but then radically altered to shock and challenge his audience's expectations. He convincingly demonstrates that the parables betray an oral origin in that they embody the narrative traits of orality, including mnemonic influences that are characteristic of spoken interchange. Indeed, C. H. Dodd, one of Jeremias' major contemporaries, also confirms this conclusion in his *Parables of the Kingdom* and *Apostolic Preaching and Its Developments*.[13] Form criticism's treatment of the parables as strictly literary forms to be arbitrarily divided into categories of similes, comparisons, allegories, fables, etc., was completely artificial, and therefore, not especially productive. The reason this was required was quite obvious to Jeremias. In first-century Palestinian Judaism, the *Mashal* incorporated *all* of these oral forms of teaching, even the riddle.

Jeremias begins with contextual analysis of the various historical influences that came to bear on these Palestinian *Mathla* in the contemporary Jewish milieu of the Palestinian church, then determines the impact that transmission must have had on these *Mathla* in the Roman-Hellenistic milieu that made up the communities outside of Palestine. Jeremias believed he could recover the original message of the parable within the contemporary life setting of Jesus.[14] To achieve this reconstruction, scholars must retrace the steps back from the church to the traditions and their original setting in the activity of Jesus. The critical and significant insights gained from *formgeschichte* revealed the history of transmission of the oral forms as they were adapted to the needs and challenges of the church. Jeremias' analysis applied the same presumption as to the influence of the church and its life setting, but once past this influence, a reliable link to the message of

---

13. Dodd was immensely influential in pressing the idea of "realized eschatology," or that the kingdom was both present and future, particularly as revealed in the parables of Jesus. As such, the proclamation of Jesus and the faith of early Christians were purely historical, as was the inbreaking and presence of the kingdom of God in history as the believer by faith encounters it. The parable reliably conveyed this core message of Jesus: "[The parables] use all the resources of dramatic illustration to help men see that in the events before their eyes . . . God is confronting them in His kingdom, power, and glory. This world has become the scene of a divine drama, in which the eternal issues are laid bare. It is the hour of decision. It is realized eschatology" (Dodd, *Parables of the Kingdom*, 159).

14. Given the results of qualitative risk analysis, such conclusions can be tested.

the historical Jesus could be found, and more importantly, the very content of this message before the crucifixion and resurrection experience could be recovered. Thus, the parables are unique literary forms in the gospel tradition and represent a reliable opportunity to reach the words and world of perilous risk and crisis of Jesus of Nazareth.

The various influences on the parabolic tradition can be delineated as a whole, from the translation of the parables from Aramaic (the native language of Jesus), to Greek (*koine*, or common Greek), to the discernable additions or changes Jeremias associates with the church, including the community influence that must have been prevalent as oral traditions were circulated and retained. Examples include the embellishment[15] of elements within the parables that would have enhanced their impact to various audiences,[16] particularly in the Hellenistic-Roman world; in crises that threatened the community's identity or existence, especially those arising from the delay of the return of Jesus;[17] and in challenges faced by itinerant missionaries, who were clearly facing dynamic situations particularly outside of Palestine. Many of the parables were transformed into allegories, which provided interpretations that can only be associated with later issues no longer connected with Jesus' historical situation. As such, they became polemics for the church against opponents or those who abandoned the community.[18] Some parables became material for preaching or paraenesis,[19] while others were blended, adapted, or conflated into consolidated stories.[20] At times, parables even had sayings appended to their endings, which completely altered[21] what seemed to be their original meaning.[22] Expanded analysis to non-canonical materials, including materials found in the *Gospel of Thomas*, rabbinical teachings, and Palestinian popular stories and anecdotes, elucidate the use of parables in contemporary settings. In addition, comparison with Aramaic and Semitic sources, folktales, traits of oral

---

15. Jeremias, *Parables of Jesus*, 27–20; Matt 25:15 on the talents given (up to twenty years'-worth of a day laborer's wage).

16. Jeremias, *Parables of Jesus*, 33–42; Matt 20:1–16 on the laborers in the vineyard.

17. Jeremias, *Parables of Jesus*, 48–66; Luke 12:29 on the thief in the night; Matt 25:1–13 on the ten virgins.

18. Jeremias, *Parables of Jesus*, 66–90; Mark 12:1–11 on the wicked husbandman.

19. Jeremias, *Parables of Jesus*, 42–48; Matt 5:25 on going before the judge.

20. Jeremias, *Parables of Jesus*, 90–96; Mark 4:21–25 on the lamp and measure.

21. Jeremias, *Parables of Jesus*, 108; Mark 12:1–9 on the wicked husbandman.

22. What Jeremias describes as the "setting" (Jeremias, *Parables of Jesus*, 97–114).

transmission, and more subtle insights into nuances of ancient "oriental" story telling (such as the emphasis on exaggeration, embellishment, and traditional story structures, including how story and anecdotal content and endings were anticipated) provide subtle insights as well. The results are sometimes stunning. Jesus may have turned contemporary tales on their heads to *shock his audience*, perhaps a common trait of his.

Combining these resources provides the "laws of transmission,"[23] which, if applied as a consistent methodology, often recovered the original form of the parable and the situation in life that gave rise to its creation or use by Jesus of Nazareth:

(1) Translating the parables from Aramaic to Greek often changed their meaning.

(2) Sometimes, elements of the original parable (such as a description of Palestinian buildings or structures) were translated into terminology or technical explanations more familiar to the Roman world to make better sense of them for a new audience.

(3) There was a tendency to embellish the parables (a phenomenon Jeremias calls "the oriental storyteller's delight"[24] in exaggeration of elements such as numbers or size).

(4) Parables that include popular folktale themes or passages of Jewish Scripture tend to influence the material. Instead of supplementing the parable, over time they become the dominant influence and so are secondary additions evident as the parable was transmitted.

(5) Parables addressed to the church were originally directed by Jesus toward his opponents and their failure to respond to him.

(6) This change in audience led to a shift away from Jesus' intense eschatological emphasis on the arrival of God in history[25] towards instructions on community rule, i.e. how the community was to behave and how practices were to be conducted in the last days.[26]

---

23. Ibid., 113–14.

24. Ibid. 28.

25. That is, the original eschatological emphasis of Jesus, a fact also confirmed by qualitative risk analysis.

26. What Jeremias calls "hortatory" parables, which exhort specific conduct as a member of the community of God according to a community rule (ibid., 42–48).

(7) As time passed, it is evident that parables were also affected by the church's specific needs in addressing its particular concerns.[27]

(8) Sometimes, adjustment to meet the needs of the church was accomplished by allegorical interpretation of the parables, which were clearly secondary additions.[28]

(9) Eventually, collections of parables were made by the church, and when this collection took place, some parables were invariably fused together or two separate parables were linked together, thereby forcing a change in interpretations and loss of the original situation in life.

(10) Form criticism's conclusions as to the secondary construction of the gospel framework are accurate, as evidenced by how parables are "dropped into" this framework, just as Eusebius had noted about Mark's random order. This finding, combined with the needs of the early church, allowed many of the parables to be inserted into a secondary narrative framework that afforded a shift to hortatory interpretations as opposed to the original eschatological setting of imminent crises and decision: the arrival of the kingdom of God.

The original setting (most likely after his exorcisms) had long been forgotten during the oral transmission of the parables. Yet, the parables exerted a powerful influence on the early church as their original, dynamic, confronting nature, which was guided by the community prophets and the Spirit and sayings of the risen Lord, was applied to challenges, threats (and as we shall see, perilous risks), and community organizational structural responses to new rules.[29] The original audience, usually Jesus' opponents

---

27. As noted above, Jeremias cites the delay of the return of Christ, the rejection of its missionaries and harsh opposition, and instructions to leaders as informing the church's needs. Here, parables such as Jesus' condemnation of his opponents' treatment of the innocent, poor, and disadvantaged are applied to directives for church leaders. They are to serve and protect the weak ones of the congregation.

28. Here, Jesus' original references to a king, landlord, or merchant were allegorically applied to Christ—or, where obscure, parables were supplied with interpretations using allegory.

29. The generations that passed, along with Paul, Cephas, and the other early witnesses, left behind the residual communities that they gathered in private homes and buildings. Eventually these communities encountered new oral traditions of Jesus, passed on by travelers and wandering missionaries. These missionaries were certainly armed with many parables (evidenced by their ability to use them to explain the harsh opposition, hardships, and rejection they experienced, which Jeremias uncovered by application of his laws—especially the change in audience). Thus, the missionaries ushered in a

and the elite, became instead the examples of errant behavior and poor comprehension. This shifted the emphasis of the parables to instructive guidance for the leaders of the church, away from unacceptable practices and toward the proper treatment of the poor, innocent, outcasts, and also apostasy. The parables provided a rich source for the development of community identity while it waited for the Parousia. It is this stage of oral transmission that became crystallized in the Synoptic Gospels.[30] Jeremias found that common themes became discernable as the original forms of the parables were recovered through application of the laws. These could be grouped together, thereby identifying the core themes of Jesus' urgent and eschatological proclamation.

We can now turn to several of these common themes detected by Jeremias' effort. In presenting these, we can then analyze findings and test their veracity by applying qualitative risk analysis to identify where the recovered themes match the countermeasures Jesus' employed to meet the perilous risk of apostasy and imperialism in his urgent eschatological proclamation to repent given God's arrival as king. Again, while the original setting we can recover was likely post-exorcism, it is certainly possible that after he cleansed the temple precincts of demons several parables were spoken over the next three-to-five days before he was executed.

## SATAN IS BEING OVERTHROWN

The first theme emerges from similes, or comparisons, which still fall under the form of *Mashal*. These similes concern Jesus' urgent eschatological call to recognize and accept that today is the "day of salvation" and repent from evil.[31] In perhaps one of his most beautiful and moving sayings, Jesus responds to the disciples of the imprisoned John the Baptist. They send messengers in desperation to ask Jesus if he is the "one to come," that is, not necessarily the Messiah, but the last herald of God who announces

---

wealth of new traditions from Jesus, including the parables, that were eagerly absorbed by these communities into their own spiritual and social fabric, providing new insights and helping to explain their situation, perhaps through allegorical interpretation, but still understood as inspired. They filled the vacuum created by the passing of the first and second generations.

30. As noted, this concern was already evident in the earliest of the New Testament writings, including the letter of Paul to the believers in Thessalonica, written perhaps twenty years before the compilation of the Gospel of Mark (1 Thess 4:13–18).

31. Jeremias, *Parables of Jesus*, 115–24.

## Jesus' Exorcisms and the Risk Context of His Mashal

and inaugurates the kingdom's arrival. The historicity of this encounter has been confirmed by qualitative risk analysis.[32] Jesus replies by quoting Isaiah: "Then will the eyes of the blind be opened and the ears of the deaf unstopped. Then will the lame leap like a deer, and the mute tongue shout for joy" (Isa 35:5–6). Isaiah, as one of the most revered Hebrew prophets who lived hundreds of years before Jesus, was known for prophesying about the return of God[33] and the unparalleled joy that would be experienced at his arrival—everything would be overturned and evil would be ended. Jesus tells his witnesses to report what they are seeing, namely his charismatic events, exorcisms, and the expulsion of evil spirits. But, as Jeremias notes, the point is not to stress that exorcisms are occurring, but that they are signs of the overthrowing of Satan and the imminent arrival of the king—precisely what Jesus said at his synagogue cleansings. This also correlates with the form criticism and related criterion's conclusions regarding the historicity of Jesus' saying regarding casting out demons by the

---

32. In the Gospel of Mark, John the Baptist never points at Jesus and says, "there he is, the messiah," such as in the Gospels of Matthew and John ("I have no need to baptize you" [Matt 3:11–12], and "behold the lamb of God" [John 1:29], respectively). Instead John says that "someone" is coming after him who is greater (Mark 1:7), and immediately afterward, Jesus arrives, is baptized, and the Spirit descends on him, signifying his special relationship with God. Clearly, the Gospel of Mark is linking the words of John with the arrival and baptism of Jesus. Later gospel writers obviously expanded this tradition. The point is that the statement of Jesus in response to the question of John is historically plausible because it does not presuppose John's identification of Jesus as the Messiah. Most significantly, this means that the question posed by John is historically reliable—namely, that John baptized Jesus and likely acknowledged him as a "lamb of God," but obviously still questioned whether Jesus was the messenger of God as the son of *Abba*, as he claimed. Jesus' answer is also historically reliable, since it *pointed to God's action in history, not his own*, as evidenced by the joyous charismatic events effected for the hopeless, dispossessed, and abandoned. God's mercy was presented in events that were indescribably gracious and loving. Jesus pointed to the work of God, and as such, *he made no titular claim for himself*. Instead, he described his love for *Abba* and the good news he had been given to proclaim to all, having received the sole and exclusive understanding of *Abba*'s will and nature. Jesus was the radical child of *Abba*, moving forward in complete faith and trust, relentless in his proclamation, his charismatic activity, and his mission to the outcasts, for it was their forgiveness and their welcome as the children of *Abba* in the kingdom that most clearly demonstrated the depth of God's love and mercy, as well as his rejection of the religious elite. Jesus, as the radical son of *Abba*, had complete trust and faith in the good news and the wondrous events unfolding as tangible signs of the long-promised entry of God and his justice into history. Truly, the day of salvation was emerging.

33. This was interpreted by some of the Jewish sects noted above as heralding the messianic age.

finger of God, as well as the findings of qualitative risk analysis regarding the charismatic events that resulted from countermeasures to the perilous risk of apostasy—the overturning of evil powers, which demands humility and repentance (Luke 11:20). Consequently, the point of this saying is not that exorcisms and healings are occurring, but instead, that they confirm the end of satanic rule and, by implication, substantiate the arrival of the kingdom of God.

Jeremias pushes the implications of the parable beyond those made available to us by qualitative risk analysis. For Jeremias, Jesus also expresses the overwhelming joy of the arrival of God's rule when he answers John's disciples—the lepers are healed and even the dead rise. This goes well beyond the promise of the revered prophet, Isaiah. As Jeremias describes, *Jesus is unequivocally stating that the long-promised day of salvation has now arrived,* "the hour is come," but more importantly, *that it exceeds all expectations.* The overturning of the powers of evil has begun; the rule of Satan is ending. This overturning of demonic forces includes all the apostate and unrepentant, particularly—as we have seen through the application of qualitative risk analysis—the Jerusalem aristocracy and religious elite, due to their complicit acceptance of a foreign king and their refusal to repent and accept the *euangelion*. For those who heed Jesus, the day of salvation is more wonderful than anyone could have imagined. It is more powerful than deeds and words can describe, for the miracles are only signs of the goodness and graciousness of God. As such Jesus' quotation of Isaiah in his reply to John's disciples about the miraculous appearance of the kingdom is historically coherent with other sayings that can be traced back to Jesus using critical analysis, and now by qualitative risk analysis. Can we accept these findings? The extension is in many ways coherent with our results.

The characterization of the "day of salvation,"[34] or deliverance from Satan, as exceeding all expectations is the cornerstone of Jesus' good news to the possessed and disenfranchised—those who have been oppressed by imperial occupation and the corrupted Jerusalem elite under the influence of Satan and his demons. The similes that echo this wonderful announcement of their renewal, such as a "wedding feast" (Matt 22:1–14), the most joyous of celebrations in Judaism; "the harvest" (Luke 10:2), the time of reaping the bounty of the work; and "the light on the lamp stand" (Mark 4:21), or the security and peace of a home free from darkness and danger. Far from being the "days of terror" for them, it is the day of joy, the day of

---

34. Jeremias, *Parables of Jesus*, 115–24.

promise, when all hopes are fulfilled, and all signs and wonders of God have already exceeded every expectation. Jesus calls to them in this context: "You are the salt of the earth; you are the light of the world," he proclaims (Matt 5:13). These sayings could find a setting in the synagogue cleansings of Jesus.

The impact of Jesus' sayings is easily lost. To imagine what this message meant to his audience in their oppressed life setting and how they considered themselves and their standing before God—the poor, the sick, the lame and crippled, the mute and blind, the pariahs of Jewish society who were considered unclean for practicing livelihoods thought to separate them from God's favor,[35] and all those denied the privilege of heritage and forced to live on the fringe of society as outcasts—excites pity, for all of these people had believed themselves forever hopeless and condemned before God. Jesus' unparalleled claim of God's acceptance of these men and women, together with his democratization of hope and righteousness through faith and trust in God's mercy, was shocking—and destabilizing. For the aristocracy and the elite, Jesus' proclamation of new reconciliation and acceptance was not only abhorrent and disgusting, it was dangerous, a threat to social stability and peace, and thus, to their safety and standing with their patrons,[36] the Romans, just as John's popular ministry had been a threat. It fostered an intense fear and hatred of Jesus, along with any Jew who raised the threat of rebellion or social unrest as an outspoken critic.[37]

---

35. See ibid., 303–12, especially the table on 304.

36. Patterson, *God of Jesus*, 62–64.

37. These include Athronges (4 BCE) (Josephus, *Ant.*, 17); Judas the Galilean (6 BCE), whose rebellion against new taxation brought about the death of thousands of Jews by the Romans (ibid., 20:5.2); and the grandsons of Judas; and Theudas (40–46 CE), to name just the well-known movements. John the Baptist and Jesus of Nazareth should be added to the list of those radicals crushed by the elite, John by Herod and Jesus by Pontius Pilate. Josephus reports that Herod feared John, primarily because he believed John's followers would do as he "commanded," which could include violent rebellion. While rebellion was seditious and worthy of death, Josephus is clear that John had nothing to do with tendencies toward violent rebellion—his motives were prophetic and religious. Nonetheless, Herod was not just concerned that the people would follow John for religious purposes; he was concerned about social destabilization, since John was calling for social transformation that bypassed the elite's hierarchical control over the class structure. John's call for piety and righteousness was dangerous. Consequently, Herod's coldly brutal murder of John was centered on the political turmoil John and his followers might cause. It is startling that Herod presumed that murdering John would end his influence, but this assumption was based on other religious and messianic movements that had disbanded when the leader was captured or killed by the Romans.

Jesus, as this history ultimately proves, was considered a perilous risk that needed to be eliminated.

This group of *Mashal* represented the powerful countermeasure to the apostasy of the elite under the influence and possession of Satan and imperialism by foreshadowing its imminent displacement through raising the fringe classes, untouchables, and outcasts to the new status of the children of God, who would be children of the kingdom, freed from evil and harm. Jesus had won them from possession through his *Mashal*, the simple country stories of a Galilean peasant and exorcist driven by John's murder to go to war with Satan. Those who responded to Jesus' message, regardless of their standing, joined in the displacement of the kingdom of Satan and his demons.

## THE PERIL OF ESCHATOLOGICAL REVERSAL

The next group of parables is "God's mercy for sinners."[38] This group of parables contains "the good news itself"[39] for those who respond to the call to abandon apostasy, and a dire warning for the elite. Jesus announced the long-promised day of salvation (after his synagogue cleansings), and had used similes to announce its joyous arrival—joy like that experienced at a wedding feast, the greatest of all Palestinian celebrations. That day had come upon his hearers with authority and power, vacating the power of God's enemy "by the finger of God." It was inbreaking upon them now, demanding a decision to embrace the *euangelion* or choose separation and radical risk of loss.

What about the Jewish aristocracy and religious elite? Was it their day as well? No, says Jesus. They fail to embrace or even consider what this day means by observing what God is doing in his exorcisms and words and what God will do *to them* or *for them* when he soon arrives. God is; he is active and present in Jesus of Nazareth and he will be fully present soon. He will know who has repented and who has resisted the herald's call; he is king, and he will act in kind. Jesus points to the expulsion of evil spirits from the sick and the elevation of the outcasts to the highest place in the kingdom as the end of the aristocracy. It is the elite who become the outcasts, omitted from the messianic banquet of God for their apostasy (Luke 14:15–21). Jesus expresses the complete eschatological reversal. It is

---

38. Jeremias, *Parables of Jesus*, 124–46.
39. Ibid., 124.

the persecuted and forgotten who are "the salt of the earth and light of the world" (Matt 5:13–16). This is what God had expected his leaders to be, but instead they have turned their backs to him, abandoned and forgotten him, having embraced foreign rule and imperialism for their own benefit. The arrival of the day of salvation is not heralded by complex theological exegesis by scholars or provided by new rituals or sacrifices, nor does becoming pious separatists bring it about. The arrival of the day of salvation is miraculous reconciliation. Jesus' day of salvation presents radical social transformation of "elite" status, providing those who humbly trust and embrace God with the most wondrous change imaginable. Only when the elite accept this transformation will they too be accepted so that they may find themselves before God as children of the king. For the elite, it is easier to seek to silence Jesus as a blasphemer.

Despite witnessing Jesus' exorcisms, these arrogant and dismissive religious leaders and aristocracy willingly reject their displacement and charge Jesus with being an agent of evil.[40] In their minds, God could never show mercy to this rabble of sinners or invite them to sit at his table—much less send a peasant exorcist from Galilee to threaten their place and standing before God!

> The parables that have as their subject the gospel message in its narrower sense as their subject are, apparently without exception, addressed, not to the poor, but to the opponents. This is their distinctive note, their *sitz im leben* . . . They are controversial weapons against the critics and foes of the gospel who are indignant that Jesus should declare that God cares about sinners . . . but at the same time, the parables are intended to win over the opponents.[41]

---

40. Ibid., 145–46.

41. Ibid., 124. Please note that Jeremias clearly asserts that his analysis can recover the *sitz im leben*, or "situation in life," in the ministry of Jesus, which both Bultmann and Koester absolutely refute and reject. We also assert that it is possible to reach the *sitz im leben* of Jesus' ministry, but through the use of qualitative risk analysis. This is where qualitative risk analysis extends the *sitz im leben* beyond the community's life situation and back to the ministry of Jesus. Helmut Koester rejects any such attempt, arguing that *sitz im leben* "refers to the situation and function of the traditions in the life of a community . . . it goes without saying that such an understanding of the situation of the tradition in the life of a community cannot be used directly for an understanding of the historical Jesus" (Koester, "Synoptic Sayings," 55). We honor this conclusion, but go further. By applying qualitative risk analysis and incorporating other tools of scholarship and contextual history, we can look behind the community to Jesus himself.

I am not convinced that they are to "win over the opponents" in this case, since qualitative risk analysis instead would suggest they are countermeasure to the elite's authority; that is, the parables are intended to humiliate the elite publicly and point out their dire situation. Their claim to rule is a façade, for their wealth and power has ironically twisted their understanding of position and merit into a sense of entitlement under the influence of Satan. It is he who influences them to accept Rome and foreign rule over God's people and his temple as necessary to sustain their place and "keep peace."[42] This entitlement and corruption of power had brought perversion to the law, justifying legalistic blindness to social justice and the demand to love the least of God's children. Demonic influence is spreading. Jesus offers a warning of what is to come to them, but "their ears do not hear, and their eyes do not see" (Mark 18:18).

## THE PARABLE OF THE PRODIGAL, OR WAYWARD SON AND THE FORGIVING FATHER

This parable is remarkable in how it captures the essence of the good news and the crisis that has come upon the elite.[43] It is clear that this is a story drawn from Palestinian life, a familiar set of events to Jesus in Galilee. It is the account of the younger of two sons. He demands from his wealthy and landed father his portion of inheritance. As the younger son, his portion would have been about a third of his father's estate in accordance with Jewish law. The father, an oriental lord, agrees and provides the son with his portion. The son then goes off from home into the Gentile Roman world and squanders his inheritance. Soon, he works for a Gentile, and worst of all, his desperation results in feeding and caring for pigs. Such actions are unclean, sinful, and abhorrent to a Jew—a stain that is irreconcilable with his heritage and place with God. He realizes in his poverty and desperation that submitting to his father as a slave or servant would at least provide for his survival. In desperation, he walks barefooted and starving back to his father.

---

42. See John 18:14 and the words of Caiaphas, the high priest, which certainly ring true to the elitist view of Jesus and the threat he and others presented to the elite and their position with the Romans.

43. See Patterson's explanation of the critical elements that form the basis of the "new empire of God" (Patterson, *God of Jesus*, 152–58).

The parable's vindication is in the son's recognition that his horrible state has come from delusion, corrupt greed, and personal gratification and entitlement, which is far worse than anything ascribed to the outcasts. He recognizes his utter hopelessness and inability to merit even the slightest consideration. Then the *Mashal* erupts in a turn of events that shocked Jesus' audience. Even as the son is seen coming in the distance the father does none of the things the elite, the Herodian Pharisees, or Jesus' own fellow exorcists might expect. The father does not turn his back, disown his son, or let him starve. Instead, Jesus describes one of the most moving scenes in all of ancient literature. As the father sees his son coming in the distance, he is moved to pity, and with all the emotion a father can have for his own wounded and hurt child, he runs down the road to him, as Jeremias says, in a most "undignified" scene for "an aged oriental" lord.[44] Thus, the father's overwhelming joy is portrayed in the shocking scene of his running down the road to greet his son, his robes flowing in the wind. "This," Jesus implies, "is who God is, what he is like; this is the good news and overwhelming joy it brings to the repentant." The elite are condemned, but are also called to repentance. As God has been merciful to the worst of outcasts, so will he be to the elite who abandon apostasy and Satan and embrace his arrival, as evidenced in the exorcisms of Jesus.

The son is given a gold ring, the signet of family membership and status. The father then kisses his son, a sign of forgiveness before all the family and servants present. He has a robe placed over him, the sign of acceptance and honor,[45] and he is given shoes, signifying that he is not a slave, but wears the shoes of a free man. The fatted calf is killed and is eaten, the sign of glorious family celebration, table fellowship, reunion, and peace. The father in his joy acts immediately, celebrates with music, dancing, and singing as if a noble or king had arrived. For the father, something much more important has occurred; his son who was dead is now alive: "The three orders given by the father are the manifest tokens of forgiveness and reinstatement, [made] evident to all."[46]

> The parable describes with touching simplicity what God is like, his goodness, his grace, his boundless mercy, his abounding love.

---

44. Jeremias, *Parables of Jesus*, 130.
45. Ibid.
46. Ibid.

> He rejoices over the return of the lost, like the father who prepared the feast of welcome.[47]

Thus, while defending the gospel preached to the outcasts,[48] Jesus chooses this parable to tell. For the Herodian Pharisees, Jesus' acceptance and compassion for the lost, his healing and socialization with outcasts and the poor, and most offensive of all, his discharge of sins or evil during his exorcisms[49] was blasphemy, proving he was himself possessed and a dangerous charlatan. They are confronted both by his words and deeds.

Jesus also introduces the issue of resurrection at the end of the first section of the parable. The Pharisees had embraced the belief in resurrection of the dead, unlike the Sadducees. Jesus compares the joy of the father's love and forgiveness to a resurrection experience,[50] which directly and intentionally confronts those who would never have accepted this as a possibility for outcasts. This combination of the joyous proclamations of the father with a comparison to the resurrection must surely have rendered Jesus' opponents speechless. This is the vindication of the gospel, as Jesus implies: "This is what the father is like, who he is, and what he wants, but what you reject. It is as joyous as the resurrection you proclaim." Jesus was taking a great risk by invoking correlation between an outcast and the resurrection. He directly challenges his opponents' conception of who will be at the resurrection. Clearly, Jesus could have ended the parable here, but he does not. Opponents would not have been won over. Now, it was time to do more than confront and challenge; it was time to win them over to the good news.

The second half of the parable is what Jeremias calls a "double-edged" parable because there are two high points.[51] The first is the return of the son and joyous celebration of mercy and forgiveness for the repentant. The second is portrayed in the response of the older son to the return of his brother and his father's love. There is absolutely no break or hesitation in

---

47. Ibid.

48. All are reconciled: those who practiced trades considered to be unclean (such as tanners), the poor, sick, and blind, the lame and deaf (supposedly being punished for some sin they had committed), tax collectors (thought to be robbers and thieves, but even worse, sympathizers to Rome), and prostitutes.

49. For the Pharisees and scribes, only God could forgive sins (Mark 2:9; Luke 5:23; Matt 9:5).

50. "But we had to celebrate and be glad, because this brother of yours was dead and is alive again" (Luke 15:32).

51. Jeremias, *Parables of Jesus*, 130.

the parable as Jesus immediately relates the brother coming in from the field, obviously from a typical, long day of work, only to hear the music and dancing. When he learns that the celebration is for his brother who has been accepted and forgiven before all, as evidenced by his father's kiss and bestowal of honors, he is indignant and angry and refuses to even go into the courtyard of the home. As he did with the younger son, the father goes out to the older (Luke 15:28), this time to plead with him. In describing this action, Jesus is stressing an even more urgent appeal that his foes should recognize—the older son is already with the father and under his love and care. There is already a different level of intimacy not recognized by the older son. Yet now, because of this very display of love, care, and forgiveness (the greatest demonstration of the depths of this love), the elder son refuses even to enter. In this way, he decides to separate himself completely from the father intellectually, socially, emotionally, and physically.

This is the point—separation by choice from the father's love, a love that was already fully given and present, but is now rejected voluntarily and completely—for the older son rejects this special love by assuming the father's actions toward the errant son meant that their relationship was never appreciated and recognized because it was not acknowledged or rewarded. The father responds by explaining that he has his love already, and it need not be demonstrated, and it certainly is not earned: "everything I have is yours—you are always with me" (Luke 15:31). Into the mouth of the son, Jesus places the rejection of his opponents. Jesus warns them of their dire situation: "But we had to celebrate and be glad, because this brother of yours was dead and is alive again; he was lost and is found" (Luke 15:31–32). As Jeremias explains:

> Jesus does not pronounce sentence [on the elite]; he still has hope of moving them to abandon their resistance to the gospel, he still hopes that they will recognize how their self righteousness and lovelessness separate them from God, and that they might come to experience the great joy which the Good News brings.[52]

It cannot escape us that the young son leaves for the Gentile world having taken wealth by entitlement and turned his back on his father intentionally, embracing the practices of the Roman world—*he has become an apostate and is empty*, doomed to be rejected. Thus, it is reasonable to offer an alternative interpretation of the parable. It is possible that this parable

---

52. Ibid., 132.

was employed as a powerful message directed at the elite, that it is they who are both the young and old son, and so are apostates and hypocrites. As the young son arrogantly commanded receipt of his inheritance before leaving for the outside Gentile-Roman world, abandoning his father, so the elite have done to God by turning their back to him. Just as the older son is infuriated that the younger brother has been accepted, so too do they reject any countermeasure of forgiveness for the outcasts, recognizing that they have been displaced. If this interpretation is correct, then it is coherent with the eschatological reversal sayings of Jesus and the findings of qualitative risk analysis, and so would reflect a devastating double indictment of the elite by delineating their perilous risk before God. Given this, it is possible that this latter interpretation actually finds greater merit than the former in the life setting of Jesus, in which he confronted his opponents with the perilous risk of their apostasy by engaging them in the countermeasure offered by this last opportunity to hear the father's voice, both as the younger apostate son and the older brother who rejects mercy.

## THE PARABLE OF THE PHARISEES AND CUSTOMS COLLECTOR

Jesus' confrontation with the elite in his desperate attempt to turn them to the good news is also powerfully portrayed in another *Mashal*, the parable of the Pharisee and Customs Collector (Luke 18:9–14). This parable unquestionably mirrors Paul's own gospel of justification by faith.[53] It is important to pause again and recall the desperate and moving historical situation in which Jesus brought this parable to life, and why the parable shatters the social and religious conception of God's will held by the religious elite, thereby displaying their own separation and desperate situation with God. It is perhaps the most powerful indictment of their arrogance and deception, which had been engendered by their apostasy and sense of security and entitlement under the power of Satan.

Jews living on the true fringes of society—socially and religiously quarantined by the label of "sinner," treated as outcasts to be shunned by the religious aristocracy, and assumed to be suffering the punishment of poverty, illness, and uncleanliness because of God's disfavor—these men and women lived and died knowing they had been judged by those entrusted with the laws of God to be in hopeless separation from his mercy.

53. Ibid., 141.

## Jesus' Exorcisms and the Risk Context of His Mashal

There were countless common folk and marginalized Jews that turned to Jesus because he absolutely rejected these characterizations, and moreover, proclaimed that the day of mercy and reconciliation, joy, and peace had come first to these disenfranchised people, not to the elite—the eschatological reversal that overthrows all expectations had come. The exorcisms freed the possessed; if only the elite could be freed from Satan's control and return to God as king. According to Jesus, God was not distant and vengeful, arbitrarily punishing the downtrodden and sick, nor was he allowing demons to invade the land. Instead, he was *Abba*, the loving father, who rejected the possession of the land under elitist control. Jerusalem and the temple were no longer essential; the deceived and corrupted rulers of a pagan king dominated both. Simple repentance and humble trust like that of a child in this wondrous message of mercy brought God's full and overwhelming response of acceptance, forgiveness, and even salvation upon his arrival in the general resurrection. Into this world of religious oppression under the rule of the elite and imperialism, Jesus declares that the demoralized, broken, and exploited to be free, and goes even further to say they are the elite of the king. This is the ultimate eschatological reversal.

The Herodian Pharisees' rejection of Jesus has already been fully described. They accuse him of apostasy and possession. Despite the existing risk, Jesus offers a devastating parable of eschatological reversal, increasing the threat to his life. As before, his intent is to confront these opponents in the hope that they will recognize their dire situation. In this *Mashal*, he redefines what is "right standing" with God as king. Once again, he takes a scene from everyday life:

> To some who were confident of their own righteousness and looked down on everyone else, Jesus told this parable: "Two men went up to the temple to pray, one a Pharisee and the other a tax collector. The Pharisee stood by himself and prayed: 'God, I thank you that I am not like other people—robbers, evildoers, adulterers—or even like this tax collector. I fast twice a week and give a tenth of all I get.' But the tax collector stood at a distance. He would not even look up to heaven, but beat his breast and said, 'God, have mercy on me, a sinner.' I tell you that this man, rather than the other, *went home justified before God*. For, all those who exalt themselves will be humbled, and those who humble themselves will be exalted." (Luke 18:9–14)

The scene is set in the temple, where two men pray to God: one a Pharisee (signaling that this parable is directed at the Herodian supporters), the other a customs collector. Both have gone to the temple at the hour of prayer, either 9:00 a.m. or 3:00 p.m. One man, the customs collector, commonly known as a "tax collector," was reviled. As noted, the customs collectors were appointed and licensed by the elite imperialists, and were known to add exorbitant fees and tariffs to enrich themselves. Although they were widely considered thieves under the protection of imperialism, there was little anyone could do to complain about the tax collectors. *They were the ultimate outcasts.* In fact, no one in Jesus' audience would have disagreed with the customs collector's characterization as a hopeless outcast, both with the people and with God. To remedy their wrongs was virtually impossible, for customs collectors could not possibly remember all those they had victimized, and to make proper recompense they were to add a fifth to the amount stolen.[54] Jesus decides on this individual because his situation was totally hopeless.

As to the Pharisee, Jesus puts on his lips a very familiar prayer. It seems shocking at first to believe that a religious person would pray in such a self-righteous way, for it seems today that Jesus is making the Pharisee seem ridiculous: "I thank thee that I am not like other men, extortioners, unjust, adulterers, or even like this customs collector [my addition, as the translation reads 'tax collector']." But this is not the case. There are two examples that date to the first century, one from the Jewish Talmud[55] and another from the Hymns Scroll.[56] In these, we find a Pharisee praying with almost exactly the same emphasis in his address to God: "I thank thee, O Lord, my God, that has given me my lot, [those] that sit in the house of learning, not with those that sit on the street corner," and "... I run towards life, they run toward the pit of destruction."[57]

Jesus' *Mashal* also shows knowledge of the temple of Jerusalem, which was destroyed contemporaneously with the composition of the Gospel of Mark in about 70 CE. For example, both men are "going up" to the temple

---

54. Jeremias states, "In the general estimation, they stood on a level with robbers; they possessed no civic rights, and were shunned by all respectable people" (ibid.).

55. A collection of rabbinic literature and teachings compiled about 200 AD, but with materials dating much earlier, certainly to the first century, and in many cases, before. See ibid., 142.

56. The Hymns Scroll, likely composed in the first century BCE, was one of the documents now known as the Dead Sea Scrolls, which were found in a cave in 1947 by a shepherd. They originated from the Essenes at Qumran, a more extreme Jewish separatist sect that moved to the shores of the Dead Sea to form their own desert community.

57. Ibid., 138–39.

## Jesus' Exorcisms and the Risk Context of His Mashal

to pray, since the temple was on an upper hill of Jerusalem across from valleys on three sides. The Pharisees tithing, "a tenth of all I get," was far more than the minimum required.[58] This is an important point, for Jesus would have only emphasized this level of piety if his audience were indeed Pharisees and scribes. Separation from sinners, even physical separation, was practiced to avoid defilement. Finally, it must have been obvious to the Pharisee that this was a customs collector, since he names him in the prayer by observing him at a distance. He was identifiable either by his clothing or some other element of appearance, which unfortunately has been lost to history. It also could simply be that he was recognized since these men were well-known because they were to be avoided and despised. Jesus' audience would know what that unique appearance must have been, for they could visualize their own local customs collector down to his face. The Pharisees understood exactly every element of this parable, and so would have been able to place themselves in the scene. It mirrors experiences described in other Jewish literature and is coherent with the life setting in first-century Palestine at the hour of prayer in the temple of Jerusalem. As has been demonstrated, it was Jesus' practice to draw in his opponents with the *Mashal* and then confront them with a surprising twist that revealed the good news and demanded a decision, thus challenging his foes to consider the gospel and nature of God.

Jesus turns his attention to the customs collector. As noted, the collector is an outcast, a sinner, and in fact considered the worst of all sinners, both to Pharisees and the common folk in the audience. He stands "far off," indicating his recognition of being unworthy to be near those he perceives as righteous or even to be in the Temple for prayer. Nearby, the Pharisee is recognizable from a distance, likely indicating he is wearing robes with tassels or other clothing to identify him: "Everything they do is done for people to see: They make their phylacteries wide and the tassels on their garments long" (Matt 23:5). Such clothes were a sign of wealth, position, and status that stood out from the dress of the common Jew. The collector recognizes his hopeless situation, alone and in terror of his fate. That he is unable to make reparations to those he wronged is painfully understood, and so is his inability to work his way into good standing. There is nothing he can do to merit being right with God. He stands condemned and

---

58. Some of the items he would buy—Jeremias points to corn, oil, and wine—are already tithed by the seller, so no tithing was required, and in fact, not all agricultural products required a tithe.

# To Be Near the Fire

powerless. His sorrow and pain are so evident that he cannot even raise his eyes to God, which is normal in prayer. Feeling unworthy to look even to heaven, "he would not even venture to do so."[59] Then he "beats his breast," meaning his chest and heart. His separation is devastating. In the moving despair of the lost and hopeless, he pleads while looking down, completely humbled, and entreats God simply as a man: "God, be merciful to me, a sinner." The contrast between the collector and the Pharisee could not be starker. The Pharisee calls on entitlement, while the hopeless customs collector can only call on the mercy of God in abasement and humility. At this point, Jesus' audience of Herodian Pharisees and scribes would have completely accepted and agreed with the accuracy of his depiction and situation before God—except that those in the audience who had no hope may have hesitated to wonder whether their own situation was suddenly any different than that of the collector. It appeared that God's judgment had been rendered. The vindication of the Pharisee was expected.

In a shocking conclusion, Jesus says it is not the Jerusalem Pharisee, but the customs collector who "went down[60] to his house justified [*Dedikaiomenos*, meaning to obtain justice, to be acquitted, or to be justified]" and not "the other." God did not accept the prayer of the Pharisee.[61] The audience must have gasped. Jeremias states: "Our passage is the only one in the Gospels in which the verb *dikaioun* is used in a sense similar to that in the way Paul generally uses it."[62] Humility before God, or unjustified but deep-felt despair coupled with hope in his mercy, yields God's compassion and justification.

Jesus leaves this remarkable, shocking statement with his audience for their consideration without further comment. But in this statement is a claim of charismatic authority that is made available to all, even the dispossessed. Jesus is plainly stating that accepting this good news and repenting is redemptive, powerful, and provides direct access to the mercy of God. It is a charismatic event without need of the religious elite or the temple because they are corrupt. Jesus' war on Satan is made complete in this provision of grace and mercy, which grants access to the father and his kingdom to any who repent. The repentant are able to access to the hope

---

59. Ibid., 143.

60. Again, because the temple was on the hill, to go home the collector would have traveled back down to the valleys, then on to his residence.

61. Ibid., 142.

62. Ibid., 141.

of resurrection when the kingdom arrives—Satan is overcome by the charismatic power of the *euangelion*. Jesus claims the authority to make such a pronouncement in the name of God—an unparalleled claim to speak for God as father, *Abba*.

Consequently, this *Mashal* of Jesus presents the essence of the charismatic power of the kingdom's *euangelion*. As Jesus exorcises demons and vacates their authority, so too does he vacate the authority of the corrupted elite, thus displacing Satan's hold over the land. This is the essence of his charismatic assault in overthrowing Satan. This *Mashal* confirms Jesus' use of the *euangelion* as the charismatic countermeasure to the perilous risk of Satan's possession of the land and corruption of its rulers by providing democratizing access to God's redemption and resurrection, thereby displacing Satan and his rule. Accepting the *euangelion* drives out Satan. Jesus is exorcising demons, cleansing the towns and villages, and emptying Jerusalem of its power with the *euangelion* as he encircles it for conquest by God the king, and the kingdom is already infiltrated and is "in their midst." The *euangelion* overcomes Satan and death, as ""for this your brother was dead and is alive; he was lost, and is found" (Luke 15:32). God is king; it is he who is coming, and the power and authority of the elite are no more. Under the analytical framework provided by Jeremias, the student of qualitative risk analysis finds a sense of what the good news meant in its historical setting[63] as well as the stunning proclamation Jesus made as the king's representative and herald who carried charismatic power. Jesus leaves no option: all must embrace the *euangelion* as a humble child, for it is the definitive eschatological act of love. Jesus' entreaty to his enemies reveals the depth of Jesus' love for the good news.[64] It is a demand for a decision, as the inbreaking of God's kingdom had arrived (Luke 17:21).

By rejecting and seeking to silence Jesus as their countermeasure to his proclamation of eschatological reversal, the elite actually helped to elucidate the countermeasures employed by Jesus, which are found in the original life setting of each parable. Jesus had warned, "He who is near me is

---

63. As described in Jeremias, *Parables of Jesus*, 115–24, 124–46, "Now is the day of salvation" and "God's mercy for sinners" provide a full understanding of the radical proclamation of Jesus of Nazareth in his contemporary setting.

64. "People were also bringing little children [or babies] to Jesus for him to place his hands on them. When the disciples saw this, they rebuked them. But Jesus called the children to him and said, 'Let the little children come to me, and do not hinder them, for the kingdom of God belongs to such as these. Truly I tell you, anyone who will not receive the kingdom of God like a little child will never enter it'" (Luke 18:15–17).

near the fire" (*Gos. Thom.* 82).⁶⁵ Jesus acknowledged that it was dangerous to be near him, for his demand was for radical change or rejection, and with it, a call to recognize both the joy and the terror of the consequences.

## REALIZED DISCIPLESHIP: SEPARATING THE RIGHTEOUS FROM THE APOSTATE

This group of parables portrays the overwhelming joy and active response to Jesus' proclamation as "realized discipleship."⁶⁶ Unlike the church, which later interpreted these parables as a call to follow Jesus (i.e., for self-surrender and "heroic" behavior), they were originally directed at Jesus' audience, the poor and outcasts of society who were still internalizing the overwhelming joy and love that they had encountered in God's work of merciful forgiveness and the eschatological reversal of their standing. Their repentance, humility, and surrender to forgiveness and love had brought them directly to God as *Abba*, their father, and to freedom from Satan, demonic possession, and a corrupted Jerusalem. There were no longer barriers or intermediaries separating them, for they had personally entered into a new relationship with God as his own child—protected, safe, and with a sure hope beyond all expectations of God's fatherhood. It was a wondrous, joyful new worldview, the eschatological reversal had begun to make clear their standing with God. Even more joyfully, he was present and immediately near: *the kingdom of God was inbreaking now.*

Qualitative risk analysis would suggest that Jesus' countermeasure to perilous risk and satanic possession, the *euangelion*, required instruction to those who embraced it so as to continue in freedom from apostasy. These are the parables of the kingdom. As such, this group of *Mashal* confirms that Jesus recognized the need for these new children to understand how to respond in kind to the near presence of God—just as radically and fully as he—and thereby know how to live as the children of *Abba* in the last days of the age. In addressing this very real situation of the repentant, Jesus constructs some of his most controversial parables of the new Way until the king arrives. Just as the reversal has begun, so too must the new child display that reversal in remarkable, public practices of love. The clearest

---

65. Patterson suggests this saying may find its origin in a Hellenistic proverb, although it neatly fits the risk context of perilous conflict (Patterson, *Gospel of Thomas and Jesus*, 89).

66. Jeremias, *Parables of Jesus*, 198–219.

example of the intent of these parables, as well as their radical and controversial nature as countermeasures to apostasy, is found in the parable of the Good Samaritan (Luke 10:25–37).[67] The parable's sweeping call for action cannot be underestimated in its historical context, and its depiction of the depth of the apostasy and contamination that imperialism has brought to the elite is shocking, as evidenced by their rejection of the practice of the king's two fundamental tenets within his law: mercy and divine love of his people. While they have "the seat of Moses," Jesus demands that the Jerusalem leadership be ignored and rejected—they are of Satan (Matt 23:2).

To explain the acceptable response to mercy and forgiveness through examples of active love (which vacate Satan's power), Jesus again constructs a parabolic scene drawn from Palestinian life. Between Jerusalem and Jericho was a long road[68] that traversed gradually down through the dangerous, dry, and hilly wilderness to the Jordan Valley. The parable accurately recalls this geographical fact: "A certain man went down from Jerusalem to Jericho."[69] It was well known to Jesus' audience that this road was potentially very dangerous. Merchants were sometimes attacked and killed by robbers who appeared out of the rolling hills alongside the road to make off with their money and goods. Travelers were thrown off the road and often left for dead, exposed to the intense heat of the Palestinian sun. While this was a major trade route to Jerusalem and was well traveled, a lone merchant or individual would be susceptible as a victim. In the parable of the Good Samaritan, Jesus tells of a severely beaten, stripped, and dying man who is obviously a Jew and lays on one side of the road, clearly visible. His wounds indicate that he had tired to defend himself.[70] His clothes were obviously of value since he had been stripped, and so he was in the worst of all conditions, being critically exposed to the severe heat and elements, crippled by the attack, and dazed. Jesus sets the scene in this way to show that this man's death would be certain without intervention.

---

67. Patterson raises important interpretive questions on the parable of the enemy who saves (Patterson, *God of Jesus*, 148–52). This study presents another approach.

68. The descent from Jerusalem to Jericho is about seventeen miles; Jericho is 800 feet below sea level, while Jerusalem is 2500 feet above!

69. I traveled down this road from Jerusalem to Jericho myself in 1974. It is a vivid memory because of the starkness of the "wilderness" desert and the dangerous rolling hills that could easily hide violent thieves adjacent to the nearby road. Their escape would be immediate.

70. Jeremias, *Parables of Jesus*, 203.

To Be Near the Fire

Eventually, a temple priest, one of the elite, comes along, likely "going down" to his residence in Jericho. He would have come to Jerusalem for his temple service, having cleansed himself in his personal *miqvaot*, a ritual bath. This detail again reflects personal knowledge of Palestinian life, geography, and behavior—both for the originator of the parable and its audience.[71] Jesus is calling on personal knowledge to form the basis of his parable. Jericho was known to have been a hub for homes of the religious elite, likely where they would go after a week of service in the temple precincts. This priest sees the wounded, lifeless man from a distance. Since he has finished his temple service, he did not necessarily need to maintain his ritual purity. Nonetheless, thinking the man might be dead, the priest actually crosses the road to get far away from him (Lev 21:1). He does not check to make sure his assumption is correct. While Jesus might be plainly showing that the priest's continued concern over ritual purity outweighed concern for the life of another,[72] his point is *much more radical*: namely, that the priest, like the elite, had been corrupted by a sense of entitlement to the wealth, power, and safety associated with imperialism, and thus had no compassion or mercy for a fellow Jew he had the duty and opportunity to help. For the priest, the complacency brought about by his elitism justified his passage. For Jesus, the priest typified the attitude of the elite toward the common Jew. For those who had experienced the overwhelming joy of the good news and forgiveness, the priest's actions would not have been entirely unexpected, but would still have been repugnant to them.

Jesus' audience would have anticipated the next traveler to be a member of the religious elite. Jesus presents a Levite, a descendant of the tribe that provide lay assistants to the temple priests, who was likely a member of the wealthy aristocracy coming to Jerusalem from his residence in Jericho. The Levite would not have been forbidden to approach the man if he were dead, unlike the priest, unless he was going to Jerusalem to perform his religious duty in the temple. If so, he would have been concerned about maintaining his ritual purity. Like the priest, he crosses over to the other side of the road to avoid the man as soon as he sees him.

At this point, the listeners would anticipate the next traveler to be a common Jew who would rescue the hopeless man. They would assume that he, like themselves, would come and assist the man to save him, giving Jesus'

---

71. Ibid. Jeremias' brilliant analysis in this section provides a wonderful array of historical insights, as does, *Jerusalem in the Time*.

72. Ibid., 203–204.

parable an anti-clerical, anti-elitist emphasis.[73] Yet, in another one of Jesus' shocking adjustments to popular stories and assumptions, he introduces instead a Samaritan, the hated enemy of the Jews, as the one who portrays the nature and will of the king, the last person anyone would have expected to assist a Jew. As such, Jesus provides a warning to the new children of God that they also should not assume standing, but that they must exhibit mercy that crosses every boundary (i.e., mercy that is a radical countermeasure to apostasy and hatred) in order to continue to remain under the protection of the king. Jesus' choice of a Samaritan was intentional and underscored the depth of personal risk and peril that must be taken to be a child of the king to counter the apostasy and pollution of the land. The act of the Samaritan evidences the total eschatological reversal of standing with the Jew, demonstrating that even the enemy must be considered one's neighbor. This complete release of hatred and evil disables the power of Satan.

The Samaritans and Jews despised each other and came to violent confrontation during the first century. The Samaritans rejected Jerusalem as the true place of God's presence, and thus the legitimacy of the temple, the priestly aristocracy, and their interpretation of the law of Moses and rights of purity. They had withdrawn to Mount Gerazim in Samaria to worship, for they claimed that this was the sacred mountain established by Joshua after entering Canaan for conquest. They asserted their legitimacy as the descendants of the tribes of Manasseh and Ephraim prior to the conquest by the Assyrians In other words, it was they who were the true Israelites (Deut 11:29, 27:12; Josh 8:33). The Jews, including Josephus, held that the Samaritans were settlers brought by the Assyrians to Israel to mix with locals. In fact, a series of events convinced the Assyrians that a Jewish priest must be brought into the region to instruct the local settlers in the law, but the result led to the Samaritan Torah, which the Jews considered to be a distortion of the Jewish Torah.[74] At the time of Jesus' ministry, many Jews from Galilee and northern regions passed through Samaria as they headed to Jerusalem for religious festivals. Often they were mistreated and sometimes even beaten. Only twenty years before Jesus' ministry, open hostility had broken out when Samaritans had scattered the bones of the dead in the temple precincts on the eve of Passover, thereby defiling the temple and making it ritually impure.[75] Josephus clearly depicts the abso-

73. Ibid., 204.
74. Josephus, *Ant.*, 9:277–91.
75. Ibid., 18:30.

lute abhorrence the Jews held for the Samaritans, and vice versa.[76] The word "Samaritan" was synonymous with a slur, a detestable individual among the Jews of Palestine.

Given Jesus' choice of a Samaritan, no one among his listeners would have known what to expect. Yet, the word Jesus uses to describe the Samaritan when he sees the Jew is "compassion" (*esplagchnisthe*). This is the same word Jesus used in his parable of the Prodigal Son when the father first saw his son coming home on the distant road, shoeless and in tattered clothes. Even though the wounded man is a Jew, his supposed enemy, the Samaritan, comes to his aid out of compassion, which overcomes all personal prejudice, cultural animosity, and hatred. It is he—the most detested of all possible heroes—who displays right action before God, demonstrating the radical eschatological love that is a countermeasure to elitist arrogance and rejection, thereby revealing the urgent crisis upon them. Far beyond legal or ritual considerations, Jesus' audience knows that the Samaritan had every reason to avoid the Jew and wish him dead. The Samaritan found a hated enemy of his people on the brink of death, and instead of jeering and taunting him, bent down and cared from him in a stunning act of compassion. As a countermeasure to the arrogance and elitism of the Jerusalem aristocracy and temple priests, Jesus' parable lays bare that those outside of the polluted temple, those whom the elite detest, are more acceptable because they exhibit the compassion and mercy of God and are righteous. Mercy and compassion evidence the eschatological reversal, and so such people displace the elite in the last days of the age—they become God's chosen. Satan is defeated.

On a historical basis, it is important to note that this Samaritan man, who was himself traveling in dangerous Jewish territory, was taking an extreme personal risk. This underscores the perils facing those who embrace the good news. For example, it was possible that other passers-by might assume he had made the attack and robbed the Jew himself, so well-known was the hatred between the Samaritans and the Jews, despite the evidence of his actions. Even if he was seen as helping the Jew, other Jews passing by might take their revenge on him simply for being a Samaritan. Despite these risks (and Jesus is very intentional with these details), the Samaritan immediately attends to his wounds using whatever materials he has as bandages, likely to stop the man's bleeding. Since he would not have been carrying bandages, he would have had to tear up his own clothing or linens

---

76. Ibid., 20:6.

to make them, likely using his head-cloth.⁷⁷ He goes even further to clean the wounds. He uses oil to help sooth the pain and clean or "mollify" the wounds (Isa 1:6.), and wine to disinfect them, thus indicating their severity.⁷⁸ The oil would help numb the pain by keeping air and friction from it. This was the immediate and critical attention that was needed. The use of oil and wine also indicate that the Samaritan was willing to use materials of some value to help the man.⁷⁹ Given these additional details, it is clear that the Samaritan comes to represent the startling end of things as they are and that those who embrace the king must engage in countermeasures to indifference and apostasy. God's coming judgment evidences the separation that has taken place between himself and the Jerusalem leadership—they are, utterly displaced and lost, for they are without compassion. The apostate Samaritan is the example of who the children of God are. Jesus' message is shocking, and yet unassailable as a remarkable call to embrace divine radicalism and achieve realized discipleship.

Can we be sure that the parable comes from the time of Jesus and that it reflects the historical situation of first-century Palestine? Here Jeremias becomes most helpful. After helping the Jew to some form of stability, the Samaritan then lifted the man and put him on his own donkey or other burden animal. It must not be forgotten that the donkey was the preferred means of transportation. A donkey demonstrated status, since kings in Judea had used the donkey from ancient times (1 Kgs 13).⁸⁰ This may have meant that he had another animal that carried his wares or trade goods, which would indicate he was a trader or merchant. Oil and wine, certainly valuable trade goods, were not necessarily commonly carried on a short journey unless they were headed for delivery or to market.⁸¹ Still more unusually, he carries the man to an inn on the road. The innkeeper must know the Samaritan, for he is willing to take care of the man, and if doing so exceeds the expense of the two *denarii*,⁸² he believes that the Samaritan will return and pay. Two *denarii* would have covered about twenty-four days

---

77. Jeremias, *Parables of Jesus*, 204.

78. Clearly, these were not just bruises, but severe wounds that were causing blood loss and the risk of infection and death.

79. Ibid., 204–205.

80. For the use of the donkey as a burden animal, see Neh 13:15.

81. Jeremias, *Parables of Jesus*, 205.

82. According to Matt 20:2 and John 12:5, it was a day's wage for a common worker, so the payments would easily cover several days of lodging and care.

of room and board—not an insignificant amount of money. All of these features provide strong evidence that the parable's elements were set in the life situation of first-century Palestine and familiar to Jesus' audience. Thus, what is remarkable and shocking to them would not just be that it was a Samaritan who saved the helpless Jew, but also the pains he took, both physically and financially, to ensure the man's recovery, over and above what anyone might suspect him to do. The compassion he felt was overwhelming and the response he gave was beyond all measure and expectation. This is realized discipleship, and it models the response in joy and faith one feels in response to the unbounded mercy of God, *Abba*. Jesus' radical twist in the expected ending democratizes the expectation of compassion by showing that it knows no boundaries and marginalizes those who claim to be the elite of God.

As such, the parable demonstrated the charismatic power of the *euangelion*. Realized discipleship bypassed ritual, presumptive separatism, and biased interpretation of the law, but more importantly, it obliterated the apostasy of the elite and their illusion of safety and standing brought about by corrupt power and imperialism under Satan's influence. It found its pure expression in helping the hopeless, the poor, and the outcast—this was the Way of *Abba* that drives out demonic forces and corruption until the king arrives. Realized discipleship rejected the corruption of the Herodian Pharisees and scribes, as well as the status, prestige, and presumed special standing of the priestly elite and wealthy aristocracy. For those who were transformed by the humility and faith stemming from their overwhelming joy in their new standing with God as *Abba*, there was the realization of what that love meant. They were free of Satan and oppression and empowered to award this same freedom to their neighbor, which was Jesus' parable now defined as any person in need, even the enemy, and even to the point of risking everything. This was not a burden, but a joy, the same joy experienced by the true disciple of *Abba*.

## JESUS THE EXORCIST AND THE MASHAL

Through qualitative risk analysis of the Jesus *Mashal*, we have been provided remarkable insight into the radically transformative religious and social impact of the eschatological reversal and divine radicalism proclaimed by Jesus of Nazareth in its contemporary setting. We encounter the perilous risk that it created for the Jewish elite, and witness how Jesus' applied these parables as a countermeasure to the perilous risk they created: the crisis of apostasy that inaugurated the inbreaking of God as king into history. They pointed to the charismatic power and authority of the *euangelion* in disabling Satan. With his arrival as king, God would abolish apostasy, end imperialism, and alleviate the corruption of the temple. The parables were warnings, as well as a call to repentance and acceptance of the kingship of God, which were specifically addressed to Jesus' opponents. They also provided eschatological instruction on how the new children of the king were to practice their special standing during their lifetimes until his arrival. What is more, the original premise of qualitative risk analysis has been confirmed through the parables, that is, when the original life settings of the parables are uncovered, we concurrently find the collision of perilous risks and countermeasures between Jesus and the elite, thereby confirming their place in the context of his charismatic activity. Furthermore, we discover the historical characteristics and modes of Jesus' actions and parabolic sayings as revealed in the Jesus tradition through his charismatic efforts.[83]

---

83. Remarkably, when we recover Jesus' voice in its life setting we are disquieted because we are too present before him and can longer be dispassionate observers. His demand to repent, love, and receive radical discipleship even as we to reject apostasy and the complacency associated with arrogant elitism is once again thrust before us. Can we comprehend the demand to show mercy like the father, or aid and love the beaten man who is our enemy at the risk of our own lives, as ones who have embraced the kingdom of God and God's rule? As such, we collide with the charismatic *euangelion* of Jesus and are forced to decide for or against the king. Of course, we can embrace the joy of freedom brought by the good news of mercy, forgiveness, and love, but that demands radical humility, not entitlement. It demands that we be willing to "bear a cross beam" (Luke 15:27) and face total separation from God in faith if needed for the sake of the gospel—just as the social outcasts, sinners, and infirm had joyously received their release from hopelessness offered by Jesus on behalf of his father, but were required to turn that same love towards others, even the enemy, and risk all by revealing that they are the children of *Abba*. We also understand the dire warnings that come with rejection of the *euangelion* in continuing to embrace elitism, as well as the risk of not only displacement, but also rejection and judgment upon the arrival of God as king on that day. Only in the collision of the perilous risks of Jesus and the elite and the countermeasures they employ can we discover the historical Jesus, the radical child of *Abba*.

# 9

## Confirming Findings
### Perilous Risk, Jesus to Paul

"Take up your cross and follow me."

—MARK 8:34B

IN ADDITION TO OUR other findings, qualitative risk analysis also confirms that Mark 8:34b,[1] "Take up you cross and follow me," is an undisputed say-

---

1. The saying in Mark (par. Matt 16:24, Luke 9:23) is inserted amidst three significant traditions, namely the confession at Caesarea Phillipi, the prediction of the passion, and the coming of *bar nasha*, the Son of Man. One is immediately struck by the significant contextualization of the sayings—the placement is strategic. Redactional contextualizations have been readily identified (Griffiths, "Disciple's Cross," 358–64). Clearly evident in this redaction is the Markan theology and emphasis on the cross (Reedy, "Gospel Ending," 188–97; Williamson, "Mark," 154). In Mark, the crucified Jesus is the redeemer from sin, the Messiah, the focus of Christian life, and the one to whom the disciple must suffer knowing the promise of future redemption. Thus, the saying, which is itself independently radical, has been redacted in the context of the Markan material and also by each synoptic editor (Matthew and Luke). Mark's redactive program, which is consciously taken up and further manipulated by Matthew and Luke, conditions discipleship as suffering for the sake of the gospel with the cross as perspective. Behind this redaction is a saying of clear oral and mnemonic quality. The saying is chiastically arranged (Crossan, *In Fragments*, 135) and the core saying is expanded (Q/Luke 14:26–27; par. Matt 10:37–38, and by daily in Luke 9:23) into a double- and triple-stich saying, is converted (Q/Luke "negative" into Matt "positive"), and then is contracted (*Gos. Thom.* 55, cross and hate combined). These variances in the core saying support oral vitality (Crossan, *In*

ing of Jesus.² It characterizes the confrontation of perilous risks between Jesus and the Jerusalem aristocracy and religious elite, whom Jesus condemns as corrupt apostates, complicit with Rome and foreign kingship.³ Jesus not only rejects the elite, but also the power of imperialism to possess the children of God. Radical trust in God as king will bring vindication with the arrival of his kingdom at any hour. The perilous risk of apostasy and imperialism—its power to annihilate rebellious Jews by crucifixion (under a curse of the law)—has been vacated, and the general resurrection of the righteous is at hand. Indeed, the emerging kingdom is already in their midst (Luke 17:21; Mark 1:15). Jesus' eschatological and charismatic proclamation of God's inbreaking rule, including its inability to destroy followers of the king, is fully evidenced by public charismatic acts, which he attributes to the "finger of God."⁴ This alone overwhelms apostasy, or for that matter, any threat. All enemies of the king are facing eternal separation and doom. Indeed, the apostate and elite will be cast out, just as the demons have been. Even Satan is falling from heaven like lightening (Luke 10:18).

Consequently in Mark 8:34b, Jesus does not call for martyrdom,⁵ or for a "vocation" of rebellion or long-enduring suffering, but rather demands

---

*Fragments*, 39). The multiple attestations alone support a pre-literary oral utilization and function, as does the fact that the saying is antagonistic, not subtle, and betrays a setting from the life of Jesus and his radical call to discipleship in his last hours. The use of the "cross" would be shocking in its contemporary setting. Overlaying qualitative risk analysis in the foregoing sections leaves little doubt that this saying can be attributed to Jesus.

2. The saying is multiply attested in the Markan tradition, Q (55b and 101; Luke 14:26–27, par. Matt 10:37–38 appear to redact Q), and perhaps even in John 12:25. Bultmann generally finds the Lukan citations of Q material to be more original (Bultmann, *History of the Synoptic Tradition*, 160–61). As noted, the multiple attestations alone support a pre-literary oral utilization and function, as does the fact that the saying is antagonistic, unsubtle, and betrays a setting from the life of Jesus and his radical call to discipleship in the last hours.

3. As our study has confirmed, Jesus charged the Jewish aristocracy with having polluted Judaism by embracing pagan kingship and facilitating the infiltration of Hellenism into Palestine.

4. "If I by the finger of God cast out demons known that the kingdom of God has come upon you" (Luke 11:20); "the kingdom of God is among you" (Luke 17:21; par. Matt 12:28); "But I say to you truthfully, there are some of those standing here who will not taste death until they see the kingdom of God" (Luke 9:27).

5. Qualitative risk analysis has confirmed that Jesus did not expect to perish before the arrival of God as king and *Abba* (although he willingly accepted that perilous risk, and even the possibility of dying under a curse on a Roman cross—the ultimate expression of complete faith and commitment to the *euangelion*). As Jeremias notes, "With regard to the expression 'bear his cross,' we generally think of a cross-bearer as one who

a trust that dangerously rejects the Jerusalem elite as the leaders of Israel and accepts solely God as king. For the sake of proclaiming the good news, the repentant child of God, now free from the influence and possession of Satan, should fear nothing (not even capricious demons), trusting in the king's redemptive power to save as the hour of justice and judgment arrives. Jesus' call to risk crucifixion was shocking in the contemporary setting of Roman-occupied Palestine; it was politically dangerous and a perilous risk to the Jerusalem aristocracy, which owed patronage to the brutal Roman rule, because it created the real possibility of destabilizing their legitimacy, thereby threatening their displacement by their patron. Thus, Jesus' call to *divine radicalism* required a high-risk decision of immense faith and trust. Yet, the risk of faith was supported by remarkable, public confirmatory actions of the charismatic Jesus.[6] As such, there was no time to waste, since the demand for a decision was now, in that moment of hearing.[7] Jesus demands abandonment of Jerusalem's authority.

Embracing the cross as a symbol of the impotency of imperialism was not only shocking, but clearly seditious in its contemporary setting. Embracing the cross as a symbol of power and salvation after the crucifixion of Jesus, while consistent with Jesus' original assurance of vindication, was also radical, and an even more perilous risk. Paul holds up to the same startling example given by Jesus: the shocking reality of faith so unbounded as to accept even a cross and the risk of total separation from God for the sake of the good news. Even more, Paul elevates the Roman cross, calling it

---

patiently accepts whatever God sends; but there is no instance of this meaning *airein ton stauron*. The word does not even carry this meaning of readiness for martyrdom. Rather does the expression envisage a concrete situation, namely, the moment when the man who had been condemned to crucifixion, with the cross-piece (*patibalum*) laid on his shoulders, must run the gauntlet of the howling, shouting crowd, as it greets him with insults and curses. The anguish of this road lies in the realization of being an un-pitied outcast from the community, and exposed to defenseless shame and scorn. Anyone who follows me, says Jesus, must expect a life as hard as the *via dolorosa* on the way to the place of execution" (Jeremias, *Parables of Jesus*, 218–19).

6. As noted, Jesus was a charismatic, an exorcist, and healer. This was undisputed, for even in the later Jewish literature (see *b. Sanh.* 107b on Yeshua ben Pantera; *t. Ḥul.* 2:22–24), there was never a dispute that Jesus was a healer, nor was there any doubt expressed in Jacob of Kefar, who came to heal Rabbi Elazar ben Damah from a snakebite in the name of Yeshua ben Pantera. This is also confirmed by Vermès, *Jesus the Jew*, 78–79.

7. "If I by the finger of God cast out demons known that the kingdom of God has come upon you" (Luke 11:20; Matt 12:28); "the kingdom of God is among you" (Luke 17:21); "But I say to you truthfully, there are some of those standing here who will not taste death until they see the kingdom of God" (Luke 9:27).

the "wisdom of God" and the validation that faith alone does provide safety and salvation (1 Cor 1:18). God's rule is assured! The cross was a "stumbling block" to the Jews (1 Cor 1:23) and considered disgusting, abhorrent, and "folly" to the Gentiles,[8] but for Paul and Jesus, it is the ultimate example of complete and loving faith and trust in what God will do—that is, render justice and mercy in response to the humble, trusting faith of his adopted children (Gal 3:26–4:20).

For Paul, his beatings and physical abuse (2 Cor 11) for the sake of the gospel are marks that he not only belongs to Jesus,[9] but that he shares in that same radical faith in God as *Abba*, the vindicator of the just (Gal 6:17). Consequently, Paul's authentic letters confirm that he not only understood, but also acted on Jesus' call in Mark 8:34b for complete trust and commitment to the good news and to God as king. Jesus pointed to the charismatic "finger of God" active in overturning apostasy, while Paul pointed to the crucifixion and vindication of the resurrection as overwhelming the enemies of God (1 Cor 15:26), as well as proof of the near arrival of the kingdom, even during his lifetime (1 Thess 4:17). Indeed, for Paul, Jesus' death on a cross was validation that his life as the son of God was authentic, for he fully laid down his life to overcome apostasy, as he demanded may be necessary, and was raised (Gal 2:20). So then, vindication of the children of God who risked all was assured, as evidenced by the first resurrection, or the "first fruits" (1 Cor 15:20) witnessed by literally hundreds, many of whom were still living when Paul wrote 1 Corinthians (1 Cor 15:1–15). Paul describes to the Corinthians (and to his opponents) the significance of the resurrection, its historicity, and the central role it holds for the believer in confirming the glorious hope of life for those who have complete faith and trust in God.

Consequently for Paul, the cross of Jesus and the resurrection were the countermeasure to the perilous risk of deadly sin and apostasy for those of faith and trust, whether Jew or Greek, male or female, slave or free (Gal 3:28). While Paul was only indirectly contending with the imperial pollution of Judaism and the Jerusalem elite, he faced the same opposition and risk of death at their hands,[10] and clearly understood that it was those forces

---

8. 1 Cor 1:18–23 is the full text of Paul's comments. For the Gentiles who found it abhorrent and foolish, perhaps a better translation is "nonsense."

9. In other words, that he fully embraces Jesus as his Lord, even sharing in the crucifixion (Gal 2:20).

10. He could not be crucified since he was a Roman citizen, but could be beheaded. They hire informants and assassins to murder him en route to trial, similar to their

that murdered *the* Son of God (Acts 22:30—23:35). Those same forces were attempting to dismantle his *ecclesiae* and must be cursed.[11] The perilous risk of apostasy was still present in Jerusalem, threatening Paul. Paul knows this firsthand, having attempted to annihilate the followers of Jesus and the Way as a minion of the high priest (Gal 1:13; Acts 8:3). Paul participated in the brutal displacement and arrest of Jesus' followers and the murder of Stephen (Acts 6:8—8:3). As a former sympathizer with the elite, Paul's life-changing revelation of the Son is even more remarkable. Paul's choice to abandon the elite, as well as their authority and power, to put his life at risk as an itinerant missionary for a crucified Jesus underscores the startling shift in the perspective of perilous risk and countermeasures. Thus, more than any individual in New Testament literature other than Jesus, Paul understood and accepted that faith in *Abba* and the arrival of his kingdom represented the countermeasure to apostasy and death, and that this alone was worthy of risking all. In this context, Jesus and Paul represent radical children of *Abba*.

---

placement of Judas in the inner circle of Jesus' followers.

11. According to Gal 1:8, these were the "judaizers" from Jerusalem "sent from James," the brother of Jesus, and leader of the Jerusalem church. While they of course cannot be compared with the corrupt Jerusalem aristocracy and religious elite, they have become enemies of the gospel and are condemned as apostates by Paul, just as those who crucified Jesus.

# 10

# Qualitative Risk Analysis and Faith

JESUS OF NAZARETH LEFT Galilee, began to announce the end of elitist rule, demanded rejection of apostasy and a recommitment to God, and radically acted by supporting John, a prophet who baptized those who cast off Jerusalem's religious authority. He democratized direct access to God, announced the arrival of a new kingdom, and expelled demons as well as apostates who occupied the temple of Jerusalem. He acted to courageously counter and end the real, perilous risk that he perceived was polluting and destroying the social and religious structure of Judaism and its temple. He did this as a poor peasant, a gifted and Spirit-possessed exorcist. The countermeasures Jesus employed to mitigate this risk were not only radical, but were fraught with personal danger. He accepted the possibility of his life's end by crucifixion, but also demanded that others recognize this same peril if they wished to enter into the just cause on behalf of God, the king and father of Israel who was about to enter history. His mentor, John the Baptist, was dead, having been murdered by Antipas, the chief patron of Rome. Now spies and informants tracked Jesus to find a basis to arrest him so they might execute him under the authority of Roman law—the ultimate countermeasure. A paid assassin infiltrated the circle of his closest followers.

Jesus abandoned his reclusive life and launched an assault on the demonic forces he believed had invaded the land, fomented by the corruption of the high priesthood and aristocracy through their complicit support of foreign kingship, that is, demonic imperialism. His primary countermeasure to terminate this demonic occupation and end the rule of a satanic kingdom was unlike any contemporary of his time: exorcism followed by a demand to recognize and accept the end of Satan's rule by embracing the good news of the inbreaking kingdom of God. The village leaders of the synagogue were to embrace the outcasts and disenfranchised with mercy while awaiting the kingdom's near and full arrival. Thus, Jesus did not advocate open and violent military rebellion, clandestine assassinations, or formation of a separatist movement. This was futile. It was Satan and his demons that were to be expelled, and with them, the end of imperialism and apostasy would come by the power of God. The eschatological reversal was underway. The outcasts of society—the poor, the dispossessed, and those who had long been oppressed and rejected by the elite—stood in their privileged place. His was the voice and will of the father, which risked making himself equal with God.

In its social context, this news of eschatological reversal and practice of this divine radicalism was overwhelming—and also dangerous. When the perilous risk of Jesus' itinerant and charismatic ministry came to Jerusalem and his radicalism was found to be a dangerously effective countermeasure to the authority of the elite at Passover, then the probability that his actions would foment public dissonance became all-too real for the threatened elite. Jesus, despite his claim that he derived his authority from God, was rejected as Satan's possessed agent, as Beelzebul, and plans were made to entrap and silence him via crucifixion as a Roman criminal who practiced magic and sedition. They wanted not only to crush him, but to annihilate him body and soul as the "rebellious son of Israel" (Deut 21:21).

It is evident, based on qualitative risk analysis, that this was the collision of perilous risks between the Jerusalem elite and Jesus of Nazareth. All sayings, dialogues, historical narratives, and controversies in the Jesus tradition can be measured against this context for validation, and to discover the original form and context of their life situation when available. These efforts provide remarkable results and insights into the activity of Jesus. But more, they afford us an opportunity to discover Jesus: the intensely passionate charismatic Jew, the young peasant of Galilee, the exorcist who expected God's arrival in his lifetime but was willing to lay down his life even under a curse (sure of death and separation from God) for the sake of the charismatic good news, the *euangelion*. As a man facing overwhelming risk and likely annihilation, we encounter a new understanding of radical faith in this complex context of perilous risks and countermeasures. We discover the striking, human fear Jesus experienced at the recognition of his peril, and yet also his overwhelming joy in announcing the end of terror and demonic rule. Jesus' charismatic events, related sayings, and *Mashal* that followed are only meaningful in this context.

The analogy Jesus consistently employs is becoming like a child. This surrender to trust in God as one's own father, *Abba*, is what connects us to the proclamation of Jesus today. We can come to that man, and approach his actions and authority over demons and Satan, not as a predestined divine being who expected to die as a sacrifice, but as one of us. In this way, we can understand Jesus as a human being living by faith in a time of crisis and peril, determined to unseat the forces of evil for a holy cause by using every countermeasure at his disposal—even his life. We too can courageously embrace God and act for him, trusting in his justice and love, as Jesus did. We attach ourselves to the authentic faith and life of Jesus of Nazareth, which was validated by God as the Way to salvation and authentic life as his child. We commit ourselves to love and act as Jesus did for the benefit of every human and in every encounter overshadowed by evil, without consideration of race, gender, social standing, citizenship, sexual preference, or religion. We provide to other humans the way to achieve real countermeasures to oppression, hopelessness, and even death through the annihilation of powerlessness and satanic torture.

God as *Abba* has given us hope for freedom from possession by fear and oppression by evil through the life and words of Jesus, the uncompromising exorcist and reluctant preacher of Galilee. We learn to act for God. He breaks into history through us, his children. Our positions in life afford certain, and sometimes specific, ways to accomplish the inbreaking kingdom by extending mercy, peace, and freedom to others. While humble before God, we, like Jesus, are also empowered to act radically by employing his example when barriers to justice and hope have been erected by the audacious elite as we too await the kingdom's arrival. We are then assured that the risks we take to confront our own generation's perilous risks in oppressing, occupying, and displacing the love of God for his children are indeed taken in the cause of *Abba*, who calls on us for the sake of his son to engage and continue to bring the kingdom of God. With the tools we are given and the gifts we have, we feed hungry mouths, heal the sick, combat mental illness, and free the oppressed and disenfranchised of society. We too will find vindication and resurrection by embracing faith in the real justice of God, who raised Jesus of Nazareth from the dead. Every countermeasure we then employ to end these perilous risks answers his synagogue call. We are cleansed and freed from oppression, possessed by the Spirit as God sees fit.

We now know the miracle of faith revealed in Jesus: that God acted and will act again—and again, and again—for his children. This is the faith of Jesus, who, like a child, listened to his father's voice, accepted the Spirit of God, and then fearlessly drove out evil. The traditional images of transformation were, however, radically altered, for we see in Jesus' choice of followers every class, social standing, gender, and religious affiliation, both in and outside of Judaism. We see also that this was and is God's radicalism. The "last are first and the first are last" (Matt 20:16; Mark 10:31; Luke 13:30); all barriers to him are a façade, and where they exist, apostasy reigns and must be ended. Divine radicalism, then, is about reversal. When we engender this reversal by laying before each person or enemy what is in our ability to create by way of peace, hope, and love—the Way of *Abba* that is beyond anything expected—we become the children of God as well as the countermeasure to apostasy and evil.

When these possibilities for action are accepted, even at perilous risk, and the countermeasures we employ to attack such a perilous risk are finally perceived as dissipating that risk, then faith and divine radicalism are activated in history, extending beyond the possible to the real. We, like Jesus, are called to eliminate obstacles to God, both as king and *Abba*, wherever they may reside, for they are the work of Satan. When the child of God acts to free others from bondage and possession brought about by elitism, prejudice, guilt, physical or mental illness, poverty, judgmental religion, or class structures, the king rules and the kingdom proclaimed by Jesus is both inbreaking and present. What God does in his own time is not our concern, just as Jesus understood his life to be on the brink of transformation even as he left the outcome to God. Knowing that God is king and that he will be with us as we challenge the perilous risks that preclude the presence of his love, mercy, and hope, we enter faith that has been historically proven to be transformative in authenticating life, both temporal and eternal. In a remarkable way, qualitative risk analysis has demonstrated the core essence of Jesus' message and shown us the way to join with him in Abba's proclamation and promise of redemption when that day comes. And so we, like Jesus, our brother and Lord, must also become the radical children of *Abba*.

# 11

# Summary

AN APPLICATION OF QUALITATIVE risk analysis suggests the following parameters are fundamentally present and represent the basic risk context encountered by Jesus, thereby providing a historical framework by which to analyze perilous risks and countermeasures.

## THE CONTEXT

Brutal and corrupt Roman rulers occupied first-century Palestine. The Jerusalem Jewish aristocracy and religious elite (including the high priestly families) were Roman patrons who participated in imperial brutality and accepted Roman rule as the will of God. Jesus was a poor, dispossessed Galilean peasant and Jewish ecstatic and exorcist. For Jesus, his exorcisms evidenced that the land was possessed by demons and the foreign gods introduced by imperialism. Imperialism and the complicit support of it by the Jerusalem aristocracy and religious elite was contrary to God's will. Exorcists were well known, but Romans considered them charlatans. Exorcism was considered to be demonic magic under Roman law and was punishable by death.

## To Be Near the Fire

### Perilous Risks and Countermeasures of Verifiable Historical Conflict between Two Entities

Jesus of Nazareth employs countermeasures to end demonic and foreign possession of the land. We know that Jesus was a young, reclusive Galilean exorcist. He left Galilee to become a disciple of John the Baptist. Upon baptism, Jesus had an ecstatic experience and was possessed by the Spirit of God. Jesus was able to command demons and angels, and thus was feared. The Jerusalem elite murdered John. Jesus fled to Galilee for safety. Jesus began an assault on Satan, exorcising demons and spirits by the "finger of God." He employed familiar techniques used by other exorcists. Jesus selected and then trained other exorcist to assist him. Most, if not all, of his inner circle was made up of exorcists. Jesus sent them out to towns and villages to expand the battle. His intent was to encircle Jerusalem, cleansing synagogues in preparation for God's arrival as king. He engaged his opponents after these exorcisms in controversy dialogues and made dire warnings about their impending risk that were expressed in the charismatic language of the *Mashal*. Waiting for the Passover, Jesus entered Jerusalem and attempted to cleanse the temple by driving demons out of its precincts. He tied his activity to the end of demonic rule and apostasy, but ultimately failed to save the temple. He announced its doom. God was coming as king and would claim his children in the powerful and transformative resurrection into the kingdom. He called on the name of John to justify his actions and publicly accused the elite of murdering God's messenger.

The Roman hegemony employed its own countermeasures to squash sedition, public criticism, or rebellion. In the context of Jesus' activity as exorcist, we know the Romans took the following view of it. Exorcism was dark magic, illegal under Roman law, and a capital crime. Jesus was therefore an outlaw under the law, not just an annoyance. Furthermore, to associate demons with Rome and the elite amounted to sedition. The Jerusalem elite, as patrons of Rome, accused Jesus of being a magician and alleged that he was possessed by the chief demon, Beelzebul. During this time, Jesus own family rejected him and publicly accused him of being mad, that is, possessed. An assassin was assigned to Jesus. Herodian spies trailed him. They waited for him to come to Jerusalem to seize him. The spy, a paid "dagger man" and assassin of the elite, would lead them to Jesus at night. Jesus recognized the man's intent and that he was in a deadly trap.

*Summary*

## Escalation, Historical Conflict, and Countermeasures to Cancel out Competing Perilous Risk

Recognizing the impending risk, Jesus openly performed charismatic acts to gather crowds in Jerusalem. He announced the end of the current demonic order. When cornered by the elite, he publicly called on the memory of John for protection. The people held that Herod murdered John and responded to his call by protecting him. Jesus' countermeasures to perilous risk worked, but only temporarily.

## Risk Outcome and Final Countermeasures

Jesus was quickly captured at night and executed in only hours, swatted like a fly. He was betrayed by a paid informant and assassin who had infiltrated his band of exorcists. Jesus' followers disbanded and fled back to Galilee. Before they left, women belonging to Jesus' band found the tomb empty. Resurrection was a phenomenon associated with magic, but not bodily resurrection. Some followers met with the risen Jesus in ecstatic encounters. These men returned to Jerusalem to await the arrival of God. As expected, their countermeasure was to call on the spirit of the risen Jesus, the Son of God, to resist. They exorcised in his name and continued his rituals and practices, which are recoverable in the gospels, while awaiting the arrival of God and his Messiah.

## CONCLUSIONS

Qualitative risk analysis can be used to identify risk-based material in the New Testament that has historical merit.[1] Using facts accepted by most scholars, a new risk-based profile of Jesus' charismatic activity and exorcisms, the controversy dialogues, and the *Mashal* emerges. Jesus is not distinct from Judaism, but wholly part of it, having risked everything to preserve it from demonic activity and the growing apostasy that threatened its very existence. For this he embraced the risk of death, trusting that God, *Abba*, was the author of his charismatic authority, having been given the Spirit of God that possessed him during his baptism by John. Jesus, a

---

1. We have demonstrated that the Gospel of Mark was the product of a community in perilous crisis, which adapted the perilous risks of Jesus' conflict with opponents to its own life situation.

radical conservative adhering solely to the kingship of God, is also the radical proclaimer of liberation, as evidenced by the risk countermeasures he employed to end demonic imperialism and oppression. Risk conflict and countermeasures to mitigate perilous risks often fail. But occasionally, conflict can yield historical change—even, for example, when such conflict led a young man to a lonely, brutal death on a cross near a deserted graveyard outside of the city that had rejected and abandoned him. The search for meaning in that life and its divine encounters is enriched by embracing the risks that led to that day.

# Bibliography

Ahearne-Kroll, Stephen. *The Psalms of Lament in Mark's Passion: Jesus' Davidic Suffering.* Society for New Testament Studies 142. New York: Cambridge University Press, 2007.
Allegro, John Marco. *The Dead Sea Scrolls.* Pelican Books A376. New York: Penguin, 1956.
Anderson, Charles C. *The Historical Jesus: A Continuing Quest.* Grand Rapids: Eerdmans, 1972.
Barr, James. "Abba Isn't Daddy." *Journal of Theological Studies* 39 (1988) 28–47.
Bauer, Walter. *The Greek-English Lexicon of the New Testament, and Other Early Christian Literature.* Translated and edited by William F. Arndt and F. Wilbur Gingrich. 2nd ed. Chicago: University of Chicago Press, 1979.
Bernstein, Peter L. *Against the Gods: The Remarkable Story of Risk.* New York: Wiley, 1996.
Black, Matthew, and Géza Vermès. *An Aramaic Approach to the Gospels and Acts.* 3rd ed. Oxford: Clarendon, 1967.
Borg, Marcus J. *Jesus: Uncovering the Life, Teachings, and Relevance of a Religious Revolutionary.* San Francisco: Harper One, 2006.
———. *The Lost Gospel of Q: The Original Sayings of Jesus.* Berkeley: Ulysses, 1996.
Bornkamm, Günther. *Jesus of Nazareth.* Translated by James M. Robinson. London: Hodder & Stoughton, 1960.
Bousset, Wilhelm. *Kyrios Christos: A History of the Belief in Christ from the Beginnings of Christianity to Irenaeus.* Nashville: Abingdon, 1970.
Bowker, John. *Jesus and the Pharisees.* London: Cambridge University Press, 1973.
Brown, Raymond Edward. *The Community of the Beloved Disciple.* New York: Paulist, 1979.
———. "Roles of Women in the Fourth Gospel." *Theological Studies* 36 (1975) 688–99.
Bultmann, Rudolf. *The Gospel of John: A Commentary.* Translated by G. R. Beasley-Murray et al. Philadelphia: Westminster, 1971.
———. *History of the Synoptic Tradition.* Translated by John Marsh. Oxford: Blackwell, 1972.
———. *Jesus and the Word.* Translated by Louise Pettibone Smith and Erminie Huntress Lantero. New York: Scribner, 1958.
———. *Primitive Christianity in Its Contemporary Setting.* Translated by R. H. Fuller. Living Age Meridian Books LA4. New York: Meridian, 1956.
———. *Theology of the New Testament.* 2 vols. Translated by Kendrick Grobel. New York: Scribner, 1951–1955.

*Bibliography*

Bultmann, Rudolf, and Karl Kundsin. *Form Criticism: Two Essays on New Testament Research*. Translated by Frederick C. Grant. Harper Torchbooks. New York: Harper, 1962.

Busse, Roger S. *The Essentials of Commercial Lending*. WKB Enterprises: 1995; primary lending text of US Bancorp (1999–2007) and Pacific Continental Bank (2002–2013).

———. "The Son of Man in the Synoptic Tradition." BA thesis, Reed College, 1978.

———. "The Temple of Dea Roma and Divus Julius in Ephesos." Presentation to Professor Stefan Karwiese, Director of the Austrian Archaeological Institute, at the Harvard Archeological Colloquium, Ephesus, Turkey, May 1995.

Cameron, Ron. *The Other Gospels: Non-Canonical Gospel Texts*. Philadelphia: Westminster, 1982.

Charlesworth, James H., ed. *Apocalyptic Literature and Testaments*. Vol. 1 of *The Old Testament Pseudepigrapha*. Anchor Bible Reference Library. Garden City, NY: Doubleday, 1983.

Chazon, Esther G. "Hymns and Prayers in the Dead Sea Scrolls." In vol. 2 of *The Dead Sea Scrolls After Fifty Years: A Comprehensive Assessment*, edited by Peter W. Flint and James C. VanderKam, 244–70. Leiden: Brill, 1999.

Chilton, Bruce. *The Temple of Jesus: His Sacrificial Program within a Cultural History of Sacrifice*. University Park, PA: Pennsylvania State University Press, 1992.

Conzelmann, Hans. *1 Corinthians: A Commentary on the First Epistle to the Corinthians*. Edited by George W. MacRae and translated by James W. Leitch. Hermeneia: A Critical and Historical Commentary on the Bible. Philadelphia: Fortress, 1975.

———. *An Outline of the Theology of the New Testament*. Translated by John Bowden. New York: Harper & Row, 1969.

———. *The Theology of St. Luke*. Translated by Geoffrey Buswell. New York: Harper & Row, 1961.

Crossan, John Dominic. *The Historical Jesus: The Life of a Mediterranean Jewish Peasant*. San Francisco: HarperSanFrancisco, 1992.

———. *In Fragments: The Aphorisms of Jesus*. San Francisco: Harper & Row, 1983.

———. *In Parables: The Challenge of the Historical Jesus*. New York: Harper & Row, 1973.

———. *Sayings Parallels: A Workbook for the Jesus Tradition*. Foundations and Facets. Philadelphia: Fortress, 1986.

Cullmann, Oscar. *The Christology of the New Testament*. Translated by Shirley C. Guthrie and Charles A. M. Hall. New Testament Library. Philadelphia: Westminster, 1963.

Daube, David. "Jesus and the Samaritan Women." *Journal of Biblical Literature* 69 (1950) 137–47.

Davies, W. D. *The Setting of the Sermon on the Mount*. London: Cambridge University Press, 1964.

Dodd, C. H. *The Apostolic Preaching and Its Developments*. New York: Harper & Row, 1964.

———. *Parables of the Kingdom*. New York: Scribner, 1961.

Drabek, Thomas E. *Human System Responses to Disaster: An Inventory of Sociological Findings*. Springer Series on Environmental Management. New York: Springer, 1986.

Du Plessis, Paul. *Borkowski's Textbook on Roman Law*. 4th ed. Oxford: Oxford University Press, 2010.

Ehrman, Bart D. *The New Testament: A Historical Introduction to the Early Christian Writings*. 3rd ed. Oxford University Press: New York, 2004.

*Bibliography*

Eisenman, Robert H. *The Dead Sea Scrolls and the First Christians: Essays and Translations.* Edison, NJ: Castle, 1996.

Evans, Craig A. "Jesus' Action in the Temple as Evidence of Corruption in the First-Century Temple." In *Jesus and His Contemporaries: Comparative Studies*, 319–44. New York: Brill, 1995.

Farmer, William Reuben. *The Synoptic Problem: A Critical Analysis.* 2nd ed. London: Macmillan, 1976.

Finkelstein, Louis. *The Pharisees: The Sociological Background of Their Faith.* 2 vols. Morris Loeb Series. Philadelphia: Jewish Publication Society of America, 1946.

Fischoff, Baruch, et al. *Acceptable Risk.* Cambridge: Cambridge University Press, 1984.

Foerster, Werner. *From the Exile to Christ: A Historical Introduction to Palestinian Judaism.* Translated by Gordon E. Harris. Philadelphia: Fortress, 1964.

Fortna, Robert Tomson. *The Fourth Gospel and Its Predecessor: From Narrative Source to Present Gospel*, Philadelphia: Fortress, 1988.

———. *The Gospel of Signs: A Reconstruction of the Narrative Source Underlying the Fourth Gospel.* Society for New Testament Studies Monograph Series 10. London, Cambridge University Press, 1970.

Funk, Robert Walter, and Roy Hoover, eds. *The Five Gospels: The Search for the Authentic Words of Jesus; A New Translation and Commentary.* The Jesus Seminar. New York: Macmillan, 1993.

Furnish, Victor Paul. *The Love Command in the New Testament.* New York: Abingdon, 1972.

Gerhardsson, Birger. *Memory and Manuscript: Oral Tradition and Written Transmission in Rabbinic Judaism and Early Christianity.* Translated by Eric J. Sharpe. Acta Seminarii Neotestamentici Upsaliensis 22. Uppsala, Sweden: C. W. K. Gleerup, 1961.

———. *The Origins of the Gospel Traditions.* Philadelphia: Fortress, 1979.

Georgi, Dieter. "Forms of Religious Propaganda." In *Jesus in His Time*, edited by Hans Jürgen Schultz and translated by Brian Watchorn, 123–31. Philadelphia: Fortress, 1971.

Griffiths, J. Gwyn. "The Disciple's Cross." *New Testament Studies* 16 (1970) 358–64.

Hengel, Martin. *The Son of God: The Origin of Christology and the History of Jewish-Hellenistic Religion.* Philadelphia: Fortress, 1976.

Hock, Ronald F. *The Social Context of Paul's Ministry: Tentmaking and Apostleship.* Philadelphia: Fortress, 1980.

Horsley, Richard A. "High Priests and the Politics of Roman Palestine." *Journal for the Study of Judaism* 17 (1986) 23–55.

———. *Jesus and the Spiral of Violence: Popular Jewish Resistance in Roman Palestine.* San Francisco: Harper & Row, 1987.

Horsley, Richard A., and John S. Hanson. *Bandits, Prophets, and Messiahs: Popular Movements in the Time of Jesus.* San Francisco: Harper & Row, 1985.

Horsley, Richard A., and Neil Asher Silberman. *The Message and the Kingdom: How Jesus and Paul Ignited a Revolution and Transformed the Ancient World.* Minneapolis: Fortress, 1997.

Isaac, E. "1 (Ethiopic Apocalypse of) Enoch (Second Century B.C.–First Century A.D.)." In *Apocalyptic Literature and Testaments*, edited by James H. Charlesworth, 5–89. Vol. 1 of *The Old Testament Pseudepigrapha.* Anchor Yale Bible Reference Library. Garden City, NY: Doubleday, 1983.

# Bibliography

Jeremias, Joachim. *Abba: Studien zur Neutestamentlichen Theologie und Zietgeschichte.* Göttingen, Germany: Vandenhoeck & Ruprecht, 1966.

———. *The Central Message of the New Testament.* Philadelphia: Fortress, 1965.

———. *The Eucharistic Words of Jesus.* Translated by Norman Perrin. 3rd ed. London: SCM, 1966.

———. *Jerusalem in the Time of Jesus: An Investigation into Economic and Social Conditions during the New Testament Period.* Translated by F. H. and C. H. Cave. Philadelphia: Fortress, 1969.

———. *Jesus' Promise to the Nations.* Studies in Biblical Theology 24. London: SCM, 1958.

———. *New Testament Theology: The Proclamation of Jesus.* New York: Scribner, 1971.

———. *The Parables of Jesus.* Translated by S. H. Hooke. London: SCM, 1972.

———. *The Prayers of Jesus.* Studies in Biblical Theology, Second Series 6. Translated by John Bowden et al. London: SCM, 1967.

———. *The Problem of the Historical Jesus.* Facet Books, Biblical Series 13. Philadelphia: Fortress, 1964.

———. *Rediscovering the Parables of Jesus.* Scribner Lyceum Library. New York: Scribner, 1966.

Kahneman, Daniel, Paul Slovic, and Amos Tversky. *Judgment under Uncertainty: Heuristics and Biases.* New York: Cambridge University Press, 1982.

Kee, Howard Clark. "Testament of the Twelve Patriarchs." In *Apocalyptic Literature and Testaments*, edited by James H. Charlesworth, 775–828. Vol. 1 of *The Old Testament Pseudepigrapha*. Anchor Yale Bible Reference Library. Garden City, NY: Doubleday, 1983.

———. *The Origins of Christianity: Sources and Documents.* Englewood Cliffs, NJ: Prentice-Hall, 1973.

Kelber, Werner H. *The Oral and the Written Gospel: The Hermeneutics of Speaking and Writing in the Synoptic Tradition, Mark, Paul, and Q.* Philadelphia: Fortress, 1983.

Kirby, Peter. "The Signs Gospel: Text." *Early Christian Writings.* June 4, 2014. http://www.earlychristianwritings.com/text/signs.html.

Kloppenborg, John S. *The Formation of Q: Trajectories in Ancient Wisdom Collections.* Studies in Antiquity and Christianity. Philadelphia: Fortress, 1989.

Kloppenborg, John S., et al. *Q-Thomas Reader.* Sonoma, CA: Polebridge, 1990.

Koch, Klaus. *The Growth of the Biblical Tradition: The Form-Critical Method.* Translated by S. M. Cupitt. Scribner Studies in Biblical Interpretation. New York: Scribner, 1969.

Koester, Helmut. *Ancient Christian Gospels: Their History and Development.* Philadelphia: Trinity Press International, 1992.

———. *From Jesus to the Gospels: Interpreting the New Testament in Its Context.* Minneapolis: Fortress, 2007.

———. "GNOMAI DIAPHOROI: The Origin and Nature of Diversification in the History of Early Christianity." In *Trajectories through Early Christianity*, by Helmut Koester and James M. Robinson, 114–57. Philadelphia: Fortress, 1971.

———. "The Historical Jesus: Some Comments and Thoughts on Norman Perrin's Rediscovering the Teachings of Jesus." In *Christology and A Modern Pilgrimage: A Discussion with Norman Perrin*, edited by Hans Deiter Betz, 123–36. Missoula, MT: Scholars Press, 1974.

———. *History and Literature of Early Christianity.* Vol. 2 of *Introduction to the New Testament.* Foundations and Facets. Philadelphia: Fortress, 1982.

*Bibliography*

———. "One Jesus and Four Primitive Gospels." In *Trajectories through Early Christianity*, by Helmut Koester and James M. Robinson, 187–93. Philadelphia: Fortress, 1971.

———. "The Structure and Criteria of Early Christian Beliefs." In *Trajectories through Early Christianity*, by Helmut Koester and James M. Robinson, 205–231. Philadelphia: Fortress, 1971.

———. "The Synoptic Sayings Gospel Q in the Early Communities of Jesus' Followers." In *Early Christian Voices in Texts, Traditions, and Symbols: Essays in Honor of François Bovon*, edited by David H. Warren et al., 45–58. Biblical Interpretation Series 66. Leiden: Brill, 2003.

Kümmel, Werner Georg. *Introduction to the New Testament*. Translated by Howard Clark Kee. Nashville: Abingdon, 1975.

Layton, Bentley. *The Gnostic Scriptures: A New Translation with Annotations and Introductions*. Garden City, NY: Doubleday, 1987.

Lewis, I. M. *Ecstatic Religion: An Anthropological Study of Spirit Possession and Shamanism*. Pelican Anthropology Library. Harmondsworth, UK: Penguin, 1971.

Longenecker, Richard N. *Biblical Exegesis in the Apostolic Period*. Grand Rapids: Eerdmans, 1975.

Lohse, Eduard. *Colossians and Philemon: A Commentary on the Epistles to the Colossians and to Philemon*. Edited by Helmut Koester and translated by William R. Poehlmann and Robert J. Karris. Hermeneia. Philadelphia: Fortress, 1971.

Marshall, I. Howard. *New Testament Interpretation: Essays on Principles and Methods*. Grand Rapids: Eerdmans, 1977.

———. *The Origins of New Testament Christology*. Issues in Contemporary Theology. Downers Grove, IL: InterVarsity, 1976.

McCrae, George. "The Jewish Background of the Gnostic Sophia Myth." *Novum Testamentum* 12 (1970) 81–101.

Meeks, Wayne A. *The First Urban Christians: The Social World of the Apostle Paul*. New Haven: Yale University Press, 1983.

Metzger, Bruce M. "The Fourth Book of Ezra." In *Apocalyptic Literature and Testaments*, edited by James H. Charlesworth, 517–60. Vol. 1 of *The Old Testament Pseudepigrapha*. Anchor Yale Bible Reference Library. Garden City, NY: Doubleday, 1983.

———. *Lexical Aids for Students of New Testament Greek*. Princeton, NJ: printed by author, 1946.

———. *The Text of the New Testament: Its Transmission, Corruption, and Restoration*. 2nd ed. New York: Oxford University Press, 1968.

Miller, Robert J., ed., *The Complete Gospels: Annotated Scholars Version*. Translated by Stephen Patterson and Marvin Meyer. Gnostic Society Library; Nag Hammadi Library. Sonoma, CA: Polebridge, 1994. http://gnosis.org/naghamm/gosthom.html.

Nickelsburg, George W. E. *Jewish Literature between the Bible and the Mishnah: A Historical and Literary Introduction*. Philadelphia: Fortress, 1981.

Ogden, Daniel. *Magic, Witchcraft, and Ghosts in the Greek and Roman Worlds: A Sourcebook*. 2nd ed. New York: Oxford University Press, 2009.

Patterson, Stephen J. *Beyond the Passion: Rethinking the Death and Life of Jesus*. Minneapolis: Fortress, 2004.

———. *The God of Jesus: The Historical Jesus and the Search for Meaning*. Harrisburg, PA: Trinity, 1998.

———. *The Gospel of Thomas and Jesus*. Foundations and Facets. Sonoma, CA: Polebridge, 1993.

*Bibliography*

Pearson, Birger A. *Gnosticism, Judaism, and Egyptian Christianity.* Studies in Antiquity and Christianity. Minneapolis: Fortress, 1990.

———. *The Pneumatikos-Psychikos Terminology in 1 Corinthians: A Study in the Theology of the Corinthian Opponents of Paul and Its Relation to Gnosticism.* Missoula, MT: Scholars Press, 1973.

Perrin, Norman. *Jesus and the Language of the Kingdom: Symbol and Metaphor in New Testament Interpretation.* Philadelphia: Fortress, 1976.

———. *The New Testament, an Introduction: Proclamation and Parenesis, Myth and History.* New York: Harcourt, Brace, & Jovanovich, 1974.

———. *Rediscovering the Teachings of Jesus.* New York: Harper & Row, 1976.

Pidgeon, Nick F., et al., eds. "The Social Amplification of Risk: A Conceptual Framework." In *The Social Amplification of Risk*, 177–87. Cambridge: Cambridge University Press, 2003.

Plummer, Alfred. *A Critical and Exegetical Commentary on the Gospel According to S. Luke.* 5th ed. International Critical Commentary. Edinburgh: T. & T. Clark, 1975.

Reedy, C. J. "Mark 8:31–11:10 and the Gospel Ending: A Redactional Study." *Catholic Bible Quarterly* 34 (1972) 188–97.

Reicke, Bo. "Galilee and Judea." In *Jesus in His Time*, edited by Hans Jürgen Schultz and translated by Brian Watchorn, 28–35. Philadelphia: Fortress, 1971.

Renan, Ernst. *Vie de Jésus.* Paris: Calmann-Lévy, 1960.

Robinson, James M. "Jesus: From Easter to Valentinus (Or to the Apostle's Creed)." *Journal of Biblical Literature* 101 (1982) 5–37.

———. *A New Quest of the Historical Jesus and Other Essays.* New York: Macmillan, 1968.

———. *The Problem of History in Mark.* Studies in Biblical Theology 21. London: SCM, 1968.

———, ed. *The Nag Hammadi Library in English.* Translated and introduced by the Coptic Gnostic Library Project of the Institute for Antiquity and Christianity. 3rd rev. ed. Leiden: Brill, 1988.

Safrai, Zeev. "The Roman Army in Galilee." In *The Galilee in Late Antiquity*, edited by Lee I. Levine, 103–114. New York: Jewish Theological Seminary, 1992.

Sanders, E. P. *The Historical Figure of Jesus.* London: Penguin, 1993.

———. *Paul and Palestinian Judaism: A Comparison of Patterns of Religion.* London: SCM, 1977.

Sanders, Jack T. *The New Testament Christological Hymns: Their Historical Religious Background.* Society for New Testament Studies Monograph Series 15. Cambridge: Cambridge University Press, 1971.

Sandmel, Samuel. *A Jewish Understanding of the New Testament.* New York: University Publishers, 1956.

Schmithals, Walter. *Gnosticism in Corinth: An Investigation of the Letters to the Corinthians.* Translated by John E. Steely. New York: Abingdon, 1971.

Schweitzer, Albert. *The Quest of the Historical Jesus: A Critical Study of Its Progress from Reimarus to Wrede.* Translated by F. C. Burkitt. Rev. ed. Albert Schweitzer Library. Baltimore: Johns Hopkins University Press, 1998.

Slovic, Paul. *The Perception of Risk.* Risk, Society, and Policy Series. Sterling, VA: Earthscan, 2000.

———. "Trust, Emotion, Sex, Politics, and Science: Surveying the Risk Assessment Battlefield." *Risk Analysis* 19 (1999) 689–701.

# Bibliography

Slovic, Paul, et al. "Risk as Analysis and Risk as Feelings: Some Thoughts about Affect, Reason, Risk, and Rationality." *Risk Analysis* 24 (2004) 311–22.

Smith, Morton. *Jesus the Magician*. San Francisco: Harper & Row, 1978.

Strauss, David Friedrich. *The Life of Jesus, Critically Examined*. Edited by Peter C. Hodgson and translated by George Elliot. Lives of Jesus Series. Philadelphia: Fortress, 1972.

Strugnell, John. "A Plea for Conjectural Emendation in the New Testament, with a Coda on 1 Cor 4:6." *Catholic Bible Quarterly* 36 (1974) 543–58.

Suggs, M. Jack. *Wisdom, Christology, and Law in Matthew's Gospel*. Cambridge: Harvard University Press, 1970.

Sunstein, Cass R. "The Laws of Fear." John M. Olin Program in Law and Economics Working Paper No. 128, 2001. http://chicagounbound.uchicago.edu/law_and_economics/544/.

Theissen, Gerd. *The Social Setting of Pauline Christianity: Essays on Corinth*. Edited and translated by John H. Schutz. Philadelphia: Fortress, 1982.

Throckmorton, Bruce H., Jr., ed. *Gospel Parallels: A Synopsis of the First Three Gospels*. 2nd rev. ed. New York: Nelson, 1957.

Tödt, Heinz Eduard. *The Son of Man in the Synoptic Tradition*. Translated by Dorothea M. Barton. New Testament Library. London: SCM, 1963.

Vermès, Géza. *The Changing Faces of Jesus*. New York: Viking Compass, 2001.

———. *The Dead Sea Scrolls in English*. 3rd ed. London: Penguin, 1990.

———. *Jesus the Jew: A Historian's Reading of the Gospels*. London: Fontana, 1977.

Wassertein, Abraham, ed. *Flavius Josephus: Selections from His Works*. New York: Viking, 1974.

White, L. Michael. "Urban Development and Social Change in Imperial Ephesos." In *Ephesos, Metropolis of Asia: An Interdisciplinary Approach to Its Archaeology, Religion, and Culture*, edited by Helmut Koester, 27–79. Harvard Theological Studies 41. Valley Forge, PA: Trinity, 1995.

Williamson, Lamar, Jr. "Mark." In *Interpretation: A Bible Commentary for Teaching and Preaching*, edited by James. L. Mays et al., 147–200. Louisville, KY: John Knox, 1983. ed. by James L. Mays, 154

Willis, Wendell Lee. *Idol Meat in Corinth: The Pauline Argument in 1 Corinthians 8 and 10*. Society of Biblical Literature Dissertation Series 68. 1983. Reprint, Eugene, OR: Wipf & Stock, 2004.

www.ingramcontent.com/pod-product-compliance
Lightning Source LLC
Chambersburg PA
CBHW071447150426
43191CB00008B/1267